Libros Esenciales

Building, Marketing,
and Programming
a Core Collection
of Spanish Language
Children's Materials

Tim Wadham

Neal-Schuman Publishers, Inc.
New York   London

Published by Neal-Schuman Publishers, Inc.
100 William St., Suite 2004
New York, NY 10038

Copyright © 2007 Neal-Schuman Publishers

Printed and bound in the United States of America.

The paper used in this publication meets the minimum requirements of American National Standard for Information Sciences—Permanence of Paper for Printed Library Materials, ANSI Z39.48–1992.

ISBN-13: 978–1–55570–575–6
ISBN-10: 1–55570–575–8

Library of Congress Cataloging-in-Publication Data

Wadham, Tim.
Libros esenciales : building, marketing, and programming a core
  collection of Spanish-language children's materials / by Tim Wadham.
     p.   cm.
  Includes bibliographical references and index.
  ISBN 1–55570–575–8 (alk. paper)
  1. Libraries—Special collections—Spanish imprints.   2. Libraries—Special
collections—Children's literature, Spanish.   3. Children's literature, Spanish—
Bibliography.   I. Title.
Z688.S68W33   2007
025.2'7808899282—dc22   2006014894

Contents

Preface

"Children can grow up with a strong, powerful culture in their home, but if they don't have that validated in the classroom, they start to feel that in order to fit in they have to leave their culture behind."

Mari Womack, Professor of Cultural
Anthropology, University of California,
Los Angeles

"For the first time, young Hispanics can find books in . . . libraries . . . about children who live in two worlds but no longer feel torn. These bilingual children do not have to look far from their neighborhoods to find the voices of writers who use and understand language in their particular way: English prose that expresses American ideas in the rhythmic cadences of Spanish."

Maria Elena Fernandez, Staff Writer,
Los Angeles Times

Latinos are the fastest growing ethnic population residing in the United States. With a cultural heritage rooted in many countries, the children of this demographic share an exciting blend of cultures. Though most of these students are bilingual, they consistently score lower on language-skills tests than their counterparts who speak English alone. As a children's librarian who has worked directly with these young people, I have seen firsthand the positive difference that librarians, teachers, and caregivers can make by facilitating their linguistic development and reinforcing their cultural heritage.

Moreover, providing readers with a sense of the beauty and richness of the Spanish language and Latin American traditions is advantageous, regardless of the country background. *Libros Esenciales: Building, Marketing, and Programming a Core Collection of Spanish-Language Children's Materials* recommends top-quality titles, provides ready-to-use programs, and offers the practical strategies to help you better serve all library users.

HOW I DEVELOPED *LIBROS ESENCIALES*

Around twenty years ago I worked as librarian in a branch that served a significant Spanish-speaking population. The range of titles in our collection dedicated to this audience was limited. Many of them were either translations of books originally published in English or had little appeal. Most critically, the translated works had little to do with the culture of the Latino kids in the neighborhood I served. In the process of exploring multi-language books, I discovered plenty of great German, French and other European children's books in translation. Exciting as this was, it made finding materials relevant to the lives of the Spanish-speaking patrons whom I was serving more urgent.

My first impulse was to find books published in Spain, Mexico, and the rest of Latin America, believing that these titles would have great resonance. Yet in the late 1980s when I first began this quest, there was virtually nothing available, making collection development a frustrating chore. Today this situation has completely changed, and with it my philosophy about providing for bilingual and Spanish-speaking readers and finding books to satisfy them.

While finding the best books has long been my first priority, my need for materials to support programming always comes in a close second. When I first arrived on the job, my Spanish was already fluent, but I soon discovered that there were few resources to help me find texts to use in bilingual storytimes and other programs. Again, I initially attempted to employ materials in my programming that were indigenous to Latin American countries instead of just using translations of material originally presented in English, and I worked to collect as many of these titles as I could. In tandem with this effort, I worked to collect rhymes, finger plays, and stories from disparate sources. I often wished for a comprehensive guide that not only would provide suggestions for books but that would also gather these other resources in a systematic fashion.

My first book, *Programming with Latino Children's Materials*, attempted to meet this need. Since its publication in 1999, I have discovered the large number of teachers and librarians hungry for book suggestions and other multicultural materials to fill an ever increasing demand. I developed this follow-up, *Libros Esenciales: Building, Marketing, and Programming a Core Collection of Spanish-Language Children's Materials* to give you the tools to create such a collection, employ the materials in programming, and market the effort to the community. It revises and updates materials of lasting value from the first book, and brings a wealth of new books, programs, and ideas.

Libros Esenciales is a resource for professionals who wish to develop a basic collection that will serve the needs of their young Spanish-speaking patrons and to see that collection used both in and out of the library. I designed it to be a user-friendly guide for new librarians finding their way as well as for veterans looking for fresh materials and inspiration. Whether you are fully conversant in Spanish, speak only English, or are somewhere in between, the only necessary requirement is a desire to celebrate a remarkable language, explore a fascinating set of cultures, and to give your library patrons what they want.

SERVING THE LATINO COMMUNITY

The well-documented explosion of the Latino population in the United States is the primary source of a profound shift in the availability of bilingual and Spanish-language books. Publishers acknowledged the reading needs of this new demographic, and, at the same time, recognized the emerging writers arising from its members. The increasing diversity of these authors' works has been reflected in and recognized in the library community with such milestones as the establishment of the Pura Belpré Award in 1996, which celebrates Latino writers and illustrators in the United States. This new wealth of literary riches led me to realize that the culturally relevant materials I had been looking for abroad could be found right in my own backyard.

I began keeping a list of titles that were both useful for programming as well as books I felt ought to be added to my branch collections. As I reviewed the list, I realized that I had several sorts of books. I assembled titles

- in Spanish from Spain, Mexico, and Central and Latin America;
- in a bilingual Spanish-English format; and
- by Latino authors in English that touched on the cultural experience of being Latino in the United States.

The primary focus of this list is to provide resources for libraries and librarians working with the U.S. Latino community.

This community's diversity necessitates that a variety of materials be considered. Providing works to represent all cultures is a daunting challenge, but it is by no means impossible, especially if one attends carefully to the particulars of local communities. For example, in New York immigrants predominantly come from Puerto Rico, the Dominican Republic and other Spanish-speaking Caribbean countries. On the opposite end of the East coast, in South Florida, the culture is largely Cuban in origin. Directly across the country in Arizona and southern California, Mexican immigrants make up much of the population. Almost anywhere, you can find enclaves of people from virtually any country where Spanish is spoken, from El Salvador to Spain. Representing the variety of these numerous communities is beyond the scope of any one book, but I have endeavored to provide you with the tools to serve all young Spanish-speaking library users, whatever their background.

BOOK ORGANIZATION

Part I, "Building and Programming with the Core Collection," offers general guidelines, suggestions for titles, and ways to use guidelines and titles in programming and marketing.

Chapter 1, "Latino Children and Their Culture," recommends works organized by format, helping you find the best items for any young library patron you set out to serve. The chapter explores fairy tales, picture books, music, chapter fiction, poetry, nonfiction, novels, short story collection and works for young adults. It features some of the classic books mentioned in my earlier manual, but is significantly updated with six years worth of new publications. The list, which forms the heart of this text, includes descriptions of each book, along with sidebar highlights.

Chapter 2, "How to Create a High-Quality Collection of Bilingual and Spanish-Language Children's Materials," focuses on the selection criteria for the core collection, and the basic rules of thumb you can use to expand on it. It also provides an overview of the context in which these works are produced.

Chapter 3, "A Recommended Core Collection," provides tools and ideas that will help guarantee the works described in the first chapter are put to good use. Ready-to-use programs for all ages, including toddlers, preschoolers, elementary and teens, are included. There are also programs for holidays, parent and caregivers, as well as intergenerational programs.

Chapter 4, "Programming with the Core Collection," covers the policies and techniques that will ensure the books you bring into the library are leveraged to best effect. It explores the basic steps of needs assessment: planning, implementation, and evaluation. It also shows how to utilize the "Six P's" of marketing. The chapter explores how to create a successful written marketing plan for a Spanish-language and bilingual book collection.

Chapter 5, "Strategic Marketing of the Core Collection," offers an in-depth discussion of the background of those we serve and its impact on how we work with them.

Part II, "Planning Programs for Bilingual and Spanish-Speaking Children," further develops the framework for providing exemplary service.

Chapter 6, "Programming with Latino Folktales and Folklore," and Chapter 7, "Programming with Latino Folk Rhymes, Riddles, and Fingerplays," follow this up by presenting some of the most well known narratives of the cultures in which our youth are born along with suggestions for how we can make use of them considers other cultural phenomenon that may be of interest to your users.

Part III, "Resources for Evaluating and Locating Books and Materials for Bilingual and Spanish-Speaking Children," provides a number of additional tools to help take your collection development beyond the core. Chapter 8, "Other Notable Selections of Books and Materials," contains a list of titles you should consider if you have the resources to make your collection larger. Chapter 10, "Major Book Awards," details the prizes given to the best texts and gives an up-to-date list of those that have won. Finally, Chapter 11, "Review Sources, Publishers and Vendors," includes information on where to go next, presenting some of the Web sites, journals and publishing houses that can best serve your ongoing development and programming needs.

An appendix featuring a copy of the Multi-Language Collection Development Policy of the Oakland Public Library, Oakland, California, ends the book.

The material in this book was developed over twenty years of planning and implementing programs for children and teens. It is informed by several years of reviewing for *Críticas* magazine and the *Horn Book Guide*. Enriching it still further are numerous experiences performing community outreach and presenting programs to children and parents in Head Start and other early childhood programs.

I hope that readers of *Libros Esenciales: Building, Marketing, and Programming a Core Collection of Spanish-Language Children's Materials* will come away with a new enthusiasm for the richness and breadth of Latino literature, and a deeper appreciation for working with Latino children. Likewise, this book is written in part as a monument to the culture these children represent and I hope that readers will take away some of my enthusiasm. If the material presented here sparks new ideas in the minds of teachers and librarians, I will consider it a success.

Note: The material quoted by Ms. Womack and Ms. Fernandez is taken from the article, *Adiós Dick and Jane: Latino Children's Books Have a Whole New Voice*, by Maria Elena Fernandez, *Los Angeles Times*, October 10, 2000.

Acknowledgments

I am grateful to Isabel Schon, Director of the Barahona Center for the Study of Books in Spanish for Children and Adolescents at California State University, San Marcos, and her colleagues Teresa Mlawer and Oralia Garza de Cortes. Thank you for your very helpful insights about the list.

I especially wish to acknowledge my wife, Penny, who is my editor-in-chief, and my daughter, Hannah, who has and will read many of these books.

Part I. Building and Programming with the Core Collection

Chapter 1

Latino Children and Their Culture

In March 2006, hundreds of thousands of Latinos took to the streets in cities all over the United States, ranging from an estimated 20,000 in Phoenix to half a million in Los Angeles to protest the threat of federal immigration legislation that would make it a felony to be in the United States illegally. Many of the demonstrators were Latino youths, quite a number of whom were skipping school to participate. These demonstrations pointed out a deep divide in this country between those who desire to keep illegal immigrants out, and the immigrants themselves and their sympathizers, who point out that Latinos make our beds, cook our food, build our homes, manicure our lawns, and perform many other menial tasks. The presence of Latino youths in these demonstrations revealed, a strong sense of cultural and linguistic unity.

The cultural and social divide unveiled by these protests raises the question, how does one begin to provide exemplary service to a community representing a particular culture, especially if one is not part of that culture? This chapter will explore the culture of Latino children from many different countries. While it is difficult to fully understand a culture if you are not part of it, it is possible to become conversant with the basic language of a culture, and become "adopted" into that culture to a certain extent. When I speak of language, I am speaking not only of a particular language, such as Spanish, but also of a cultural language that manifests itself in dress, gestures, celebrations, and other practices.

In March 1997, Judith Ortiz Cofer, accepting the first Pura Belpré Award for fiction, said that people of different cultures represent "a universe of little islands connected by visions and dreams." That metaphor is especially appropriate when you realize that one of the primary ways that these culturally disparate islands can be connected is through literature, which represents the visions and dreams of these respective communities. Unfortunately, there are still too many boundaries, both national/political and mental/spiritual between cultures. One of the tasks facing the professional working with Latino children is to construct bridges between these "little islands." The poet Naomi Shihab Nye has said, "We have no borders when we read" (7). Literature can be the key to forging connections between teachers/librarians and children of different national origins, and between the children themselves. To make these connections, the professional must have what D. Bryan Stansfield calls "ethnic competence," which is a concept ". . . that includes knowledge and skills with cultural heritages and their values" (550). I would add to this that, besides developing an empathy for a culture that is not your own, ethnic competence means an ability to go beyond an "us vs. them" mentality and to appreciate the universal qualities of humanity that transcend national origin. I realize that many readers of this book are already working in Latino neighborhoods and are well aware of the cultural issues surrounding the children they serve. There are also many Latino teachers and librarians who have firsthand cultural competence. My goal is to convey, from the point of view of someone who has spent a great deal of time with Latino children, some cultural observations which others might find helpful.

POPULATION ESTIMATES OF THE LATINO COMMUNITY

It has been frequently noted that Latinos are the fastest growing ethnic group in the United States, increasing by 50 percent between 1990 and 2000, with a purchasing power of more than $590 billion a year (Andrade 1–2). In 2005 the U.S. Census Bureau announced that Texas had become the fourth "majority minority" state, along with Hawaii, California, and New Mexico. Reaching this milestone was primarily due to the growth in the Latino population in Texas. There are five states, including Arizona and New York, that have more than 40 percent minority population, and are set to become majority minority states in the not-too-distant future (Bernstein 1990). The two factors that contribute to the Latino increase are the immigration rate and a birth rate higher than the rest of the population.

In fact, the birth rate for Latinos is a major reason for professional librarians to examine and expand their services to Latino children. A recent article from the *Washington Post* indicates that Latinos represented 49 percent of the population growth in the United States between 2004 and 2005. Seventy percent of this growth is accounted for by children younger than five years. This is a preview of a definite demographic shift that will have significant implications for public and school libraries (Cohn and Barhampour 2006).

While the Latino population continues to be centered in California, Texas, and New York, there is an increasing dispersion throughout the United States. Yolanda J. Cuesta writes about what this means for teachers and librarians: "Many states not known previously for significant concentrations of Hispanics, including Alaska, Hawaii, Idaho, Maine, Massachusetts, Nevada, New Hampshire, Oregon, Rhode Island, South Carolina, Vermont, and Washington, showed population growth exceeding 100 percent. This dispersion has serious implications for librarians. We can no longer view services to the Spanish-speaking population as a concern of libraries only within specific geographic areas" (26).

Latinos now make up an estimated 5 percent of the population of North Carolina. The Latino population in the state capitol, Charlotte, alone numbers more than 50,000 (Mildenberg 2006). Latinos now number an estimated 30,000, and these immigrants come not only from Mexico, but also from El Salvador, the Dominican Republic, Guatemala, and Columbia (Sámano 2004). As the Latino population grows, so does the need for culturally sensitive library services to Latino children. In the past, the term Latino has been used to refer to Spanish-speaking people. Lately, the term Latino has come into favor as more accurately describing this community, and will be used throughout this manual, with the exception of quotations in which the term "Hispanic" is used.

WHO IS THE LATINO CHILD?

The key word in attempting to understand the Latino child is diversity. There are cultural differences as well as differences in language. As you look over a group of children during storytime, you might see children who have recently arrived from any number of countries with little or no knowledge of the English language. Next to them may be a family who speak English better than Spanish—perhaps the grandparents immigrated here, but the parents grew up in an English-language environment, and the child may speak no Spanish at all. Behind them could be a family who immigrated a few years ago. The parents speak no English, but the children have learned English in the public schools and are fully bilingual. Each of these children has a different socioeconomic status and brings a particular set of cultural values from his or her native land, or in the case of a child born here, the Latino-American culture. For professionals to begin forming bridges between themselves and these children, and to facilitate bridges being built between the children themselves, it is important to understand their cultures, and the differences and similarities between those cultures. The differences are manifested primarily through language variations and issues relating to national origin.

LANGUAGE VARIATIONS

Latino peoples are linked and separated by the Spanish language. Spanish is now one of the world's major languages, spoken by more than 400 million people, yet there is constant disagreement on what constitutes "bona fide" Spanish (Preston 1997, 1A, 12A). The differences in spoken and written Spanish from country to country and within regions can be compared to the disparity between the English spoken in England and that spoken in North America and the accents and slang of regional speech found across the United States. All Spanish traces its roots to Castilian, which originated in the Provence of Castilla in northern Spain. Since many of the colonists, conquistadors, and sailors who settled in Latin America during the sixteenth and seventeenth centuries came from the southern part of Spain, they brought with them the grammar and pronunciation spoken in that region of Spain during that time period. Over time hundreds of Indian words such as *chocolate* and *chile* entered the Spanish vocabulary, especially in countries with large Indian populations such as Bolivia, Ecuador, Peru, Bolivia, Guatemala, and Mexico. It is important to note that the existence of separate and distinct Indian languages accounts for wide variations in word meanings in different parts of Latin America. Latinos have learned to celebrate these language differences and generally have little trouble understanding each other. The common thread, as noted in an article about Spanish personal names by Roberto Cabello-Argandoña, is that "Virtually all Hispanic Americans (81 percent) believe that Spanish language is the aspect of their tradition that is most important to preserve" (1983, 3). Many cultural differences are reflected in the use of language, and maintaining the language in a new country helps maintain a sense of identity.

To understand how language differences translate into cultural differences we need to understand how language reflects culture. Mexican culture, for example, has a laid back attitude as far as the concept of time is concerned. The Spanish word *ahora* is translated as "now." In the American culture which is ruled by the clock, we would understand it to mean this exact moment in time. In Mexican culture, the concept more loosely means "today." Their scope of time is much broader. In order to specify this exact moment in time, you would say *ahora mismo* or "right now."

Another example found in Mexican culture is a certain fatalism as reflected in a common response to requests for commitments. If I'm asking someone if they will be able to make it to a particular program, the response might very well be "Si Dios quiere" or "If God wills it." This reflects a heightened awareness in the culture of the uncertainty of life, and the inevitability of death. In Tómas Rivera's novel . . . *y no se lo trago la tierra* (*And the Earth Did Not*

Part) he comments that "Sólo la muerte nos trae el descanso a nosotros" or "Only death brings us rest" (46).

Cultural attitudes toward public libraries manifest themselves through language as well. Since there is no strong tradition of free public library service in many Latin American countries, a Latino patron will likely refer to the public library as a *librería* which refers to a bookstore instead of *biblioteca* which refers to a library. This is often an obstacle to be overcome in serving these patrons. In some cases it will be necessary for you to make them aware of your services and that most public library services are of no cost to the patrons. Other cultural attitudes which may create barriers include a notion that the public library is designed solely for the use of children, or that it is an ". . . artificial service structure designed for someone else" (Stansfield, 550). These barriers can be overcome through outreach into the Latino community by dedicated and enthusiastic librarians who can articulate what the library is and how it is relevant.

Once you have been among Spanish-speakers for a period of time, it is possible to pick up on differences in speech between nationalities. Latinos themselves are aware of these differences and each national group insists in a spirit of friendly rivalry that theirs is the correct way of speaking. Regionalism does not have to become a barrier in building bridges. Alma Flor Ada has said, "The children can learn regionalisms from the different Latin American countries and they should have the opportunity to get exposed to a multitude of cultures that constitute their *patria grande*" (Aguirre, 287). For the librarian, this raises the issues of the type of Spanish language used in books and of the quality of translations. These issues will be addressed in Chapter 5 on collection development.

NATIONAL ORIGINS

It is important to immediately separate ourselves from negative stereotypes when discussing issues of national origin. One of the most commonly observed is the generalization that all people of Latino origin are from Mexico, or that "Mexican" refers to all Latinos. This could not be farther from the truth. Recognizing the diversity represented in national origin is extremely important when working with Latino children. There are in fact some major differences in Latino cultures. A common thread in the history of Mexico and Central and Latin America is the story of native peoples conquered by the Spanish and then assimilated with them. This has led to populations that are of mixed origin living alongside those native peoples who managed to maintain their identity. Countries such as Argentina and Uruguay exhibit a great deal of European influence, whereas countries such as Guatemala,

Bolivia, and Peru are shaped more by Indian influences. The native cultures continue to thrive in these countries. Mexican culture is a mixture of Spanish and Indian (Stansfield, 549). I will focus primarily on the three most prominent Latino cultures in the United States: Mexican, Puerto Rican, and Cuban.

Mexican Culture

Naomi Shahib Nye said Mexico ". . . has always been a country of spirit, a country where magic feels close and possible, a country of passionate color and deep ties" (7). You can probably trace the genesis of much of Mexican culture to its roots in the Spanish culture brought to the new world by the conquistadors. Whatever you may think of the morality of this conquest, the results cannot be changed and have indelibly stamped the culture. This conquest left Mexico as a racially mixed country, with native European Spaniards, Mexican-born Spaniards, people with Indian and Spanish blood, and the Indians. This racial mixture created societal classes which remain in Mexico to this day and are a continuing source of tension. The native Indian peoples still exist on the lowest tier of society. This is also a fusion of cultures which creates what Isabel Schon has called a "marvelous richness" of heritage (*Bicultural Heritage* 92).

Politics is yet another source of tension. The continuing effects of the Mexican Revolution are still felt. The Mexican Revolution was about a call for social justice and the toppling of dictatorial regimes and bringing democracy to the country. The Institutional Revolutionary Party, or PRI, came about as a group embodying the revolution's call for social justice. As the PRI became the governing party to the exclusion of any opposition, the specter of what caused the revolution in the first place has always been present. The continuing calls for social justice in Mexico are made in the name of the revolution.

As we realize how the trajectory of Mexican history is primarily a reaction to the conquistadors, it is important to remember that the conquistadors were, in fact, involved in a primarily religious crusade. The Catholic religion that they brought with them has been and continues to be an abiding influence on the culture of the Mexican people. Given a new set of deities that they were commanded by the Spanish invaders to accept, the Indian people of Mexico managed to synchronize them with their native religion, creating a unique blend of Christian faith and Indian practice.

The more recent history of Mexico continues to reflect the struggle between classes and, particularly, the extreme poverty of the indigenous Indian peoples. It is this very poverty that has been the primary motivating factor encouraging emigration, both legal and illegal, to the United States. Much of this immigration has been young males trying to find work in order to send money back to their families. They move often, to follow the flow of seasonal work or to stay ahead of immigration officials. The fact that they are willing to do manual labor, such as agricultural work, for low wages, has made it difficult for the tide of immigration to be halted. Many companies whose bottom line would be severely affected without the cheap labor costs afforded by these workers tacitly make it possible for illegal immigration to continue.

The issues of Indian heritage and immigration continue to resonate in literature created by Latinos. A children's book that beautifully demonstrates the mixture of religion and culture is *Spirit Child: A Story of the Nativity* (Morrow 1984), translated by John Bierhorst from a manuscript written by Aztec poets. In reading this lovely story you can feel the rhythms and poetry of Aztec speech. Barbara Cooney has illustrated the story as taking place completely within a native Aztec frame of reference, demonstrating visually how the Christian story and the Aztec culture become mixed together. While the story follows closely the biblical account, it adds details that are clearly brought from Aztec culture. The place where the devil takes people who follow him is referred to as the "Dead Land" where "there is nothing but hunger and arguments all the time, and sickness, and hard work." Barbara Cooney's accompanying illustration shows a scene of dancing skeletons straight out of a Day of the Dead celebration.

In Victor Martinez's autobiographical National Book Award–winning novel, *Parrot in the Oven: Mi Vida* (HarperCollins 1996), he speaks of the sense of heritage that had been instilled in him as a child of migrant farm workers in Fresno, California, and the pride that can be derived from that heritage: "We were descendants of Indians blessed with a color that was as necessary as dirt to the earth, as important as the sun to all the trees. We had treasures buried deep inside our blood, hidden treasures we hardly knew existed" (119). The autobiographical character that Martinez creates, Manuel Hernandez, gets this sense of heritage and culturally defining stories from people like his grandfather, an immigrant whose only memory at the end of his life was ". . . of the desert he crossed to plant his foot in this country" (81).

Cuban, Puerto Rican, and Other Latino Cultures

Much of the story of Cuba and Puerto Rico is similar to that of Mexico—a story of domination by and subsequent revolution against the Spanish government. Both these countries were conquered and colonized by Spain, beginning with the discovery of Puerto Rico, then called *Boriquén* by Christopher Columbus. (*Boriqua* is still a name which some Puerto Ricans use to refer to each other, as well as to the island itself.) In both countries there were several revolts against the Spanish regime during the 1800s. The Puerto Rican revolution began in 1868 when Dr. Ramón Emeterio Betances organized a rebellion against the Spaniards, which was put down. In the case of Cuba, a rebellion also began the same year, 1868, and the rebels were harder to defeat. A series of revolts continued until 1898 when Spain's heavy-handed attempts to quell the unrest led to the sinking of the USS *Maine*, which in turn led to the four-month Spanish-American War. This conflict ended with a treaty that made Cuba and Puerto Rico territories of the United States.

Puerto Rico has, in the ensuing years, gained a great deal of independence though it is still in many ways under the control of the U.S. government. Cuba, on the other hand, after becoming independent from American control in 1933, experienced a series of dictators and revolutions that ended with the takeover of the government by Fidel Castro in 1959. Castro's Communist government and the economic conditions, as well as the political repression it created, have been the motivating factor for the large numbers of Cuban immigrants to the United States; they have settled primarily in the Miami, Florida, area, as well as in New York and New Jersey. With an area known as Little Havana, Miami is the main base for Cuban political exiles actively seeking the end of Castro's rule. While the immigration from Cuba was due primarily to the political climate, immigration from Puerto Rico was motivated by economic conditions on the island; furthermore, its ties to the United States make immigration easy.

Beyond Cuban and Puerto Rican, the cultures a librarian or teacher working with Latino children is most likely to encounter are those from Central American countries that were part of Mexico until the 1800s. Because of this, the cultural traditions are similar. These countries, particularly Guatemala and El Salvador, have been rife with political strife and difficult economic conditions. Different ideological factions battle for control of the governments, and innocent citizens, particularly children, are caught in the crossfire. Because of their geographical proximity to Mexico, people from Honduras, El Salvador, and Guatemala can easily cross their own borders to escape this turbulence and follow the path that leads to the United States. Generally, immigration has occurred when either political or economic conditions have made it necessary for people to seek a new situation. For example, there was a surge of immigration from El Salvador during the early 1980s, because of the civil war in that country: primarily young men trying to escape conscription into the army.

The terror of political oppression is well portrayed in Frances Temple's book, *Grab Hands and Run* (HarperCollins 1993), in which a young boy, Felipe, has nightmares about the soldiers coming to his village, calling everyone out of their homes, and forcing them to put their hands over their heads (14). Death is an everyday occurrence, just something taken for granted. As Felipe is driving with his brother and sister down a dirt road, they see something that first appears to be a log, but upon closer inspection it turns out to be the body of a woman. Their driver explains in a matter-of-fact tone that "The military, the *escuadrones*, throw people they've killed in the road to make it look like a traffic accident . . . You'll see more" (43). Children who grow up in these situations obviously have a maturity of experience that has to be taken into account as we plan programs and share literature with them.

CHICANO AND AMERICAN LATINO CULTURES

All of this turbulent history has filled the United States with deep-rooted Latino influences. Many city and place names, particularly in the border states of California, New Mexico, Arizona, and Texas, as well as in Florida and New York, reflect Latino origin. At least 400 Spanish words such as "rodeo," "patio" and "plaza" have entered the English vocabulary (De Varona xvii). Latin culture has always been a part of the United States. California, Nevada, Utah, Arizona, New Mexico, Texas, and parts of Colorado, Kansas, and Oklahoma were once part of Mexico. There have been Spanish-speaking residents in the United States since the 1500s. Spanish settlements, whose remnants can be seen in the remaining missions, dot areas like San Antonio and the Pacific coast. Latino culture is an essential part of the heritage of all Americans.

Beyond history, the presence of Latinos in this country has given rise to cultures that have come, not from a blending of Spanish and Indian culture, but from a combination of Latino and North American cultures. Many groups identify themselves through names that reflect their national heritage. Tejano refers to Mexicans of Texan descent. Puerto Ricans born in New York refer to themselves as Nuyoricans. Chicano is someone of Mexican descent, born in America. The term Chicano carries with it overtones of radicalism and activism associated with the Chicano movement that was born in the ferment of the 1960s. This movement gave rise to some wonderful literature and theatre by authors such as Tomás Rivera, Rudolfo Anaya, and Rolando Hinojosa.

LATINO HOLIDAYS AND TRADITIONS

One of the most important expressions of a country's culture is its holidays and traditions. The most well known Latino holidays in the United States are of Mexican origin. They reflect all of the influences we have talked about before—Spanish, Indian, and Catholic.

Major Holiday Celebrations

CINCO DE MAYO

May 5th is a celebration of the battle of Puebla in 1862. The forces of Napoleon III had advanced on this small Mexican town on their way to Mexico City to support a French effort to establish a monarchy in Mexico. They did not recognize the government of Benito Juarez. The French forces believed they would have an easy march from the port city of Veracruz to Mexico City. In this decisive conflict, the outnumbered Mexican army heroically defeated the French army force led by veteran General Charles Ferdinand Latrille de Lorencz.

The victory halted the French advance and provided a rallying point for the Mexican people to continue fighting for their freedom. *El Cinco de Mayo* is now celebrated as an official holiday in Mexico with festivals, military parades, and official gatherings of elite social and political leaders. In the United States, it is commemorated less formally. Most communities with a large Latino population have celebrations that might include community parades, mariachi bands, or folkloric dancers. Schools in the U.S. generally use this opportunity for teaching units on Mexico. This is the most popular Latino holiday, even if there are many who would be hard pressed to tell you exactly what it commemorates. Regardless, it provides Latinos with the opportunity to touch base with their cultural heritage.

DÍA DE INDEPENDENCIA

Mexicans celebrate September 16 as the day they began to gain their independence from the Spaniards. This is the day that Father Miguel Hidalgo y Castillo rang the bell of his little church in Dolores, Mexico, and spoke to his congregation, asking them to oppose of Spanish rule. He decried the oppressive government of the Spaniards, and appealed to their sense of pride in what was indigenously Mexican. "¡*Viva la Virgen de Guadalupe!*" he cried, "¡*Viva México!*" This "*grito de Dolores*" or "cry from Dolores" was the beginning of Mexico's war to win its independence. It is celebrated like *Cinco de Mayo*, with patriotic orations, parades, and picnics. The importance of this date has led the celebration of Hispanic Heritage Month in the United States (from September 15th through October 15th). These celebrations, September 16 and *Cinco de Mayo*, are both related to political events and underscore the huge impact that the fight against Spanish rule had on Mexican culture.

DÍA DE LOS MUERTOS

The Day of the Dead is actually a two-day celebration, November 1 and 2, which incorporates the Catholic All Saints' Day along with a particularly

Mexican sensibility about death. Over this period, altars are created in homes with pictures and favorite effects of departed loved ones. Food is placed on the altar, and is also included in the offering that is taken to the cemeteries. Food and other items are left on the tombs of the departed so that their spirits can partake. The decoration of graves is primary to this celebration.

The Mexican Day of the Dead is marked with unique artistic and culinary creations. The major motif is the skeleton. Edible skulls are created from sugar. These are not viewed as morbid—a little girl preparing to do a Day of the Dead art project in a library program asked if she could draw her grandfather's skeleton. During the same program, a mother expressed her lament that the day was no longer celebrated as it had once been in Mexico. Mexicans in the United States who no longer have access to their family cemeteries in Mexico often express dissatisfaction and disappointment in the holiday and its less spiritual U.S. transformation. The good news is that this holiday seems to be growing in popularity in the United States, as the influence of Latino culture grows. San Antonio is now noted for its observances, and there are other major celebrations in Chicago and Los Angeles (Schwiesow 1996, 110).

LAS POSADAS

The Christmas season is marked by nightly processions from December 16 to December 24. These processions reenact the journey of Mary and Joseph into Bethlehem. Groups go from house to house carrying candles, asking for lodging. As they go from place to place, they will sing the traditional songs of Las Posadas. At each house they will be told that there is no room. This pattern continues until they are welcomed into a house where a party is held. The party will traditionally include breaking a piñata, although the use of a piñata is not limited to Christmas time. Tamales are a chore to make so they are often reserved for special occasions, usually for Christmas Eve. They might be accompanied by *buñuelos*, fried flour tortillas sprinkled with cinnamon. Midnight on Christmas Eve is the magic hour when presents are opened. An excellent recounting of this traditional celebration can be found in Marie Hall Ets' Caldecott-winner *12 Days Before Christmas*.

In Mexico, the Christmas season is also celebrated with *Pastorelas*, plays which describe the journeys of pilgrims or shepherds to pay homage to the Christ child. These journeys are almost always delayed or made difficult by devils and other hindrances. In a story about the *Pastorelas* done for National Public Radio, reporter David Welna noted that at the beginning of the production he saw, the narrator pointed out that this play was a celebration of

Indian and Spanish cultures, highlighting again how this sense of bi-culturalism is at the heart of the Mexican soul.

In Latin cultures, Christmas Day is traditionally celebrated as a religious holiday. The day for presents, however, in many Latino cultures, particularly those of the Caribbean and Puerto Rico, is January 6th, *Día de los Reyes* or Day of the Kings. In Christian tradition, this is the day that the Three Kings arrived at the stable. Instead of Santa, the Three Kings bring presents to the children. Children may put their shoes out to provide a receptacle for treats. In Mexico, families might prepare a special bread filled with almonds, coins, or a doll representing the baby Jesus. Cubans might eat roast pig, black beans, and rice.

Día de los Niños/Día de los Libros: April 30th is celebrated as *Día de los Niños* (Day of the Child/Day of Books) in Mexico, as part of the United Nations Children's Day observance. (Some Latin countries, such as El Salvador, celebrate this event on October 1 instead of April 30, but the intent is the same: to celebrate children and childhood). Pat Mora, poet and children's book author, has been the moving force to create this tradition in the United States, and to create a focus on literacy by calling it *Día de los Niños/Día de los Libros* (Day of the Child: Day of the Book). The year 2006 marks the tenth anniversary of the *Día* celebration in the U.S. In 2006 the Association for Library Service to Children (ALSC) became the home for the *Día* celebration. More information and a toolkit can be found at the official Web site: http://www.ala.org/ala/alsc/projectspartners/DiaFactSheet.htm.

Those who work with Latino children and their families can celebrate *Día de los Niños/Día de los Libros* and promote programs and activities that support children, books, and literacy. Some excellent suggestions for celebrating this day, along with a letter from and poem by Pat Mora can be found on the Texas State Library Web site: http://www.tsl.state.tx.us/ld/projects/ninos/index.html. Other Web sites devoted to *Día*:

REFORMA (National Association to Promote Library and Information Services to Latinos and the Spanish-Speaking)
http://reforma.org/resources/ninos/dia.html
REFORMA sponsors the Estela and Raúl Mora Award established by Pat Mora in honor of her parents, and given annually to the library that sponsors the most exemplary program celebrating *Día*.
El Paso Public Library
http://www.elpasotexas.gov/kidszone/kidszone_library/diadelosninos/diadelosninos.htm

QUINCEÑERA

Perhaps the most important day in the life of a Mexican girl is her fifteenth birthday. This is the day that she becomes a woman and can start dating. The day is generally marked by attendance at Mass and a huge party. This is a once-in-a-lifetime event and often no expense is spared by the parents. The girl celebrating her quinceñera is most often accompanied by fourteen *madrinas* (bridesmaids) and their escorts. The madrinas all have matching dresses, and the celebrant wears a white dress and a crown. There is dancing and food.

Each of these holidays and traditions have deep roots in the political and religious history of the countries and say much about the souls of the Latin people. Understanding the significance of these days can open up a window into understanding their hopes and dreams.

FINDING COMMON CULTURAL GROUND

I have observed that there are also some general cultural traits that bridge national and language barriers. Generally, Latin people exhibit a courteousness and graciousness, often not seen in other cultures. They will feed you, even at times giving up their own food to be gracious. The warm hospitality of the Latin people is extremely notable. If you were to visit someone's home, you might be told, "*Esta es su casa*" (This is your house), or "*Mi casa es su casa*" (My home is your home). In general, as Suzanne Romaine reports, it can be said that "Spanish statements are personalized while English reflects more distance" (150). This cultural conditioning is likely to make a Latino child more shy and reserved. While this is not a universal generalization, in many cases both Latino adults and children are more passive in terms of accepting whatever vicissitudes they may face. This same trait produces a tendency to avoid confrontation and to accept criticism.

The Extended Family

The concept of extended family is extremely important to understanding Latino culture. There is general agreement that "The extended Mexican and Mexican-American family is a constant source of support and encouragement to all its members" (*A Bicultural Heritage* 1978, 48). In working within Latino communities, programs that involve the entire family are the most successful. Most Latino parents need a program to which they can bring siblings of different ages. Single caregiver/single child programs are rarely successful because they are not an option for Latino parents with larger families. The overriding concern is always for their children and their children's education.

Practical programming ideas that involve families are discussed in the chapter on programs.

BILINGUALISM, CULTURE, AND LANGUAGE

I have made the point that culture cannot be understood except as expressed through language. In North America, the language spoken by much of the Latino population has become a mixture of Spanish and English, and within the Latino population there is a great difference in the level of competence with one or the other language. Bilingualism has become a hot button at the heart of controversies such as "English-only" or "English as the official language of the United States" as opposed to those who favor bilingual education, and believe "that developing literacy in the first language can make a substantial contribution to literacy development in the second language" (Schon 1978, 393). There has been a great deal of argument and discussion in the professional literature, regarding the relative merit of bilingual education in the schools. It is difficult to keep the political issues separate from the purely linguistic issues. While it is not within the scope of this manual to provide a complete overview of these arguments, a few comments seem necessary.

Even within the debate over bilingualism, there is disagreement as to the goals of bilingual education. Sonia Nieto has stated that "The commonly accepted objectives of bilingual education in the United States are fairly straightforward: to develop skills in English *while at the same time* learning content through the native language" (1986, 5). Roberto Cabello-Argandoña notes that if content is not taught at the same time as the new language, children ". . . find themselves far behind their classmates and unable to catch up. Gradually, a slow learner group develops in most schools in Hispanic neighborhoods teaching Spanish-speaking children, followed by social stigma and poor ethnic identity. Knowledge of Spanish, the mother-tongue, is not seen as an asset but rather as a liability for those children" (1983, 8). On one side is the idea that bilingual education should be truly bilingual. That is, both languages should be used throughout a student's education. This is known as the "maintenance" approach (Nieto 6).

The other point of view is that bilingual education is temporary, that it should only be used until a student is fluent in English. This, Nieto says, is the "transitional" method (6). This second view of bilingual education is described, interestingly enough, using the same bridge metaphor as author Judith Ortiz Cofer used. As Nieto says, "In effect, it is much like using their language as a bridge—and then burning the bridge" (6). Transitional programs try to assimilate students into a situation where English is spoken exclusively. The idea is that bilingualism can be used to build bridges to another language and culture, without burning the bridge behind you. Nieto speaks of classrooms where English and Spanish are used interchangeably, and where students, regardless of cultural background, learn cultural sensitivity, and where Latino students feel less isolated (6). Lori Carlson has put it eloquently: "Speaking more than one language, I have found, enriches life, broadens perspective, extends horizons of opportunity, and makes us more sensitive to nuance, difference, contrast" (1994, xiv).

What bilingualism creates is a new language that goes back and forth between Spanish and English, or that creates new words that are a mixture of both languages. In Texas for example, it is called Tex-Mex. Sometimes it is manifest in the Latinization of an English word such as a truck being referred to as a *troque* instead of the standard Spanish *camion*. The bilingual person might *parquear* (park) instead of *estacionar* his *troque*. As explained by Suzanne Romaine, this is a classic example of borrowing verbs from one language and making them fit another. She says "Borrowed verbs are often slotted into the most common verb class of the language. Spanish, for example, puts loanwords into the class of verbs ending in *ear* (e.g., *checkear*—to check)" (64). This bilingualism can also be made manifest in sentences spoken in English with a few Spanish words thrown in, or the other way around. Listen to the radio in a place like San Antonio, and you might hear something like "*La Fabulosa*, the station with the most tejano music, *para ustedes!*"

Sonia Nieto says that "because of the interrelationship of language and culture, students' cultural heritage is an equally important aspect of bilingual education" (1986, 5). By encouraging rather than discouraging bilingualism, a much richer culture develops, through a *mezcla* or mixture of cultures. The author Alma Flor Ada, born in Cuba, has devoted much time to her concern that Spanish not disappear from the "everyday life" of Latino children (Aguirre 1986, 287). Ada speaks of how, after coming to this country, she tried to speak to Latino children in Spanish. They refused to speak to her in that language, and denied they even knew it (287). I have seen a similar attitude in young library patrons who can speak Spanish fluently, but prefer to speak English. Sometimes it seems that Spanish becomes something that is only part of their insular family life and not a part of their larger social interaction outside the family. A bilingual child can "switch codes" or go back and forth between languages and ". . . step out of one language system and . . . view it in the perspective of the other" (Romaine 1989, 205). Some of the issues a bilingual child faces are very clearly expressed in the book *Pepita Talks Twice* by Ofelia Dumas Lachtman, a daughter of Mexican immigrants. In the story, Pepita gets tired of being the one who has to translate because she is bilingual. She feels like she has to say everything twice, and so she refuses to speak Spanish. She even begins calling her dog, *Lobo*, by the English equivalent, Wolf. It is only when Lobo does not respond to his English name in a perilous situation that Pepita realizes the important part that the Spanish language plays in her identity. It is interesting how much language and names play a role in the personal identity of Latino children.

A child's identity as a Latin American speaking English as his or her primary language is much easier to develop if the child is born in this country. Alma Flor Ada speaks eloquently to the loss of cultural identity in her story *My Name Is María Isabel*. In this short novella, she writes of a young girl from Puerto Rico. On her first day of school in the United States she is told that since there are already two Marías in her class, that she will be called Mary López. María Isabel does not recognize herself in this "strange new name" (1993, 12). She has always loved her name because she was named for her father's mother and for her Puerto Rican grandmother. María's desire to regain her identity is poignantly expressed in a paragraph she writes for her teacher on the theme, "My Greatest Wish":

> . . . I think my greatest wish is to be called María Isabel Salazar López. When that was my name, I felt proud of being named María like my papa's mother, and Isabel like my Grandmother Chabela. She is saving money so that I can study and not have to spend my whole life in a kitchen like her. I was Salazar like my papa and my Grandpa Antonio, and López, like my Grandfather Manuel. I never knew him but he could really tell stories. I know because my mother told me.
>
> If I was called María Isabel Salazar López, I could listen better in class because it's easier to hear than Mary López. (49–51)

WHAT DOES THIS MEAN FOR THE PRACTICING PROFESSIONAL?

The primary goal of bilingual programming can be found in this statement by Elaine Golen: "Bilingual storytimes and puppet shows for children of various ages improve their mastery of their own languages as well as ties to their culture through the use of folklore, song and rhyme. The children will eventually learn English in school bilingual education programs and from their peers, but the function of library programming and collections is to help children become integrated into American society while enabling them to maintain cultural ties with their ethnic group" (1985, 94). So often the needs of the Latino community focus on immediate survival issues such as food, shelter, jobs, and learning to speak English that it is difficult to get Latino parents to support bilingual storytimes or other programs which focus on literature and art, which are perceived as nonessential to survival. The challenge in schools and libraries is to provide opportunities to reinforce the cultural heritage of children, to instill a love and familiarity with literature that is sometimes difficult to achieve for a bilingual child struggling to read and communicate in two languages, and to bring families closer together in the process. Hopefully, the information presented here will give professionals empathy for the Latino child, and the cultural background necessary to locate appropriate materials for whatever group they are working with, as well as planning programs that mesh with the culture and lifestyle of the community being served.

FURTHER READINGS

Carlson, Lori, ed. *Cool Salsa: Bilingual Poems on Growing Up Latino in the United States.* New York: Holt, 1994.

Cockroft, James D. *Latinos in the Making of the United States.* The Hispanic Experience in the Americas Series. New York: Watts, 1995.

Culturegrams: The Nations Around Us. Volume 1: The Americas and Europe. Provo, Utah: David M. Kennedy Center for International Studies, Brigham Young University, 1996.

De Varona, Frank. *Latino Literacy: The Complete Guide to Our Hispanic History and Culture.* New York: Holt, 1996.

Meltzer, Milton. *The Hispanic Americans.* New York: Crowell, 1982.

WORKS CITED

Ada, Alma Flor. *My Name Is Maria Isabel.* Trans. Ana M. Cero. New York: Atheneum, 1993.

Aguirre, Rosainés. "The Dragons Came on a Hot Summer Day: A Word With Alma Flor Ada." *Lector* 3, no. 6, 1989: 287.

Andrade, Juan. "Waking the Giant." *Profiles in Diversity Journal.* September 2003. March 19, 2006. http://www.diversityatwork.com/articles/andrade.pdf

Bernstein, Robert. "Texas Becomes Nation's Newest 'Majority-Minority' State Census Bureau Announces." *Newsroom*, March 19, 2006. U.S. Census Bureau, 2005. http://www.census.gov/Press-Release/www/releases/archives/population/005514.html.

Bierhorst, John. *Spirit Child: A Story of the Nativity.* Illustrated by Barbara Cooney. New York: William Morrow, 1984.

Cabello-Argandoña, Roberto, and Roberto Peter Haro. "General Considerations of Spanish Personal Names." *California Spanish Language Data Base*, 1983.

Cohn, D'Vera, and Tara Barhampar. "Of U.S. Children Under 5, Nearly Half Are Minorities." Washingtonpost.com. Accessed: Wednesday, May 10, 2006.

Cuesta, Yolanda J. "From Survival to Sophistication: Hispanic Needs = Library Needs." *Library Journal*, May 15, 1990: 26–28.

De Varona, Frank. *Latino Literacy: The Complete Guide to Our Hispanic History and Culture*. New York: Holt, 1996.

Golen, Elaine P. "Developing Library Collections to Serve New Immigrants." *School Library Journal*, October 1985: 93–97.

Lachtman, Doris. *Pepita Talks Twice*. Illustrated by Alex Prado de Lange. Houston: Piñata (Arte Público), 1995.

Martinez, Victor. *Parrot in the Oven: Mi Vida*. New York: HarperCollins, 1996.

Mildenberg, David. "UNC Expert: Latino Influx Poses Challenge." *Charlotte Business Journal*, April 1, 2004. Accessed 31 March 2006. http://char lotte.bizjournals.com/charlotte/stories/2004/03/29/daily39.html

Nieto, Sonia. "Equity in Education: The Case for Bilingual Education." In *Bulletin of the Council on Interracial Books for Children*. vol. 17, no. 3 and 4, 1986: 4–8.

Nye, Naomi Shihab. *The Tree Is Older Than You Are: A Bilingual Gathering of Poems and Stories from Mexico with Paintings by Mexican Artists*. New York: Simon and Schuster, 1995.

Preston, Julia. "Spain losing command of the king's Spanish." *Dallas Morning News*, April 20, 1997: 1A, 12A.

Rangel, Enrique. "Immigrants being lured to Alaska by tales of riches." *Dallas Morning News*, November 11, 1996: 10A.

Rivera, Tómas. *. . . y no se lo tragó la tierra* (. . . and the Earth did not Part). Houston: Piñata (Arte Público), 1996.

Romaine, Suzanne. *Bilingualism*. New York: Basil Blackwell, Inc., 1989.

Sámano, "Latinos in the 'Last Frontier.'" *Pacific News Services: News for the New America*, August 16, 2004. *Noticiero Semenal*, March 31, 2006. http://news.pacificnews.org/news/view_article.html?article_id=3961ae 152a6778b5ae475874b09182bd.

Schick, Frank L., and Renee Schick. *Statistical Handbook on U.S. Hispanics*. Oryx Press, 1991.

Schon, Isabel. *A Bicultural Heritage: Themes for the Exploration of Mexican and Mexican-American Culture in Books for Children and Adolescents*. Metuchen, NJ: Scarecrow Press, 1978.

———. "Latino Children's Books." In *Children's Books and Their Creators*, edited by Anita Silvey. Boston: Houghton Mifflin.

Schwiesow, Deirdre R. "A Growing Respect for the Day of the Dead." *USA Today*, November 1, 1996: 11D.

Stansfield, D. Bryan. "Serving Hispanic Person: The Cross-Cultural Border Experience at Fabens." *RQ* vol. 27 no. 4 (Summer 1988): 547–561.

Temple, Frances. *Grab Hands and Run.* New York: HarperCollins, 1993.

Welna, David. "Christmas Celebrations in Mexico." *Morning Edition Saturday*, NPR, December 21, 1996.

Chapter 2

How to Create a High-Quality Collection of Bilingual and Spanish-Language Children's Materials

The 100 essential titles highlighted in this manual form the foundation of a collection to serve Latino children, whether they are bilingual, Spanish-dominant or English-dominant. Many of the titles will be useful in programs for preschoolers, grade school children and young adults. Beyond that, they will provide all children with a framework from which they can understand the Latino culture. This chapter will provide a background for selection, with a brief outline of the history and current state of Spanish and bilingual book publishing for children. It will focus on the criteria used to develop the core collection. It will also discuss the basic criteria for the selection of Spanish-language and bilingual materials in general.

To provide a context from which to understand collection development issues for Latino children, it is important to have an understanding of the literature that is produced for this audience. Latino children's literature is as diverse in character and theme as Latino children are themselves. In general, children's literature reflects a certain shared humanity, regardless of the culture from which it comes. More specifically, children's books by Latino authors provide a panorama that is every bit as colorful as the sights and sounds of Spain, Mexico and other Latin American countries. In one sense, the history of children's literature for Spanish-speaking readers reflects the history of attitudes toward children in the various countries in which it originates. In the United States, it is also the history of the changing attitudes toward Latino culture and people.

OVERVIEW OF LATINO CHILDREN'S LITERATURE

The history of children's literature begins in Spain and has been duplicated in other Spanish-speaking countries. Up until the twentieth century, there was really no literature written specifically for young people. However, Spain is rich in traditional stories and folklore, which have always been a part of the lives of Spanish children. While not necessarily written or published for children, these stories have been told to children and been embraced by them. In addition to indigenous folklore, youngsters in Spain have grown up with translations of the world's folklore—the Grimms, Joseph Jacobs, Andersen, and Perrault. In this century, a large portion of the literature for children published in Spain has been European and American classics in Spanish translation. The development of a purely Spanish children's literature by Spaniards is fairly recent, only in the latter half of this century. Even then, some of this literature is extremely didactic, written for purely educational purposes, rather than as art. This comes out of a prevalent mindset that children's books are primarily of educational rather than recreational value.

There are, however, treasures to be found. Over the years a couple of works have stood out as being children's classics. Cervantes' *Don Quixote de la Mancha* is the touchstone of Spanish literature. Much of it is accessible to children, and the core list highlights some excellent newly illustrated and abridged editions for children. Don Quixote is actually part of a tradition that began with *Lazarillo de Tormes*, which is the first of the Spanish picaresque tales that would influence so much Spanish literature and folklore. This work by an unknown author, first published in 1553, portrays Lazarillo as a rogue. His adventures with a series of employers form the barest thread of what can hardly be called a plot. Lazarillo cheats some of his employers in his endless search for food and money. The priest thinks rats have gotten into his larder, when it is simply Lazarillo who is gnawing holes in the bread to make it appear that rats had found it.

Up until the 1970s, the majority of children's books (with some notable exceptions) that included Latino characters and settings were created by non-Latinos, who attempted to articulate the Latino experience to young children. The problem was that these books reflected the attitudes of an Anglo culture looking in on the Latino world. They promoted the separatism of cultures with the notion that somehow Anglos had to come in and rescue Latinos from their poverty, a condition that afflicted all Latinos in the United States.

In a perceptive article called "Paternalism and Assimilation in Books About Latinos," Opal Moore and Donnarae MacCann point out how most of these books reflect what they call "classic 'liberal' attitudes of the 1950s variety: that privileged whites have a moral obligation to uplift and improve the world's unfortunate" (1987, 99–100). These books propose ". . . condescending liberalism as a virtue" (100). The authors suggest, with some insight, that perhaps these attitudes, especially towards Latinos as reflected in children's literature, arise from the American experience of intervention in Latin America (157). America has intervened in the affairs of Latin American countries throughout this century, taking on what Moore and MacCann call a "managerial" role. Some of the books which they mention that fall into this category are: *Viva Chicano* (Dutton 1970) by Franck Bonham; *The Street of the Flower Boxes* (Coward McCann 1966) by Peggy Mann; *Maria Luisa* (Lippincott n.d.) by Madison Winifred; and *A Shadow Like a Leopard* (Harper 1981) by Myron Levoy.

The primary problem is that these books present Latino culture as inferior and quaint, and Latino people who are fine at heart but need to adopt superior Anglo ways. They sometimes present stereotypes as the norm. Especially when a book has a Latin American setting during this period, stereotyping can present problem. A book like *The Story of Pancho and the Bull With the Crooked Tail* (Macmillan 1942) by Berta and Elmer Hader shows a sombrero and tortilla view of Mexican village life. The story itself is delightful and shows a child succeeding where adults cannot. Hader drew from her personal experience living in Mexico, but the stereotyping mars an otherwise delightful story.

In the sixties, as cultural attitudes changed, awareness of the Latino community became more heightened. Cesar Chávez was fighting for the rights of migrant workers, and the Chicano movement was visible. During this same period there was certainly an emerging awareness of Latino culture in literature, even if many of the well-intentioned books, which reflected this concern, actually marginalized it. There were some books, however, which managed to transcend the prevalent social attitudes. Four Newbery award-winning books, published between 1953 and 1966, reflected and respected Latino life. Interestingly enough, these books received the award in pairs and they are all coming-of-age stories of young men. Ann Nolan Clark's *Secret of the Andes* in 1953 was followed the succeeding year by . . . *And Now Miguel* by Joseph Krumgold. Maia Wojciechowska won the Newbery medal in 1965 for *Shadow of a Bull*. The following year the award went to *I, Juan de Pareja* by Elizabeth Borton de Treviño. While none of these authors were Latino, they do show a respect for Latino life and culture that rose above condescension.

Secret of the Andes portrays the tension so prevalent in Latin American life between indigenous Indian peoples and the mixed-race Mestizos. The boy, Cusi, lives with the ancient llama herder, Chuto, in a valley hidden amidst the grandeur of the Andes mountains. He knows nothing of his parentage, or why he lives with Chuto. It is only after making a journey into the city of Cusco and learning of discrimination and then returning to his valley that he is given the secret of which he is to be the guardian for the rest of his life. . . . *And Now Miguel* is set in New Mexico and chronicles Miguel's desire to be considered a man and to be able to go with the other men into the mountains with the sheep. *Shadow of a Bull* is a story set in Spain about a young man who by his birthright is expected to be a great bullfighter, but who ends up following his own path. Each of these books paved the trail for the changing of attitudes by presenting children dealing with universal concerns.

Anglos were writing the majority of books dealing with Latino culture during the 1950s, 1960s and 1970s; however the situation has changed completely. In the 1990s the number of bilingual and Spanish-language children's books being published in the United States began to skyrocket. The explosion of Latino authors, such as Columbian Gabriel Garcia Marquez, onto the worldwide literary scene in the 1970s was known as the "boom." This would also be an apt term to apply to what has happened to Latino children's literature in the United States since 1990. This new "boom" is a result of several factors. Since publishing is driven by economics, one of the primary factors has been that with the increasing Latino population in the United States, publishers now see that it makes economic sense to reach out for this market. The demand for books that reflect our multicultural society has grown exponentially. As Isabel Schon notes in her article on "Latino Children's Books" in Anita Silvey's *Children's Books and Their Creators,*

> The statistics are difficult to ignore: The U.S. Hispanic-origin population is approaching 25 millions—an almost 60 percent increase from the 1980 census. The U.S. Department of Education estimates that Hispanic children make up 73 percent of the two million children in the United States who have limited proficiency in English. In addition, it is important to note that Spanish is now the second language in the Western world . . . These numbers, coupled with the fact that the field of children's literature in many Spanish-speaking countries is barely developing, may be the catalyst for the constantly improving selection in the quality and quantity of books for and about Hispanic children. (Schon 392–393)

The United States is now "the fifth-largest Spanish-language market in the word, after Spain, Mexico, Argentina and Columbia" (Taylor 1996, S3). Publishing for Latino children has grown by leaps and bounds. Starting in the early 1970s independents such as Harriet Rohmer of Children's Book Press began to fill the need that they saw for bilingual and multicultural books, which at that time was not being met by mainstream publishers. Children's Book Press began in 1975 and focuses on bilingual traditional and contemporary stories. Reflecting this growth, in the past six years many of the major U.S. publishing houses, such as HarperCollins, Farrar, Straus and Giroux, Penguin, and Scholastic have begun Spanish-language imprints. The Houston-based Arte Público Press has established a children's imprint, Piñata Books, and has become a major force in publishing English-language and bilingual fiction and picture books by Latino authors. They are engaged in a publishing project: Recovering the U.S. Hispanic Literary Heritage, which is bringing back into print some previously unknown classics by Latino writers. While these imprints have primarily been outlets for Spanish translations of books on their lists, the number of books by Latino authors being published has grown as well. Scholastic, Inc., recently acquired the distributor Lectorum Publications, which will certainly provide wider distribution and awareness for titles by Latino authors, especially those from outside the United States. Publishers in Latin American countries are thinking in terms of all Spanish-language markets, for instance, by publishing books in a generic Spanish that can be understood everywhere. When they bring out children's books, there should be an increasing presence of these books in the United States (Taylor S3). Latin American publishers, of course, are also acquiring rights to publish American books in Spanish, such as the *Goosebumps* series. Disney books are also extremely popular. For the librarian and teacher, this means that there will be an increasing number of American children's books available in Spanish translations.

Increased awareness of the need for children to see their own cultures in their literature has been another driving force behind the increasing numbers of U.S. Latino authors now publishing books for children. This is not to say that there aren't still problems. There could be much more Latino children's literature than there now is. Even with the current boom, the proportion of Latino writers to that of other groups is still low. Too many books celebrating Latinos' cultural heritage focus on the exotic celebrations and native costume, and perpetuate the stereotypes that have always plagued Latinos.

A WORD ABOUT PRIZES

There are numerous prizes awarded to Spanish-language children's books throughout the Spanish-speaking world. It is very difficult to keep track of all these awards—many are awarded by publishing houses rather than by organizations devoted to the promulgation of Spanish-language children's books. New awards sprout up, and others are discontinued. In general, you need to be careful in assigning any Spanish-language prize the same status as the Newbery and Caldecott awards in the U.S. Individual books need to be examined for their child appeal and quality. Selection decisions based solely on the fact that a book has won a prize can prove to be catastrophic. Many times these prizes are given for reasons other than child appeal, and focus on didactic or religious content.

The establishment of the Premio Lazarillo in Spain in 1958 has given increased visibility to children's literature in the Spanish language. This prize honors both authors and illustrators. It is probably the premier prize given for Spanish-language children's literature, and the closest in intent to the Newbery and Caldecott awards. A list of the winners of this award, as well as information on the qualifications and governing body, can be found in the Appendix. The other award considered most prestigious, and perhaps beginning to eclipse the Lazarillo in importance is the El Barco del Vapor prize given by the Fundación Santa María, which is a foundation of SM publishers. There are a number of other prizes for children's literature in Spain. Unlike U.S. literary prizes for children's literature, which come through the American Library Association or the National Book Foundation, publishers give many of these prizes. The best source for annual lists of all these prizes is the April issue of *CLIJ* (*Cuadernos de Literatura Infantil y Juvenil*), which is the premier magazine for information on Spanish-language children's literature. A subscription to *CLIJ* can be easily obtained through U.S. jobbers such as Ebsco.

Some of the important Spanish prizes:

Premio El Barco del Vapor given by the Fundación Santa María, which is a foundation of SM publishers;

Premios Nacionales (National Prizes) given by the Spanish Ministry of Culture;

Premio Ala Delta given by Editorial Edelvives Publishers;

Premio Destino Infantil Apel-les Mestres given by Ediciones Destino Publishers;

Premio Edebé given by Editorial Edebé Publishers;

Premio Internacional de Literatura Infantil y Juvenil Anaya given by Editorial Anaya Publishers and Ambito Cultural; and

Premio Leer es Vivir (To Read is to Live) given by Grupo Everest Publishers in collaboration with Ayuntamiento de León.

The now-defunct "Antoniorobles" prize was named after an important figure in Mexican children's literature. It was administered by the Asociación Mexicana Para el Fomento del Libro Infantil, the Mexican section of the International Board on Books for Young People (IBBY), and discontinued because of lack of funding. It honored outstanding children's books of Mexico. This organization now simply publishes an annual list of recommended books.

In 1993, the national Consortium of Latin American Studies Programs (CLASP) instituted the Américas Book Award for Children's and Young Adult Literature. This award recognized books in English or Spanish that "authentically and engagingly portray Latin America, the Caribbean, or Latinos in the United States" (www.uwm.edu). The value of the Américas Book Awards is that in addition to a winner, they also provide an extended list of recommended books on an annual basis.

In 1995 the College of Education at Texas State University—San Marcos established the Tomás Rivera Mexican Children's Book award. Celebrating the life of writer and University of California administrator Tomás Rivera, this award encourages the creation of books that "authentically reflect the lives of Mexican American children and young adults in the United States." The Web site for the Rivera award is www.education.txstate.edu/subpages/tomasrivera.

In August 1996, during the Conference of REFORMA in Austin, Texas, the first biennial Pura Belpré Awards for text and illustration were presented. Named after the first Latina storyteller at the New York Public Library and spearheaded by Oralia Garza de Cortez, then of the San Antonio Public Library, these awards fill a longtime need similar to the Coretta Scott King awards for African-American authors and illustrators in the United States. The purpose of the Pura Belpré award is to honor "Hispanic writers and illustrators whose works best exemplify authentic cultural experience in a work of literature for children and youth." As with other American Library Association division-sponsored children's book awards, recipients must be U.S. residents. Books must exhibit cultural content, or in other words be about something relevant to Latino culture. The establishment of this prize has now given Latino children's literature in the United States a credibility and impetus that it has never before experienced.

CRITERIA FOR SELECTING A CORE COLLECTION

Before addressing the specific criteria used to select the core collection presented in this book, it is important to examine the more basic question, which is what exactly represents a core collection? What are "core" titles? The best source that I have found that addresses this question is Carol Alabaster, in *Developing an Outstanding Core Collection: A Guide for Libraries*. I highly recommend this book for anyone doing collection development. In her book, Carol Alabaster defines core titles as books that people assume they will find in their library (10). This is as good a definition as you are likely to find. However, it is not entirely the case with the titles I recommend here. It will probably be the case that clients will not know about many of these books, much less expect that they can be found in their libraries. Another way of looking at "core" titles is to think of them as classics, or as Alabaster states as her premise: ". . . the essential classics that are read by generation after generation as well as the seminal works that shed light on the events of humankind" (9). There is a school of thought that a "core" title represents something of lasting value, and that it must be included in the collection. The difficulty becomes defining what represents a "classic," and there are many schools of thought on this issue. Alabaster throws another wrench into the works when she declares core titles must circulate. In other words, they need to be popular titles, titles that are in demand. Ultimately, because of the subjectivity involved in making such selections, one might argue against the idea of "core collections."

Certainly a "core" list is not set in stone, but is ever-changing. Books will go out of print. Outstanding new books will be published. But this does represent an attempt to define the best-loved and most useful titles that should be known and used by librarians working with Latino children. I recognize that my judgment is as subjective as anyone else's. For the purposes of this list, my definition of "core collection" is a middle ground between customer expectations and classic titles. These are books of note and lasting value, as well as books that will be useful to librarians and hopefully read and enjoyed by children and their parents and caregivers. The choice to select the 100 best titles for the core list was for the most part, but not entirely, arbitrary. This list was originally presented at the 2002 Public Library Association conference held in Phoenix, Arizona. In preparing that list I selected what I felt were the best and most useful books at that time. The list was fairly large, and so I indicated some titles that I felt were the most essential. When I looked at that smaller list, it turned out to be about 100 titles. With some additions and revisions, those are the titles that are in the core collection. At the end of this manual there is a list of additional titles, which represent some excellent books that would be useful in larger collections.

CREATING A CORE COLLECTION

The selection of the core collection presented in this book was based on the following suggested Core Collection Development Statement prepared for the Collection Development Policy of the Maricopa County Library District: "Spanish language and bilingual children's books will be actively collected for the communities that have a high Spanish-speaking population. All branches will collect a set of core Spanish and bilingual titles. Core titles will reflect classic authors and literature as well Latino folklore. Standard titles will also include basic titles to provide staff with resources for Spanish and bilingual storytimes and programs. Quality of translation, format, and binding quality will be considered in making selection decisions."

This statement was designed to provide a basic guide for the Maricopa County Library District, which serves a very diverse group of customers over a very large area. The basic idea was that our Spanish-speaking population is so large that all branches should have some titles in Spanish, but that those branches in more heavily populated Spanish-speaking communities would have expanded collections. Currently the Library District has fourteen libraries and a Bookmobile service that operates out of one of the large regional libraries. The communities served by the Library District are spread out. Two of the smallest communities, primarily Latino, are 95 miles, or an hour and a half drive, from the Library District's administrative offices. Spanish speakers are a factor in virtually all of the libraries. We look at our branches in three tiers: Large regional libraries, intermediate size branches, and small "baby" branches in many of the outlying areas of the community. At least five branches in the communities of Aguila, Gila Bend, El Mirage, Guadalupe and Surprise, Arizona, and to some extent Queen Creek serve primarily Spanish-speaking populations. In general, it is the smaller branches that have a higher density of Spanish-speaking customers.

Consequently, the need for collections in Spanish became very evident. At the beginning of this project, we looked at the average collection size of our three large regional libraries, which was estimated at 163,966 volumes. The average size of the Spanish collection was 1,628 volumes. One of our regional libraries, in an urban area of Phoenix, near a very large Latino community had 2,632 volumes in Spanish. Our two intermediate branches at the time had an average collection size of 40,517 volumes, with only 207 in Spanish. These two branches did not serve large Latino populations. Our eight smallest branches had an average collection size of 9,412 volumes with 735 in Spanish. It was clear that we could better serve our Latino customers, and especially the children.

Given the fact that our libraries serve very different, specific, and sometimes geographically isolated communities, the criteria for selecting the core list had to include a wide variety of materials. To meet the needs of the various communities served by the library district, I realized that I had to expand my list with titles that I had not previously focused on, specifically, some Spanish translations of picture books that originally appeared in English. I realized that many Mexican, Latin American and Spanish children's books treated universal themes, and had no specific cultural context for the Latino experience other than the Spanish language itself. Of course, language *is* culture, or at least it is the way people express their culture. Much of the Latino culture finds its expression in vivid and beautiful language. It was an experience at an international book fair in Guadalajara, Mexico, that solidified in my mind the need for Spanish-speaking children to hear stories in their own language. At the book fair, I attended a children's program that took place under a very large tent. Hundreds of Mexican schoolchildren in their uniforms had gathered to see a puppet show presented by a well-known puppeteer from Spain, which was the featured country at the book fair that year. One of the stories he presented with puppets I immediately recognized as the story "The Very Tall Mouse and the Very Short Mouse" from Arnold Lobel's book, *Mouse Tales*. I'm not sure if the puppeteer mentioned the source of the story, but it was an amazing moment watching him perform. As I watched, I realized that here was a Spanish puppeteer performing the work of an American author for Mexican children. His performance made the story seem like folklore, a tale for all cultures and all countries.

In creating this list, I was trying to include a number of different types of books. The following represents some specific selection criteria I used:

- Books in Spanish, bilingual books, translations of books that originally appeared in English, and books available only in English, but by Latino writers, with Latino cultural content would be included. Cultural content was not necessary for books in Spanish by Spanish, Latin American or Mexican writers.
- The books should have a special spark, something that sets them apart.
- Books that can be used with kids, have reader appeal, and have the potential to make an impact on children's lives.
- Books with songs and fingerplays, the "Mother Goose" stuff of Latino culture, as a basic collection for programming.
- Award-winning books, including the Pura Belpré award and the Américas Book Award.
- Latin American authors should be represented, including such authors as Alma Flor Ada, Francisco Alarcón, and Gary Soto.

- Well-known "classic" Spanish and Latin American writers should be represented. I've included at the end of the manual, a list of such "classic" books. I noticed in researching the in-print status that several of my old favorites had been reissued in new editions. The classic authors include such literary luminaries as Frederico García Lorca, Juan Ramon Jímenez, Gabriela Mistral, and Asun Balzoa.
- Best-loved titles, based on popularity with kids, should be included.
- Well-known picture book versions and collections of Latino folktales should be represented.
- Publishers who have pioneered in presenting bilingual books will be represented, such as Harriet Rohmer and her groundbreaking Children's Press.
- Important books that cover Latino festivals and cultural events.

The following is a list of the primary magazines, award lists and Web sites used to develop the core list. More information about these along with the many other collection development tools for Spanish-language materials can be found at the end of this manual.

Américas Book Award
Críticas magazine (now an online journal, *Críticas* is published monthly on the web with two print issues a year, in June and November)
CLIJ *Cuadernos de Literatura Infantil y Juvenil* Magazine
Editorial Ekare Publishers: www.ekare.com/
Pura Belpré Award
Spanish "Amazon.com": www.tematika.com.ar/ and www.tematika.com .mx/
Spanish Books in Print www.leer.nisc.com

UNIQUE STANDARDS FOR SELECTING SPANISH-LANGUAGE MATERIALS

General collection development policies remain the same regardless of the language in which a piece of material is written or the ethnicity of the author. There are, however, several criteria that are unique to dealing with collection development of Latino literature that had to be addressed in the development of this core collection, and that will need to be addressed as you work to build your own collection and expand on the list.

There are guidelines to help in selecting books; and avoiding a haphazard approach. The temptation with Spanish-language materials can be to grab up anything you can get your hands on, since they are often difficult to find.

Rather than making random, careless, thoughtless purchases, teachers and librarians must exercise discrimination in the materials they select. The American Library Association's Library Services to the Spanish-Speaking Committee has adopted official guidelines for the collection and selection of materials. These appeared in the Summer 1988 edition of *RQ* (*Reference Quarterly*, pages 491–493). They apply to both adult and children's materials. The following are ideas to help in establishing general guidelines for the selection of Spanish-language materials specifically for children, considering the issues unique to these books.

The Oakland Public Library Multi-Language Collection Development policy

Appendix A contains the complete text of the Oakland Public Library's Multi-Language Collection Development policy. It is a terrific model for anyone wishing to develop a written policy that addresses the specific needs of collection development in Spanish.

Considering the Community

Before you can know what to buy, you need to know for whom you are buying. This means that you need to know your community. Who lives in it? What kind of materials do they need? For teachers in schools the children are in front of you every day, and their language abilities and needs are readily apparent. In library settings, you can get a sense of your clientele as you work the reference desk on a regular basis. But, in order to make intelligent purchases, you have to be able to go on more than just a gut feeling based on the children you have talked to. There is also the issue of how to serve those who are not coming into the library. The first step is to check census information. This will probably confirm what you have already guessed in terms of the concentration of Latinos in your community. This data becomes the core of any collection development policy. Another approach to get a better sense of community needs involves outreach in the community, whether it be in a school, grocery store, or recreation center. It is particularly important to find out the language skills and preferences of the children in your community. Are they fully bilingual or Spanish-dominant? Do they prefer reading in Spanish or English? What do they want to read about? What are their informational reading needs? What are their reading ability levels? What are the primary Latino cultures represented in the community? This information will help you balance

the collection between Spanish-language materials, bilingual books, and books in English with cultural relevance. It can be obtained by formal or informal surveys, which can be done both in-house and through schools—with children in the classroom as well as parents in PTA settings.

Establishing Selection Goals and Objectives

What goals and objectives do you want to meet in building your Spanish-language children's collection? Your collection development goals should be congruent with your institution's mission statement, or the overall goals of your organization. Certainly, the overall goal will be to meet and to continually respond to the changing recreational and informational reading needs of Latino children; it must also acknowledge and provide validation for their cultural heritage and background. Any selection policy should recognize the tremendous diversity in the Latino community and strive to reflect that diversity in the collection. A good Spanish-language collection for children, like any collection, should include standard titles, which is what I try to identify in this manual. Isabel Schon has said, "Just as any Anglo child grows up appreciating the language of Shakespeare, so should Spanish-speaking children grow up appreciating the language of Cervantes (1995, 120). The classics in Spanish have a place in the collection. In addition to the standard titles, there should be titles that meet specific community needs. The ability to achieve collection development goals will be limited by available budget, so you will have to exercise considerable discretion.

Additional issues to be considered in goal-setting will be the availability of Spanish-speaking staff to articulate the collection and services to the Spanish-speaking community, as well as staff to process the materials. If bilingual catalogers are not available, then distributors who offer pre-cataloged materials should be sought. Bilingual access to the collection should be considered. There should be tools within the library's bibliographic databases as well as signage and printed materials in the facilities themselves in Spanish.

Once the general goals have been defined, you can then set objectives to meet them. Methods of acquisition need to be approved. The budget parameters need to be specified. The actual age levels for which materials are needed must be defined. Make sure you have a mechanism for including community needs, desires, and requests in your selection decisions. This can be as simple as a box at the information desk where requests are noted. Weeding should be a part of the policy, and efforts should be made to keep the collection up-to-date.

EVALUATING THE MATERIAL

In a recent conversation with Isabel Schon, she outlined four basic, very simple critieria to keep in mind when evaluating Spanish-language books, bilingual books and translated books:

Literary Quality
Artistic Quality
Reader Appeal
Quality of Translation

Since her first two criteria apply to any materials, I shall address them briefly. Of course, any book, regardless of its language, should be judged on its literary and artistic merit. For an overview of the basic literary and artistic standards that should be applied to the evaluation of children's books, I strongly recommend Kathleen Horning's book *From Cover to Cover: Evaluating and Reviewing Children's Books* (HarperCollins 1997). This is *the* definitive resource for book evaluation. Anyone wishing to understand the basic standards for book evaluation should study this book. In regard to books in Spanish, literary quality is harder to judge if you do not speak the language. Artistic quality can be judged pretty fairly, even by someone who does not speak Spanish, particularly in the case of picture books, where the illustrations and design of the book should be evaluated by the consistent guidelines in Horning's book. For fiction in Spanish, perhaps the best thing to do is to use reviews, such as those in *Críticas*, or on Isabel Schon's Web site or in her many books.

Reader Appeal

Reader appeal is a subjective matter and merits being considered separately. It is easy to see when books appeal to readers: they fly off the shelves. But different books appeal to different readers; what appeals to one may not appeal to another. Reader appeal is a tricky thing to gauge, but important to take into account in the selection process. On the one hand, some books that appear at first glance not to have reader appeal may in fact be the sorts of books that, if given a chance, would have a profound impact on the right reader. On the other, some may just simply be dull. In particular, many of the Spanish-language books I see coming from outside the United States may use unfamiliar expressions and be too dense in their language to be understood, even by Spanish-speaking children here in the U.S. The other difficulty lies in how to balance literary appeal with the criteria of literary and artistic quality. The twain may not always meet. Experience shows that the best course may be to err on the side of reader appeal. Particularly with reluctant Spanish readers, any reading they can do is a small victory.

Quality of Translations

When considering the issue of translations as part of book selection, I am speaking primarily of bilingual books where the text appears in English and Spanish as well as materials with Latino cultural content that has been translated into Spanish. There are two issues involved when considering translations. First is the quality of the translation itself. It is important that there is no grammatical, spelling, or typographical errors. The text should be clearly understood and be free of awkward or incorrect sentence constructions. I have seen books translated into "Spanish" where a Spanish-sounding suffix has simply been added to the English words. There are also translations where the Spanish makes no real sense whatsoever; this problem becomes especially apparent when you attempt to read the book aloud. If you are unqualified to make this sort of judgment, then use review sources, such as *Booklist*, which take these problems into consideration, or find someone who has Spanish-language skills to review the translation for you.

The other issue is that of regional and national dialects. While most current Spanish-language publishing attempts to use a neutral dialect, there are still many books that use a form of Spanish more tied to a particular country. You can find regionalisms that are difficult to understand by someone who is not from that region. You will probably come across books written using the *vosotros* form of address. An otherwise excellent book does not have to be rejected because of this problem. If you choose to read a book that uses the *vosotros* form, you can simply substitute *ustedes*, the mode of address that is more widely used. For the definitive treatment of this issue, the selector should consult Isabel Schon's article "Spanish Language Books for Young Readers—Great Expectations, Disappointing Realities" which appeared in the October 1, 1995, issue of *Booklist* magazine.

OTHER COLLECTION DEVELOPMENT ISSUES

Besides Isabel Schon's criteria, there are a couple of other issues to be considered when selecting Spanish-language and bilingual books. They are the quality of the binding and the cultural sensitivity of the text.

Binding Quality

Binding quality has been a constant complaint whenever books from Latin American publishers have been discussed. This has been a legitimate concern for a long time, since Latin American publishers have lacked the resources their

North American counterparts have had to produce books with quality library bindings. This, however, is changing. According to Sally Taylor in *Publisher's Weekly*, "printing technologies have improved enormously in the last three years, in Mexico and elsewhere in Latin America. Lifting of tariffs on printing equipment under NAFTA and the presence of a number of U.S. printers in these markets helped spur the upgrade, as did the need to compete against editions from Spain" (1996, S4). This means that more and more, the books being imported from Latin America will equal the quality of books being published here. In the case of poor bindings that will not last more than a precious few circulations, one option is to initially send the material to a commercial binder for a library binding. This way, quality books, marred only by the binding, can be added to library collections.

Cultural Sensitivity

At a speech I attended by the author Pat Mora, she mentioned that to an outsider Latino culture is fiestas, piñatas, folklórico dance, and bright costumes. But she cautioned against seeing the culture only through the viewpoint of celebrations. Culture goes much deeper than that; when selecting books to use with Latino children, you need to be sensitive to cultural issues. Avoid books that present a stereotyped view of Latino life. This is what I call the sombrero and tortilla school: books that portray only a world of poverty and traditional costumes. Books should respect the Latino culture, and not portray it as inferior to Anglo culture. Try to find books that represent the cultures of the children you are working with, if possible written by authors from those cultures. Try to find folktales that come from their native lands. There are some tales that have spread throughout the Latin American world. However, there have been collections published which contain tales from specific countries. Some of the best can be found in the core collection and the list of general titles. Ultimately, books that honor and respect Latino culture should build up the child's sense of cultural identity. Using these guidelines, you can develop Spanish-language and bilingual collections that will nourish the souls of Latino children.

WORKS CITED

Alabaster, Carol. *Developing an Outstanding Core Collection: A Guide for Libraries*. Chicago: American Library Association, 2002.

Moore, Opal, and Donnarae MacCann. "Paternalism and Assimilation in Books About Latinos: Part One of a Two-Part Essay." *Children's Literature Association Quarterly*, vol. 12. no. 2. Summer 1987.

Schon, Isabel. "Spanish-Language Books for Young Readers—Great Expectations, Disappointing Realities." *Booklist*, October 1, 1995: 318–319.

Taylor, Sally. "Big Changes South of the Border." *Publisher's Weekly*, September 23, 1996: S3–S20.

Chapter 3

A Recommended Core Collection

OVERVIEW OF THE LIST

This list is the heart of the book. It provides detailed information about each book and sidebar information about authors, publishers, and other pertinent information. The books are presented organized by genre, beginning with picture books for preschoolers, on to young adult novels. Within each genre the books are presented alphabetically by author.

This list includes books written in both Spanish and English. Some are bilingual and include both the Spanish and English texts in the same volume. In other cases the original Spanish or English text has been published, and then a translation published in the other language as a separate volume. For the purposes of clarity in the bibliography, books in English, Spanish and bilingual books are distinguished in the following way:

- If a book is available only in Spanish, the title has been translated and placed in parentheses.
- If the book is bilingual, the Spanish and English titles are separated with a "/".
- If there is an English or Spanish translation of a book published separately, the Spanish and English titles are separated with a "/" and "dual edition" is noted. The publication information on the translation is noted only if it is different from the main citation. For example, if only the title is listed then the publisher and publication date are the same.

While the books are arranged by format and age level, I have also included this information after each citation. The following are the designations used and a brief explanation of the genres into which this list is divided.

- **Board Book**: A storybook for children from birth to 3 years. Printed on heavy cardboard.
- **Picture Book**: A storybook where the pictures are equally as important as the text. Appropriate for ages 18 months to 7 years (preschool through grade 2).
- **Picture Book Anthology**: An anthology including different types of literature such as poetry and folk tales. Appropriate for ages 18 months through 7 years (preschool through grade 2).
- **Music**: An illustrated book of songs, which includes both the music and lyrics. Appropriate for all ages.
- **Chapter Fiction, 7–11**: Shorter novels with content appropriate for ages 7–11 (grades 2–5).
- **Poetry, 7–11**: Poems for grade-school children (grades 2–5).
- **Nonfiction, 7–11**: Nonfiction for grade-school children. Many of these books are heavily illustrated photo essays, with plenty of color pictures (grades 2–5).
- **Novels, 8–12**: Novels (fiction) for slightly older grade-school children (grades 3–7).
- **Young Adult**: Fiction appropriate for ages 12 and up. It sometimes includes mature content (grade 6 and above).

RECOMMENDED CHILDREN'S SPANISH/ BILINGUAL CORE COLLECTION

Board Books

All About Baby/Todo sobre bebé.
New York: DK, Inc., 2004.
ISBN: 0756604362
Different things that a baby can do are presented bilingually with DK's trademark photos.

Note: The board books listed here were selected for our local implementation of a program developed by the Arizona State Library called "Building a New Generation of Readers" that was designed to use the Public Library Association's "Every Child Ready to Read @ Your Library"® material in workshops for parents and caregivers. The PLA Web site for this program can be found at: www.pla.org/ala/pla/plaissues/earlylit/earlyliteracy.htm. These books are very useful for adults desiring to introduce infants to language.

Bebé/Baby (Stroller Book).
New York: DK, Inc., 2004.
ISBN: 0756606284 (board book)
This book of images of babies is designed to clip to a stroller so that babies can look at it while they are on the move.

Benjamin, Alan.
Let's Eat/Vamos a comer.
New York: Little Simon, 1992.
ISBN: 0671769278
Different foods are labeled with their English and Spanish names.

Christian, Cheryl.
¿Dónde está el bebé? (Where Is the Baby?)
New York: Star Bright Books, 1999.
ISBN: 01887734260 (board book)
This lift-the-flap board book shows an object, such as a chair or a tub.
When you lift the flap, you see a baby in the object.

Dwight, Laura.
¿Y ahora que pasará? (What Happens Next?)
New York: Star Bright Books, 1999.
ISBN: 01887734279
This is a lift-the-flap book that shows a baby what will happen next.

Intrater, Roberta Grobel.
Besitos y abrazos (Hugs and Kisses).
New York: Scholastic, 2002.
ISBN: 0439390796 (board book)
All in Spanish, this shows mothers hugging and kissing their babies.

My First Spanish Farm Board Book/Mi primer libro de la granja.
New York: DK, Inc.
ISBN: 00789495228 (board book)
Things you might find on a farm, from machinery to animals to plants, are labeled bilingually.

Parr, Todd.
Blanco y negro (Black and White).
Mexico, D.F.: Ediciones Serres (Abrapalabra Editores), 2004
ISBN: 08484881458 (board book)
Allows infants to explore positive and negative images.

Shott, Stephen.
El mundo del bebé (Baby's World).
New York: Dutton, 1992.
ISBN: 00525448462 (board book)
Objects that are familiar in a baby's world are labled.

Suen, Anastasia.
Toddler Two/Dos años.
New York: Lee and Low Books, 2002.
ISBN: 158430054X
The rhythmic text talks about things that a two-year-old has two of, such as hands and feet.

El Tractor/Tractor (Stroller Book).
New York: DK, Inc., 2004.
ISBN: 0756606276 (board book)
Introduces infants to that all time favorite topic, heavy machinery.

Zagarenski, Pamela.
How Do I Feel?/¿Cómo me siento?
New York: Houghton Mifflin, 2001.
ISBN: 00618169318 (board book)
Bright pictures help infants gain a vocabulary.

Picture Books

Picture Book: A storybook where the pictures are equally as important as the text. Appropriate for ages 18 months to 7 years (preschool through grade 2).

Fairy Tales in Spanish

Here is a selection of new fairy tale adaptations from two publishers, Chronicle Books and Combel Editorial. The Chronicle Books titles are bilingual, and the Combel series is Spanish only. The Chronicle Books series is somewhat uneaven in quality, and I've highlighted the two newest titles that I reviewed for the *Horn Book Guide* with a list of the other available titles. Combel's version of the Cucaracha Martina story, *La ratita presumida*, is an instant storytime classic. On the whole, these books are an excellent choice to introduce the universally known fairy tales into a storytime.

Adapted by Abeyà, Elisabet.
Hansel and Gretel/Hansel y Gretel. Illustrated by Cristina Losantos.
San Francisco: Chronicle Books, 2005.

ISBN: 0811847942 (picture book)
Hansel and Gretel is presented with European illustrations in the style of Asterix, which should appeal to the audience.
Adapted by Ros, Roser.
The Musicians of Bremen/Los músicos de Bremen. Illustrated by
   Pep Montserrat.
San Francisco: Chronicle Books, 2005.
ISBN: 0811847950 (picture book)
The illustrations in this edition are simple, stylized, but highly effective, and complement the readable and accessible text.

Other Bilingual Fairy Tales from Chronicle

Cinderella/Cenicienta, 2001.
ISBN: 081183090X
Goldilocks and the Three Bears/Ricitos de oro y los tres osos,
   1998.
ISBN: 0811818357
Jack and the Beanstalk/Juan y los frijoles mágicos, 1998.
ISBN: 008118 18438
The Little Mermaid/La sirenita, 2003.
ISBN: 0081183 9117
Little Red Riding Hood/Caperucita Roja, 1999.
ISBN: 0081181825620
The Princess and the Pea/La princesa y el guisante, 2004.
ISBN: 0081181844528
Puss in Boots/El gato con botas, 2004.
ISBN: 0081181839249
The Sleeping Beauty/La bella durmiente, 2003.
ISBN: 0081181839125
Thumbelina/Pulgarcita, 2004.
ISBN: 0811839281
The Ugly Duckling/El patito feo, 2004.
ISBN: 0811844544

Fairy Tales, Spanish Language Only

Adapted by Orihuela, Luz.
La ratita presumida (The Conceited Little Mouse). Illustrated by Rosa
   M. Curto.
Barcelona, Spain: Combel Editorial, 2003.
ISBN: 8478647635 (picture book)

A take on the familiar folktale of "Perez and Martina." In this version, the little rat receives marriage proposals from a number of animals, and finally accepts the cat's proposal. The cat promptly eats her. This is actually a lot of fun and the illustrations are charming.

Special note: In Fall, 2006, Scholastic publishers issued "spinner rack" paperback editions of five of the Combel titles for the U.S. market. Scholastic offerings are:

El patito feo/The Ugly Duckling. ISBN: 0439773768

La ratita presumida/The Conceited Little Rat. ISBN: 0439773792

La lechera/The Milkmaid. ISBN: 0439773776

Los tres cerditos/The Three Little Pigs. ISBN: 0439773822

Caperucita Roja/Little Red Riding Hood. ISBN: 043977375X

Adapted by Orihuela, Luz.

El león y el ratón (The Lion and the Mouse).

Illustrated by Subi.

Barcelona, Spain: Combel Editorial, 2003.

ISBN: 8478647848 (picture book)

A retelling of the familiar Aesop's fable, with appealing illustrations.

Titles in the al Galope series:

Como la sal (Just Like Salt).

Illustrated by Max.

ISBN: 8478647864

A retelling of the folktale known variously as "Love Like Salt" and "Cap O'Rushes." A king's daughter tells her father that she loves him like meat loves salt. She is banished until the king is able to understand what she meant.

El zapatero y los duendes (The Shoemaker and the Elves). Illustrated by Sebastià Serra.

ISBN: 8478647856

A retelling of the familiar fairy tale with illustrations reminiscent of J. Otto Seibold's computer work.

Los músicos de Bremen (The Bremen Town Musicians). Illustrated by Petra Steinmeyer.

ISBN: 847864783X

A great retelling of the familiar folktale with delightful energetic illustrations that are a cross between Tomie dePaola and Dav Pilkey.

Titles in the al Trote series:

La vieja del bosque (The Old Woman of the Forest).

Illustrated by Mabel Piérola.

ISBN: 8478647767
A young girl finds a ring in a witch's house that releases a prince and many others from the witch's enchantment.
La bella durmiente (Sleeping Beauty). Illustrated by Jordi Vila Declòs.
ISBN: 8478647759
This adaptation has very traditional illustrations.

Titles in the al Paso series:

El patito feo (The Ugly Duckling). Illustrated by Irene Bordoy.
ISBN: 8478647643
Hans Christan Andersen's autobiographical fable is retold here very simply for very young readers, accompanied by luminous illustrations.
Los siete cabritillos y el lobo (The Seven Little Goats and the Wolf). Illustrated by Marta Montañá.
ISBN: 847864766X
A folktale similar to the "Three Little Pigs." The goats' revenge against the wolf is to fill his stomach with stones, after which he drowns in the river.
Los tres cerditos (The Three Little Pigs). Illustrated by María Rius.
ISBN: 8478647651
The three pigs in this retelling are extraordinarily cute.

Ada, Alma Flor.
Gathering the Sun: An Alphabet in Spanish and English. Illustrated by Simón Silva. English translation by Rosalma Zubizarreta.
New York: Lothrop, 1997.
ISBN: 0688139035 (picture book)
Pura Belpré Illustrator Honor Book, 1998.
A series of poems that celebrate migrant farmworkers, and their champion César Chávez.

Ada, Alma Flor.
Mediopollito: Cuento tradicional en español y inglés/Half Chicken: A Folktale in Spanish and English. Illustrated by Kim Howard. Translated by Rosalma Zubizarreta.
New York: Doubleday, 1996.
ISBN: 0385446373 (picture book)
Américas Award, 1995.
This cumulative tale explains how weather vanes came to be. Mediopollito, the one-legged chicken, helps the river, fire, and wind, among others, on his way to see the Viceroy. When the Viceroy wants his chef to use

Mediopollito as the main ingredient in a soup, Mediopollito's friends come to his aid.

Altman, Linda Jacobs.
El camino de Amelia (Amelia's Road). Illustrated by Enrique O. Sánchez.
Spanish translation by Daniel Santacruz.
New York: Lee & Low Books, 1993, 1994.
ISBN: 1880000105 (picture book)
Amelia is a migrant child who never has any place to call home. Her calendar is the crops. It is only after a teacher notices her that Amelia finds a way to make a place she can call her own by burying a metal box filled with treasures under a large shade tree.

Alvarez, Julia.
A Gift of Gracias. Illustrated by Beatriz Vidal.
New York: Knopf, 2005.
ISBN: 037582425 (picture book)
Julia Alvarez retells a legend from her native Dominican Republic about *Nuestra Señora de la Altagracia* (Our Lady of Thanks), who appears to a girl named María, afraid of having to leave her farm after the olive crop fails.

Anzaldúa, Gloria.
Prietita and the Ghost Woman/Prietita y la llorona. Illustrated by
  Christina Gonzalez.
San Francisco, CA: Children's Book Press, 1996.
ISBN: 0892391367 (picture book)
When Prietita searches for an herb, *La curandera* that the local healer, needs for her mother, she meets *la llorona*.

Anzaldúa, Gloria.
Friends from the Other Side/Amigos del otro lado. Illustrated by Consuelo Méndez.
San Francisco, CA: Children's Press, 1993.
ISBN: 0892391308 (picture book)
Prietita meets Joaquin, who has just come across the great river to America.

Barbot, Daniel.
Rosaura en bicicleta (Rosaura on a Bicycle). Illustrated by Morella Fuenmayor.
Caracas, Venezuela: Ediciones Ekaré, 1990.
ISBN: 9802570559 (picture book)
Rosaura is a chicken. For her birthday, she asks for a bicycle. A man arrives in town, and makes a bicycle for Rosaura. But there is only one problem. It doesn't have brakes.

Bierhorst, John (translator).
Spirit Child: A Story of the Nativity. Illustrated by Barbara Cooney.
New York: Sea Star, 2001.
ISBN: 1587170884
Spanish edition: **El niño espíritu: Una historia de la Navidad**.
ISBN: 1587170892 (picture book)
An Aztec version of the birth of Christ.

Latina and Latino Singers, Painters and Poets

Here are some books about some Latina and Latino artists for very young readers. Use these to inspire your own budding artists. These books can easily be tied in with craft or creative writing projects.

Brown, Monica.
My Name Is Celia: The Life of Celia Cruz/Me llamo Celia: La vida de Celia Cruz. Illustrated by Rafael López.
Flagstaff, AZ: Rising Moon (Northland Publishing), 2004.
ISBN: 087358872X (picture book)
The life of Cuban salsa singer Celia Cruz is presented for young readers with a lively text and vivid, colorful illustrations.

————.

My Name Is Gabriela: The Life of Gabriela Mistral/Me llamo Gabriela: La vida de Gabriela Mistral. Illustrated by John Parra.
Flagstaff, Arizona: Rising Moon (Northland Publishing), 2005.
ISBN: 0873588592 (picture book)
The life of Nobel Prize-winning Chilean poet Gabriela Mistral is presented for younger readers with a poetic language suiting its subject, and striking illustrations.

da Coll, Ivar.
¡Azucar! (Sugar!)
New York: Lectorum Publications, 2005.
ISBN: 1930332653 (picture book)
A poetic celebration of Celia Cruz's life.

Winter, Jeannette.
Josefina.
San Diego: Harcourt, 1996.
ISBN: 0152010912
Jeanette Winter introduces children to the clay sculptor Josefina Aguilar.

Winter, Jonah.
Diego. Illustrated by Jeanette Winter.
New York: Knopf, 1991.

ISBN: 0679819878 (picture book)

This book explores the childhood of Mexican muralist Diego Rivera, who was famously married to the subject of the book below.

————.

Frida. Illustrated by Ana Juan.

New York: Scholastic, 2002.

ISBN: 0439331188 (picture book)

In very simple language, Jonah Winter tells young children about the life and art of celebrated Mexican painter Frida Kahlo.

Carlin, Joi.

La cama de mamá (Mother's Bed). Illustrated by Morella Fuenmayor.
  Caracas, Venezuela: Ediciones Ekaré Volcano Press, 1989, 1994.

ISBN: 9802571679 (picture book)

Mother's bed is the best place to be. During the day the children use it for their imaginative adventures, and, at night, they can come and share the bed so that they are not afraid.

————.

Chumba la cachumba. Illustrated by Carlos Cotte.

Caracas, Venezuela: Ediciones Ekaré, 1995.

ISBN: 9802571148 (picture book)

What skeletons do at each hour of the night. A picture book based on a traditional song.

Carling, Amelia Lau.

Mama and Papa Have a Store.

New York: Penguin Putnam, 1998.

ISBN: 0803720440 (picture book)

Pura Belpré Illustrator Honor Book, 2000.

A Chinese girl observes a typical day in her parents' general store in Guatemala City.

Delacre, Lulu.

Arrorró, mi niño: Latino Lullabies and Gentle Games.

New York: Lee & Low, 2004.

ISBN: 1584301597 (picture book)

Pura Belpre Illustrator Honor, 2006.

Lulu Delacre includes all of the most well known lullabies from the Latino culture, a veritable Latino Mother Goose. The rhymes are presented bilingually and the English versions are literal translations of the original Spanish. Delacre's oil wash illustrations capture many lovely scenes of mothers and grandmothers with young children.

———.
Rafi and Rosi.
New York: HarperCollins, 2004.
ISBN: 0060098953 (picture book)
Rafi and Rosi are two Puerto Rican tree fogs who are brother and sister. Rafi says he can do magic. The "magic" he performs is, in reality, science. The "stars" that he claims have fallen from the sky are actually algae in the ocean that create a bioluminescent light. Spanish words and phrases are used throughout, with a glossary appended.

A sequel.
Rafi and Rosi Carnival! 2006.
ISBN: 006073597X
These new Rafi and Rosi stories are set around preparations for a Carnival parade.

Delgado, María Isabel.
Chave's Memories/Los recuerdos de Chave.
Houston: Piñata (Arte Público), 1996.
ISBN: 1558850848 (picture book)
Chave leaves the city behind to visit his grandparents in Mexico. His experiences on his grandparents' rural ranch become a magical time for him.

dePaola, Tomie.
The Lady of Guadalupe.
New York: Holiday House, 1980.
ISBN: 0823403734
Spanish edition: **Nuestra Señora de Guadalupe**. Translated by Pura Belpré.
ISBN: 0823403742 (picture book)
This retelling of the story of the appearance of the Virgin Mary to the peasant Juan Diego is enhanced by dePaola's simple and respectful illustrations.

———.
The Legend of the Poinsettia.
New York: Putnam, 1994.
ISBN: 0399216928
Spanish edition: **La leyenda de la flor de nochebuena**.
ISBN: 039922789X (picture book)
Lucinda is unable to finish her gift for the baby Jesus on time, but receives a miracle and is able to offer the poinsettia as her gift.

Dorros, Arthur.
Abuela (Grandmother). Illustrated by Elisa Kleven.
New York: Dutton, 1991.

ISBN: 0525447504
Spanish edition: **Abuela**. Translated by Sandra Marulandra Dorros.
ISBN: 0525454381 (picture book)
Rosalba imagines flying with her grandmother high above the city streets.

————.
Isla. Illustrated by Elisa Kleven.
New York: Dutton, 1991.
ISBN: 0140565051
Spanish edition: **La isla**. Translated by Sandra Marulandra Dorros.
ISBN: 0525451498 (picture book)
In this sequel to **Abuela**, Rosalba and her abuela fly to the Caribbean island where Abuela grew up.

Ehlert, Lois.
Cuckoo/Cucú. Translated by Gloria de Aragón Andújar.
San Diego, CA: Harcourt, 1997.
ISBN: 015200274X (picture book)
Cuckoo is lazy, until a fire threatens the seed crop, and she is the only one who can save it.

————.
Moon Rope: A Peruvian Tale/Un lazo a la luna: Una leyenda peruana.
   Translated by Amy Prince.
San Diego, CA: Harcourt, 1992.
ISBN: 0152553436 (picture book)
Fox and Mole try to climb up to the moon on a rope woven of stars.

Elya, Susan Middleton.
Fairy Trails: A Story Told in English and Spanish. Illustrated by Mercedes McDonald.
New York: Bloomsbury, 2005.
ISBN: 1582349724 (picture book)
Miguel and María go to visit their auntie, and encounter a host of fairy tale characters. The story is told in rhyme, using Spanish words throughout. A glossary is included.

————.
Estaba el Señor Don Gato (There Was Mr. Cat). Illustrated by Carmen Salvador.
Caracas, Venezuela: Ediciones Ekaré, 1993.
ISBN: 9802571342 (picture book)
Song about the death and resurrection of Señor Don Gato, who wakes up

smelling like sardines after everyone thinks he is dead. A traditional song, part of the Clave del Sol Collection from Ediciones Ekaré.

Ets, Marie Hall.
Gilberto and the Wind.
New York: Viking, 1963.
ISBN: 0670340251
Spanish edition: **Gilberto y el viento**.
New York: Lectorum (Scholastic), 1995.
ISBN: 1880507161 (picture book)
Gilberto plays alone and imagines the wind to be his playmate.

Fancy, Colin.
Los cocodrilos no se cepillan los dientes (Crocodiles Don't Brush Their
    Teeth). Illustrated by Ken Wilson–Max. Spanish translation by Chris-
    tiane Reyes.
Barcelona: Ediciones Juventud, 2005.
ISBN: 8426134491 (picture book)
Animals don't take care of themselves or use good manners, but little chil-
dren do. A perfect book for toddlers.

Garza, Xavier.
Lucha Libre: The Man in the Silver Mask: A Bilingual Cuento.
El Paso, TX: Cinco Puntos Press, 2005.
ISBN: 093831792X (picture book)
Carlitos and his dad go to a *lucha libre*, a Mexican professional wrestling
match. They are supposed to meet Carlitos's Uncle Rodolfo at the match, but
he does not show up. In the ring that night is El Santo, the Man in the Silver
Mask. He looks oddly familiar, and even picks Carlitos out of the crowd and
smiles at him. You can guess the rest.

González, Lucia M.
The Bossy Gallito/El gallo de bodas: A Traditional Cuban Folktale.
New York: Scholastic, 1997.
ISBN: 059046843X (picture book)
Pura Belpré Author and Illustrator Honor Book, 1996.
    The Gallito dirties his beak on the way to the wedding of his Uncle Parrot,
but no one will help him clean it, until he calls on his friend, the sun. The il-
lustrations set the tale in Miami's "Little Havana."

Gonzalez, Ralfka, and Ana Ruiz.
Mi primer libro de dichos/My First Book of Proverbs.

Emeryville, CA: Children's Book Press, 1995.
ISBN: 0892391340 (picture book)
Contains familiar proverbs and others not so familiar.
"Pig out while you have the chance/Atáscate ahora que hay lodo"; and "If you hang out with wolves you will learn how to howl/El que anda con lobos a aullar se enseña."

Griego, Margot C., Besty L. Bucks, Sharon S. Gilbert, and Laurel H. Kimball, Selected and Translated.
Tortillitas para Mamá and Other Nursery Rhymes/Spanish and English. Illustrated by Barbara Cooney.
New York: Holt, 1981.
ISBN: 0805002855 (picture book)
This classic should be in the collection of any librarian or teacher working with Latino children. Includes some of the most common rhymes.

Gusti.
La mosca en "un día perfecto puede llegar a ser una pesadilla" (The fly in "A perfect day can turn into a nightmare").
Mexico, D.F.: Ediciones Serres (Abrapalabra Editores), 2005.
ISBN: 9709705032 (picture book)
The fly decides it is a great day to take a bath, but he does so in a toilet bowl, with near tragic results.

Guy, Ginger Foglesong.
¡Fiesta! Illustrated by Rene King Moreno.
New York: Greenwillow, 1996.
ISBN: 0688143318 (picture book)
Also available in board book format, ISBN: 0060092637
A bilingual counting book that follows children preparing for a party. Children can count the number of objects in each picture, and are encouraged to turn the page with the recurring question, "¿Que más?/What else?".

———.
Siesta. Illustrated by Rene King Moreno.
New York: Greenwillow, 2005.
ISBN: 0688143318 (picture book)
In this sequel to *¡Fiesta!*, the concept of colors is developed through a story of a brother and sister gathering items to take to the backyard, where they make a tent for their afternoon nap.

Hayes, Joe.
The Terrible Tragadabas/El terrible tragadabas. Illustrated by Lucy Jelinek.

Santa Fe, NM: Trails West, 1987.
ISBN: 0939729024 (picture book)
Great monster story in a cumulative tale. Three sisters, one by one, get scared up into climbing a tree by the Tragadabas. The Tragadabas gets stung by a bee and the girls return home safely to their grandmother.

Herrera, Juan Felipe.
Calling the Doves/El canto de las palomas. Illustrated by Elly Simmons.
Emeryville, CA: Children's Book Press, 1995.
ISBN: 0892391324 (picture book)
The author recalls his farmworker parents, who inspired him through singing.

Isol.
Cosas que pasan (Things That Happen).
Mexico, D.F.: Fondo de Cultura Económica, 1998.
ISBN: 9505573294 (picture book)
A little girl wants to be different. A genie appears, and the girl wishes for everything. But "everything" is not in the genie's book.

———.

Un regalo sorpresa (A Surprise Present).
Mexico, D.F.: Fondo de Cultura Económica, 1998.
ISBN: 9681657179 (picture book)
Nino discovers his birthday present in his parents' closet. He imagines all the things it could be, and is disappointed to learn that it is a book—until he opens the book. This is a perfect book for parent presentations and for introducing kids to the joy of reading.

Jaramillo, Nelly Palacio.
Grandmother's Nursery Rhymes: Lullabies, Tongue Twisters, and Riddles from South America/Las nanas de abuelita: Canciones de cuna, trabalenguas y adivinanzas de Surámerica. Illustrated by Elivia Savadier.
New York: Henry Holt, 1994.
ISBN: 0805025553 (picture book)
The author, who hails from Colombia, collected these to share after the birth of a grandchild. This book provides English versions of the rhymes which non-Spanish speakers will find helpful. Includes "Aserrín Asserán" with an explanation of the wordplay.

Johnston, Tony.
Day of the Dead. Illustrated by Jeanette Winter.
New York: Harcourt, 1997.

ISBN: 0152024468 (picture book)
A small format picture book that details Day of the Dead celebrations.

Krull, Kathleen.
Harvesting Hope: The Story of César Chávez. Illustrated by Yuyi
  Morales.
New York: Harcourt, 2003.
ISBN: 0152014373
Spanish edition: **Cosechando esperanza: La historia de César Chávez**.
Translated by F. Isabel Campoy and Alma Flor Ada.
ISBN: 0152047557 (picture book)
A picture book retelling of the life of César Chávez. A vivid, engaging text
describing the events of Chavez's life is accompanied by evocative illustrations.

Kurusa.
La calle es libre. Illustrated by Monika Doppert.
Caracas, Venezuela: Ediciones Ekaré/Banco del Libro, 1981.
ISBN: 9802570508
English edition: **The Streets Are Free**. Translated by Karen Englander.
Toronto: Annick Press, 1985.
ISBN: 0920303099 (picture book)
The true story of a group of kids who, with support from the neighbor-
hood librarian, take matters into their own hands when the government re-
fuses to supply a park to play in instead of the streets.

Lee, Héctor Viveros.
Yo tenía un hipopótamo (I Had a Hippopotamus).
New York: Lee & Low, 1996, 1997.
ISBN: 1880000970 (board book)
In this predictable tale, the narrator tells the fate of each of his pets, until
he comes to the cat, which he keeps. A natural choice for storytime.

Leon, Georgina Lazaro.
El flamboyan amarillo (The Yellow Flame Tree). Illustrated by Lulu
  Delacre.
New York: Lectorum Publications, 2004.
ISBN: 1930332556
On a walk with his mother, the beauty of a yellow flame tree amazes a boy.
He takes a seed home, plants it, and cares for it over the years as it grows.

Levy, Janice.
**The Spirit of Tío Fernando: A Day of the Dead Story/El espíritu de
  tío Fernando: una historia del día de los muertos**. Illustrated by
  Morella Fuenmayor.

Morton Grove, IL: Albert Whitman, 1995.
ISBN: 0807575852 (picture book)
A young boy remembers his uncle as he and his mother prepare to cele-
brate the uncle's memory on the Day of the Dead.

Lionni, Leo.
Frederick.
New York: Knopf, 1967, 1995.
ISBN: 0394810406
Spanish edition: **Frederick**. Translated by Teresa Mlawer.
New York: Lectorum Publications, Inc., 2005.
ISBN: 1930332815 (picture book)
This is one of those rare classics, a quiet lovely book with elegant language
and spare, but perfect, cut paper illustrations. This little miracle of a book
tells the story of mice preparing for the winter. Rather than storing up food,
Frederick stores up rays of the sun, colors and words. Teresa Mlawer's Span-
ish translation takes Lionni's original English text and creates a version in
Spanish that recreates the rhythm and feeling of the original.

―――.

Swimmy.
New York: Knopf, 1963, 1991.
ISBN: 0394917138
Spanish edition: **Nadarín**. Translated by Teresa Mlawer.
New York: Lectorum Publications, Inc., 2005.
ISBN: 1930332807 (picture book)
Universal in its David vs. Goliath theme. This book works particularly
well when told aloud, and is one of my favorites.

Lobel, Arnold.
Mouse Tales.
New York: HarperCollins, 1972.
ISBN: 0060239417
Spanish edition: *Historias de ratones*. Translated by Xosé Manuel Gonzáles.
Pontevedra, Spain: Kalandraka, 2000.
ISBN: 8495123959 (picture book)
Seven stories, one for each of papa mouse's seven sons.

Lomas Garza, Carmen.
Family Pictures/Cuadros de familia. Translated by Rosalina Zu-
    bizaretta.
San Francisco, CA: Children's Book Press, 1990, 2005.
ISBN: 0892392061 (picture book)

Pura Belpré Illustrator Honor Book, 1996.

Pictures of growing up Latino in Kingsville, Texas. This book feels like a family album with its folk art illustrations. The accompanying text is equally conversational. A 15th anniversary edition of this classic book was released in 2005. This anniversary edition includes a new illustration and a new introduction by Sandra Cisneros.

———.

In My Family/En mi familia. Edited by David Schecter. Spanish translation by Francisco X. Alarcón.
San Francisco, CA: Children's Book Press, 1996.
ISBN: 0892391383 (picture book)
Pura Belpré Illustrator Honor Book, 1998.
This follow up to *Family Pictures* is another bilingual picture book that celebrates Mexican-American culture. Some of the memories Lomas Garza shares about her childhood in Kingsville, Texas, include an encounter with horned toads, eating cactus and empanadas, and having a birthday barbecue.

Marti, Jose.
Los zapaticos de Rosa (Rosa's Shoes). Illustrated by Lulu Delacre.
New York: Lectorum, 1997.
ISBN: 1880507331 (picture book)
Two worlds meet as a privileged young girl decides to gift her precious shoes to an ill child she meets on the beach one day. Marti's poetry, along with Delacre's gorgeous illustrations, makes this a classic.

Montes, Marisa.
Juan Bobo Goes to Work: A Puerto Rican Folk Tale. Illustrated by Joe Cepeda.
New York: HarperCollins, 2000.
ISBN: 0525675752 (picture book)
Pura Belpré Illustrator Honor Book, 2002.
Retelling of traditional Puerto Rican folktales starring the classic folklore character, Juan Bobo.

Mora, Pat.
Doña Flor: A Tall Tale About a Giant Woman with a Great Big Heart. Illustrated by Raúl Colón.
New York: Knopf, 2005.
ISBN: 0375923373 (picture book)
Pura Belpré Illustrator Award, 2006.
Pura Belpré Author Honor Book, 2006.
In this original tall tale, Doña Flor is a giant who is very helpful to the

people of the village where she lives. When a puma threatens the village, it is Doña Flor who must save the day.

————.

Listen to the Desert/Oye al desierto. Illustrated by Daniel Lechon.
New York: Clarion, 1994.
ISBN: 0395672929 (picture book)
A bilingual chant about the sounds of the desert.

————.

Pablo's Tree. Illustrated by Cecily Lange.
New York: Macmillan, 1994.
ISBN: 0027674010 (picture book)
Every year on his birthday, Pablo goes to his grandfather Lito's house. Lito decorates a special tree in Pablo's honor, which was planted when he was adopted. Each year Lito uses something different to decorate it—chimes, balloons, paper lanterns, or tiny birdcages.

————.

Tomás and the Library Lady. Illustrated by Raúl Colón.
New York: Knopf, 1997.
ISBN: 0679804013
Spanish edition: **Tomás y la señora de la biblioteca**.
ISBN: 0679841733 (picture book)
This is based on the true story of Tomás Rivera, who grew up to be the first chancellor of the University of California system. Tomás hears stories from his grandfather, who then takes him to the library for more. The "Library Lady" becomes an important influence in his life.

Morales, Yuyi.
Just a Minute: A Trickster Tale and Counting Book.
San Francisco: Chronicle Books, 2003.
ISBN: 0811837580 (picture book)
Death comes to the door in the form of a skeleton. Grandma Beetle puts him off by having him wait and count her housecleaning tasks. By the time he is done, Death ends up as one of the invited guests to Grandma Beetle's birthday party.

Niera, Maria, and Anna Wennberg.
Mamá oca y el pastel (Mother Goose and the Cake). Illustrated by Irene Bordoy.
Barcelona, Spain: Combel Editorial, 2000.
ISBN: 8478644032 (picture book)
Mother Goose bakes a cake, but someone unexpected eats it.

Mamá Oca y la luna (Mother Goose and the Moon).
ISBN: 8478644016
Mother Goose and the cat build a tower of stories to reach the moon.

Mamá Oca y la tormenta (Mother Goose and the Storm).
ISBN: 8478644040
Mother Goose hides during a storm, then gets dirty playing in the puddles it leaves behind.

Mamá Oca y las vocales (Mother Goose and the Vowels).
ISBN: 8478644024
Mother Goose tries to help a dog to read, but the vowels escape from his book.

Orozco, José-Luis.
Diez deditos and Other Play Rhymes and Action Songs from Latin America. Illustrated by Elisa Kleven.
New York: Dutton, 1997.
ISBN: 0525457364 (picture book)
This is still one of the best collections of rhymes and songs to use in storytimes and programs. Included are the rhymes in Spanish and English, with line drawings to illustrate how to do the actions. Includes all the most well-known rhymes such as "Este compró un huevito," and many others.

Pellicer Lopez, Carlos.
Juan y sus zapátos (Juan and His Shoes).
Mexico: Promexa, 1982.
ISBN: 9681670213 (picture book)
A terrific little book about Juan who gets sick and has to stay in bed. His shoes begin to walk and talk. They take him on an adventure. He goes to a bell tower and sees the night creatures. The shoes allow him to hear the voices of nature that speak of dreams and stories.

———.
Julieta y su caja de colores (Julieta and Her Box of Paints).
Mexico, D. F.: Fondo de Cultura Económica, 1993.
ISBN: 9681641272 (picture book)
Awarded the Antoniorobles prize in 1983.
A reprint of a book originally published by Editorial Patria in 1984.
Julieta opens up her box of paints and discovers that through her imagination and her paintings, cities, animals, fruits, and even dreams can magically appear.

Ramos, Mario.
¡Mamá!
Barcelona, Spain: Editorial Corimbo, 2004.
ISBN: 848470145X (picture book)
The minimal text here hardly needs translation. A boy looks through every room in the house, calling out for his mother. In each room there are animals. As he leaves the house he shouts, "Mama, there's a spider in the house!" This is also a counting book.

Reiser, Lynn.
Margaret and Margarita/Margarita y Margaret.
New York: Greenwillow, 1993.
ISBN: 0688122396 (picture book)
Perfect for bilingual storytime. Margaret speaks only English, Margarita speaks only Spanish. They meet in a park.

Robles Boza, Eduardo.
Cuatro letras se escaparon (Four Letters Escaped). Illustrated by Rebeca
    Cerda.
Mexico: Editorial Trillas, 1986.
ISBN: 9682419379 (picture book)
Four letters escape from a page and try to form a word.

Ryan, Pam Muñoz.
Mice and Beans. Illustrated by Joe Cepeda.
New York: Scholastic, 2001.
ISBN: 0439183030
Spanish edition: **Arroz con frijoles . . . y unos amables ratones**.
ISBN: 0613455193 (picture book)
Rosa María is a grandmother preparing for the birthday of her grand-daughter. When items for the party begin to disappear, she sets out moustraps that also disappear. The mice finally redeem themselves by filling the birthday piñata with candy.

———.
Nacho and Lolita. Illustrated by Claudia Rueda.
New York: Scholastic, 2005.
ISBN: 0439269687 (picture book)
Nacho, a rare *pitcacoche* bird comes to San Juan Capistrano and meets a swallow named Lolita. After an unsuccessful attempt to migrate with the swallows, he ultimately finds a self-sacrificing way to guide the swallows back.

Salinas, Bobbi.
The Three Pigs/Los tres cerdos: Nacho, Tito and Miguel. Translated
   by Amapola Franzen and Marcos Guerrero.
Oakland, CA: Piñata Publications, 1998.
ISBN: 0934925054 (picture book)
Tomás Rivera Mexican-American Children's Book Award 1998. A South-
western version of the popular nursery tale.

Sánchez, Mireia.
Arriba del árbol (Up the Tree). Illustrated by Pau Estrada.
Barcelona, Spain: Combel Editorial, 2000.
ISBN: 8478644237 (picture book)
Children kick a ball up a tree, and end up rescuing a cat. This is one of my
favorite recent series. I love that these books are very simple. They are perfect
for one-on-one sharing or for storytime and have lots of child appeal.

SERIES: AL PASO. OTHER TITLES IN THIS SERIES:

Dentro del cajón (Inside the Box).
ISBN: 8478644245
A child steals a piece of candy but is found out.

En el suelo (On the Floor).
ISBN: 8478644210
A little girl's toy city gets knocked down by her brother.

Sobre la arena (On the Sand).
ISBN: 8478644229
A day at the beach is ruined by rain.

Sandin, Joan.
Coyote School News.
New York: Holt, 2003.
ISBN: 080506558X (picture book)
Historical fiction about Latino life in the Southwest in the late 1930s. This
is a first person tale told by Monchi Ramírez about his work on the school
newspaper and includes many Latino celebrations.

Sastrías, Marta.
El sapo que no quería comer (The Toad That Refused to Eat). Illustrated
   by Francisco Nava Bouchaín.
México: D.F.: Fondo de Cultura Económica, 1998.
ISBN: 9681657586 (picture book)
The Frog King goes to the palace of the Turtle Queen, but he will not eat

anything she serves him, until it is discovered that what he wants to eat is insects.

Shannon, David.
No, David!
New York: Blue Sky Press, 1998.
ISBN: 0590930028
Spanish edition: ¡**No, David!** Translated by Teresa Mlawer.
Leon, Spain: Editorial Everest, 1998.
ISBN: 842418114X (picture book)
It is hard to think of another English title that works as well as this translation of David Shannon's popular book. This is as perfect a storytime choice as there is for Spanish-speaking kids.

Soto, Gary.
Chato's Kitchen. Illustrated by Susan Guevara.
New York: Putnam, 1995.
ISBN: 0399226583
Spanish edition: **Chato y su cena**. 1997.
ISBN: 0698116011 (picture book)
Pura Belpré Illustrator Award, 1996.
Chato, a cool, low-riding cat, invites the mice who've moved in next door over for dinner. Chato and his friend, Novio Boy, prepare a feast of tortillas and guacamole to lure the mice, but the mice also bring a surprise with them.

SEQUELS TO *CHATO'S KITCHEN* BY GARY SOTO:

Chato and the Party Animals. Illustrated by Susan Guevara.
New York: Putnam, 2000.
ISBN: 0399231595 (picture book)
Spanish edition: **Chato y los amigos pachangueros**. Translated by Teresa Mlawer.
New York: Puffin, 2004.
ISBN: 0142400335
Pura Belpré Award for Illustration, 2002.
Chato plans a surprise birthday party for Novio Boy.

Chato Goes Cruisin'. Illustrated by Susan Guevara.
New York: Putnam, 2005.
ISBN: 039923974X (picture book)
Chato and Novio Boy win a cruise, but find that the passengers on the cruise ship are dogs. This title is enhanced with the addition of pen and ink comic strips to Guevara's wonderful realization of these characters.

Picture Book Anthologies:

An anthology is a collection including different types of literature such as poetry and folk tales. The two recommended here are appropriate for ages 18 months through 7 years (preschool through grade 2).

Ada, Alma Flor, and F. Isabel Campoy.
Mamá Goose: A Latino Nursery Treasury/Un tesoro de rimas infantiles. Illustrated by Maribel Suárez.
New York: Hyperion, 2004.
ISBN: 0786819357 (picture book anthology)
An anthology of nursery rhymes, lullabies, songs, riddles, and other treasures presented bilingually with appealing illustrations.

———.
¡Pio Peep! Traditional Spanish Nursery Rhymes. English adaptation by Alice Schertle. Illustrated by Viví Escrivá.
New York: Rayo, 2006.
ISBN: 0061116661 (picture book anthology)
This special bilingual edition collection of traditional rhymes includes a CD with songs from the book.

———.
Tales Our Abuelitas Told: A Hispanic Folktale Collection. Illustrated by Felipe Dávalos, Viví Escrivá, Susan Guevara, and Leyla Torres.
New York: Atheneum, 2006.
ISBN: 0689825838 (picture book anthology)
Spanish edition: **Cuentos que cantaban nuestras abuelas: Cuentos populares Hispanicos**.
ISBN: 1416919058 (picture book anthology)
With a who's who of Latino illustrators, this collection provides not only excellent resource for parents, but also for librarians looking for tales to add to their repertoire.

Syverson-Stork, Jill, and Nancy Abraham Hall.
Los pollitos dicen: Juegos, rimas y canciones/The Baby Chicks Sing: Traditional Games, Nursery Rhymes and Songs from Spanish-Speaking Countries. Illustrated by Kay Chorao.
Boston: Little Brown, 1994.
ISBN: 0316338524 (picture book anthology)
Traditional songs, rhymes, and games present a bilingual format. Includes "A la víbora de la mar."

Music

The following illustrated books of songs, which include both the music and
lyrics, are appropriate for all ages.

Delacre, Lulu.
Arroz con leche: Popular Songs and Rhymes from Latin America (Rice
with Milk).
New York: Scholastic, 1984.
ISBN: 0590418874 (music)
The Spanish and English lyrics to these songs are enhanced by Delacre's
lovely illustrations. The music is included at the back of the book. Includes
"Aserrín, asserán."

———.
Las Navidades: Popular Christmas Songs from Latin America.
New York: Scholastic, 1990.
ISBN: 0590435485 (music)
Selected and illustrated by Lulu Delacre. English lyrics by Elena Paz. Mu-
sical arrangements by Ana-María Rosado.

Orozco, José-Luis.
De Colores and Other Latin-American Folk Songs for Children. Illus-
trated by Elisa Kleven.
New York: Dutton, 1994.
ISBN: 0525452605 (music)
Selected, arranged, and translated by José-Luis Orozco. Orozco includes
background on the origins of the songs as well as some related games.
   Includes "El chocolate," "La araña pequeñita"/"The Eensy, Weensy Spi-
der," and "Los Pollitos."

Chapter Fiction

Shorter novels with content appropriate for ages 7–11 (grades 3–5).

Ada, Alma Flor.
My Name Is María Isabel. Illustrated by K. Dyble Thompson. Trans-
lated by Ana M. Cerro.
New York: Atheneum, 1993.
ISBN: 068980217X
Spanish edition: **Me llamo María Isabel**.
New York: Simon and Schuster, 1996.
ISBN: 0689810997 (chapter fiction 7–11)

The teacher calls her Mary Lopez because there were so many Marias in the class, but María Isabel wants her new teacher to call her by her real name.

Osorio, Marta.
El caballito que queria volar (The Horse Who Wanted to Fly). Illustrated by Santos Heredero, María Jesús.
Leon, Spain: Gaviota Junior (Editorial Everest), 2000.
ISBN: 8439281110 (chapter fiction 7–11)
This is a beautiful story about a wooden carousel horse that wants to become a bird so that he can fly. He is the only horse on the carousel that is different. When he was made, he came from the carpenter's last piece of tree trunk, which had a large open gash. He finally gets his wish.

Don Quixote

2005 marked the 400th anniversary of the publication of *Don Quixote*, one of the greatest novels ever written. Publishers celebrated with numerous new editions and adaptations, many directed at children. Here are three takes on Cervantes' timeless classic, two from the same publisher, that all attempt to bring the tale to 21st century children.

De Cervantes, Miguel.
Don Quixote de la Mancha (Don Quixote of La Mancha). Adapted by Eduardo Alonso. Introduction by Martín de Riquer. Illustrated by Victor G. Ambrus.
Barcelona, Spain: Vicens Vives, 2004.
ISBN: 8431673966 (chapter fiction 7–11)

———.

Don Quixote de la Mancha (Don Quixote of La Mancha). Adapted by Agustín Sánchez. Illustrated by Svetlin.
Barcelona, Spain: Vicens Vives, 2004.
ISBN: 843167637X (chapter fiction 7–11)

López, Alberto Conejero.
El libro loco del Quijote (The Crazy Quijote Book). Illustrated by Joma.
Spain: SM, 2005.
ISBN: 846750384X (nonfiction 7–11)

The Alonso adaptation reduces Cervantes' original by a third, keeping much of the original text. In fact, it seems to be more of an edited version of the text than truly an adaptation. This is actually a good thing in that it retains much of

Cervantes' original language, while making this admittedly sprawling work more accessible to young people. The adaptation by Agustín Sánchez is much shorter but also retains much of the original language. While the story is, of necessity, highly abridged, Sánchez makes Quixote real for very young readers. Both volumes contain color illustrations. The Alonso version also includes an informative introduction about the life of Cervantes, and the history of the book itself, along with a note from Eduardo Alonso describing how he approached the adaptation. Editoral Vicens Vives has made an important contribution in keeping the legacy of Cervantes and his Quixote vibrant for a new generation of Spanish-speaking readers. Finally, *El libro loco del Quijote* is sort of like a DK Publishers version of the Quijote for kids. The book explores what seems like every possible angle of Quijote in a very entertaining way. It goes from games and a Quixote zodiac to recipes inspired by the book.

Rodríguez, Luis J.
It Doesn't Have to Be This Way: A Barrio Story/No tiene que ser así: una historia del barrio. Illustrated by Daniel Galvez.
San Francisco, CA: Children's Book Press, 1999.
ISBN: 0892391618 (fiction 7–11)
While this is a picture book, the content is mature and not for preschoolers. This is a gang story about Mochi, a ten year-old, who becomes involved in a gang despite the warnings of his cousin, Dreamer. A tragedy on the night of his gang initiation shows him the reality of gang life.

Ryan, Pam Muñoz.
Becoming Naomi León.
New York: Scholastic, 2004.
ISBN: 0439269695
Spanish edition: **Yo, Naomi León**.
ISBN: 0439755727 (chapter fiction 7–11)
Naomi lives with her grandmother and younger brother in a California trailer park. When Naomi's mother shows up, Naomi and her brother have to confront their family situation. They end up on a journey in the trailer to Mexico where Naomi meets her father, a talented wood-carver.

———.
Esperanza Rising.
New York: Scholastic, 2000.
ISBN: 0439120411
Spanish edition: **Esperanza renace**. Translated by Nuria Molinero.
ISBN: 0439398851 (chapter fiction 7–11)
Pura Belpré Author Award, 2002.

Esperanza's world is torn apart after her father is killed. She is forced to flee secretly with her mother and begins a new life in California as a farm-worker.

Sepúlveda, Luis.
Historia de una gaviota y del gato que le enseñó a volar.
New York: Arthur A. Levine (Scholastic), 2003.
ISBN: 0439560268
English edition: **The Story of a Seagull and the Cat Who Taught Her to Fly**. Translated by Margaret Sayers.
ISBN: 0439401860 (chapter fiction 7–11)
Zorba the cat helps a dying seagull by promising to watch over the incubating egg and to teach the chick how to fly. Zorba learns what caring is about as he enlists the help of his feline friends and even a human poet, to whom he speaks, breaking an important cat taboo.

Poetry

Poems for grade-school children (ages 7–11).

Alarcón, Francisco X.
Angels Ride Bikes and Other Fall Poems/Los angeles andan en bicicleta y otros poemas de otoño. Illustrated by Maya Christina Gonzalez.
San Francisco: Children's Book Press, 1999.
ISBN: 089239160X
Alarcón has written a series of outstanding books of bilingual poetry that vividly evoke the sights, sounds and smells of the seasons. Each of the books is excellent. The other books in this seasonal series include the following:

From the Bellybutton of the Moon and Other Summer Poems/Del ombligo de la luna y otros poemas de verano. Illustrated by Maya Christina González.
San Francisco: Children's Book Press, 1998.
ISBN: 0892391537
Pura Belpré Author Honor Book, 2000.

Iguanas in the Snow and Other Winter Poems/Iguanas en la nieve y otros poemas de invierno. Illustrated by Maya Christina González.
San Francisco: Children's Book Press, 2001.
ISBN: 0892391685
Pura Belpré Author Honor Book, 2002.

Laughing Tomatoes and Other Spring Poems/Jitomates risueños y otros poemas de primavera. Illustrated by Maya Christina González.
San Francisco: Children's Book Press, 1997.

ISBN: 0892391391
Pura Belpré Author Honor Book, 1998.

Bernier-Grand, Carmen T.
César: ¡Sí, se puede!/Yes, We Can! Illustrated by David Diaz.
Tarrytown, NY: Marshall Cavendish, 2004.
ISBN: 0761451722
Poems pay tribute to the life of the migrant-worker leader and organizer,
César Chavéz.

Herrera, Juan Felipe.
Laughing Out Loud, I Fly: Poems in English and Spanish. Illustrated
    by Karen Barbour.
New York: HarperCollins, 1998.
ISBN: 0060276045
Pura Belpré Author Honor Book, 2000.
A book of whimsical poetry from this award-winning writer.

Schon, Isabel.
Tito, Tito: Rimas, adivinanzas y juegos infantiles (Tito, Tito: Rhymes,
    Riddles and Children's Games). Illustrated by Violeta Monreal.
Mexico: Editorial Everest, 1995.
ISBN: 842413351X
Isabel Schon collects the rhymes games she loved the best as a child. The
book is complimented by beautiful watercolor illustrations.

Nonfiction

Nonfiction for younger grade-school children. 7–11 (grades 2–5). Many
of these books are heavily illustrated photo essays, with plenty of color
pictures.

Ancona, George.
Barrio: José's Neighborhood.
New York: Harcourt, 1998.
ISBN: 0152010491 (nonfiction 7–11)
Pura Belpré Illustrator Honor Book, 2000.
José lives in San Francisco's mission district. Ancona photographs him en-
gaging in his daily activities, as well as some significant cultural celebrations.
In doing so, he evokes what it is like to grow up Latino.

———.

The Piñata Maker/El piñatero.
San Diego, CA: Harcourt, 1995.

ISBN: 0152000607 (nonfiction 7–11)
Don Ricardo makes piñatas for all the village events.

Perl, Lila.
Piñatas and Paper Flowers: Holidays of the Americas in English and Spanish/Piñatas y flores de papel: Fiestas de las Américas en inglés y español. Translated by Alma Flor Ada.
New York: Clarion, 1983.
ISBN: 089919155X (nonfiction 7–11)
Describes the Latino holidays celebrated in the United States, as well as those observed in Latin America.

Novels

Novels (fiction) for slightly older grade-school children (ages 8–12).

Laura Gallego García
Laura Gallego García is one of the most exciting new talents to emerge from Spain. In 2005, Arthur A. Levine books published the first translation of her work in English, making her one of the very few Spanish children's writers to have broken into the English market. What makes her so special? Her fantasy writing has universal appeal. She published her first novel at age 21; and it won the prestigious El Barco de Vapor prize. Her works are bestsellers in Spain. She was featured on the cover of the January/February 2003 issue of *Críticas* magazine.
La leyenda del rey errante. Spain: Ediciones SM, 2005. ISBN: 8434888181 English edition: **The Legend of the Wandering King.** New York: Arthur A. Levine (Scholastic), 2005. ISBN: 0439585562.
An incredible story of redemption. Prince Walid has organized a poetry contest and is shamed when he loses to a carpet weaver named Hammad. In retribution, he gives Hammad some impossible tasks that Hammad manages to complete, but which drive him to his death. One of the tasks Walid gave Hammad was to weave a carpet that shows the future of human resources. Walid is consumed by guilt, and when the carpet is stolen, he tries to find redemption by embarking on an epic journey to find it.

El valle de los lobos.
Spain: Ediciones SM, 2004.
ISBN: 8434873613
English edition: **The Valley of the Wolves.**
New York: Arthur A. Levine (Scholastic), 2006.
ISBN: 0439585538
Dana accepts the invitation of a character called "Maestro" to go and study sorcery in the Valley of the Wolves.

Short Story Collections

Short stories for older grade-school children, ages 8–12 (grades 3–7).

Jiménez, Francisco.
The Circuit: Stories for the Life of a Migrant Child.
Boston: Houghton Mifflin, 1999.
ISBN: 0395979021
Spanish edition: **Cajas de cartón: relatos de la vida peregrina de un niño campesino.** Houghton Mifflin, 2002.
ISBN: 0618226168
Poignant short stories about the life of a child of migrant farmworkers in California. These simple stories are realistic, and do not shrink from portraying the unpleasant aspects of Jiménez's life.

Soto, Gary.
Baseball in April and Other Stories.
San Diego, CA: Harcourt Brace, 1990.
ISBN: 015205720X
Spanish edition: **Bèisbol en abril y otras historias.**
Mexico, D.F.: Fondo de Cultura Económica. 1995.
ISBN: 9681638549
Pura Belpré Author honor book 1996.
Includes "No-Guitar Blues," upon which a film was based.

Young Adult

Fiction appropriate for ages 12 and up (6th grade and above). They sometimes include mature content.

Anaya, Rudolfo.
Bless Me, Ultima.
New York: Warner, 1999.

ISBN: 0446675369
Spanish edition: **Bendíceme, Ultima**.
ISBN: 0446601772
Six-year-old Antonio becomes a friend and apprentice to the *curandera*, or healer, named Ultima. Antonio's life is full of questions and doubts. Each chapter includes a dream sequence in which his worst fears are given a voice.

Canales, Viola.
The Tequila Worm.
New York: Wendy Lamb (Random House), 2005.
ISBN: 038574674
Pura Belpré Author Award, 2006.
A spectacular first novel that weaves the threads of Latino culture and family relationships into the story of Sofia, who is faced with the choice of leaving her family for a boarding school where she can pursue her dreams.

Jiménez, Francisco.
Breaking Through.
Boston: Houghton Mifflin, 2001.
ISBN: 0000
Pura Belpré Author Honor Book 2002.
Continues the autobiography begun in *The Circuit*, focusing on Jiménez's adolescent experiences.

Martinez, Victor.
Parrot in the Oven: Mi vida.
New York: HarperCollins, 1996.
ISBN: 0060267062
Spanish edition: **El loro en el horno**.
Barcelona, Spain: Noguer y Caralt Editores, S.A., 1998.
ISBN: 8427932383
Pura Bepré Author Award, 1998.
National Book Award.
Manuel Hernandez tries to find his way in the world and with his family in this series of vignettes.

Ortiz Cofer, Judith.
An Island Like You: Stories of the Barrio.
New York: Orchard, 1996.
ISBN: 0531068978
Pura Belpré Author Award, 1996.
Twelve stories about young people in a New Jersey barrio struggling to reconcile their Puerto Rican heritage with their American life.

Chapter 4

Programming with the Core Collection

STORYTIME AND THEME PROGRAM GUIDELINES

Programming can be a highly rewarding experience, particularly with a Spanish-speaking or bilingual audience. One of the first books I found that was useful in programming was *Cuatro letras se escaparon* by Eduardo Robles Boza. This tale of letters that escaped from a book turned out to be perfect for creative dramatization in a parent/child program. A second, and still one of my all-time favorites, was *El caballito que quería volar* by Marta Osorio. It was one of those books you might not think would appeal to readers, but this magical story of a carousel horse that wanted to fly enchanted a group of children who held on to every word of the rich Spanish used in the book. At another time, I worked with older kids who did not speak English and were recent immigrants. We did a play with these kids based on the Pedro de Ordimalas folktale in which he tricks his way into heaven. This familiar story helped these children feel more comfortable in an unfamiliar environment.

This chapter will cover programs that you can do in a school or library setting with Latino children. In preparing to do programs, it is important to remember, as I have emphasized throughout this book, that not all Latino kids speak Spanish, and if they do, they may not speak it as their first language. The conflict this presents can be solved. To use storytime as an example, if two storytimes are offered, do one in English and one in Spanish or bilingual. If you speak Spanish, then it is easy. If you do not, find a volunteer such as a parent who can help you. Working with parents is crucial. Latino parents are concerned for the welfare of their children. Because the culture is so family oriented, you must have them on your side to be able to reach the children.

Latino parents can be a wealth of knowledge—they may know stories, rhymes, or games from their childhood, but before they can share their culture with you, they must be reached.

Why Bilingual Storytimes?

The anecdotes above should make it clear that there is a very important reason for doing bilingual storytimes. Besides making kids feel comfortable and giving them something familiar, using Spanish also helps children understand that their language is important and helps them feel a sense of validation. Those who are not Latino can also experience the culture and the language through these programs. Bilingual storytimes in English and Spanish should not just be for Latinos only. Hopefully one biproduct of bilingual storytimes would be a greater understanding of cultures and a sense of our shared humanity.

Earlier in this manual I mentioned attending a speech by Pat Mora in which she cautioned against equating Latino culture solely with celebrations and the very visible colorful manifestations of Latino culture. In this chapter I do include some programs and books that deal with celebrations and Latino holidays. I have tried to include a balance of storytime themes and programs that touch on more universal themes along with those that are more specific to Latino culture. While the basis of culture is language, and not celebrations, celebrations are undeniably important in Latino culture. I remember a Latino parent telling me how sad she felt that many of the traditions she had celebrated in Mexico, such as the Day of the Dead, were being lost here in the U.S., and that her children would not experience those traditions. Storytimes and library programs are a way to keep cultural traditions alive.

STORYTIMES AND THEME PROGRAMS

The following are suggested bilingual storytimes that can be used individually or in a series. I have grouped the storytimes by age, toddler first, and then preschoolers. I have also included program ideas for elementary school programs, as well as some booktalks from the core collection for young adults. The programs for elementary-age children includes ideas for special occasions and holidays. I also describe some intergenerational programs that can involve parents and children. Full bibliographic information for the books can be found either in the core collection, or in the list of additional titles. I have tried to include most of the core collection in these programming ideas, supplementing them with additional titles. These ideas are meant primarily to get you started in terms of beginning to put together themes, and hopefully will be a jumping-off point for you to add your own favorite books, crafts, and activity ideas. A terrific resource for programs for all ages can be found at the Texas State Library Web site where you can access a document called "Digame un cuento/Tell Me A Story: Bilingual Library Programs for Children and Families." The URL is http://www.tsl.state.tx.us/ld/pubs/bilingual/index.html.

Books and Fingerplays for Toddler Programs

It is difficult to have specific theme programs for toddlers, since the titles appropriate for this age group in Spanish are so limited. To present bilingual or Spanish language storytimes for toddlers you have to think beyond books in Spanish. Most toddler-appropriate books in English have simple enough texts that they can easily be translated. You can also use wordless books and describe them in Spanish. The following are suggestions of poems and fingerplays that could be combined for toddler times. These can also be used effectively with groups of older preschoolers as well. Remember that with the toddler age group, 15 minutes is usually the maximum attention span. For preschoolers, you can usually go up to 30 minutes.

SUGGESTED BOOKS FOR TODDLER TIME AND PRESCHOOL STORYTIME

Gusti. **La mosca en "un día perfecto puede llegar a ser una pesadilla."**
Guy, Ginger Foglesong. **Siesta.**
Lee, Héctor Viveros. **Yo tenía un hipopótamo.**
Menéndez, Margarita. **Un abrigo crecedero.**
Sánchez, Mireia. **Arriba del árbol.**
Shannon, David. **¡No, David!**
Poetry:
Arrorró, mi niño: Latino Lullabies and Gentle Games, illustrated by
    Lulu Delacre, which includes some of the rhymes below.

TODDLER TIME BOOK SUGGESTIONS

Books on Counting:
• Guy, Ginger Foglesong. **¡Fiesta!**
• Mora, Pat. **Uno, dos, tres: One, Two, Three.**
• Morales, Yuyi. **Just a Minute: Trickster Tales and Counting Book.**

Books about Mother:
• Carlin, Joi. **La cama de Mamá.**
• Ramos, Mario. **¡Mamá!**

Books about Colors:
- Guy, Ginger Foglesong. **Siesta**.
- Marcos, Subcomandante. **The Story of Colors**.

SUGGESTED FINGERPLAYS FOR TODDLERS

Simon Bribon   *Lazy Simon*

(Children pretend they are eating a melon)

Simón Bribón	Lazy Simon
comió me melon	ate my melon
y luego me dijo	and later said to me
¡Que calveron!	How greedy I was!

Los Ninos Traviesos   *The Mischevious Children*

(A Latin equivalent of Eeny, Meeny, Miney, Moe)

Este pide pan	This one asks for bread
Esta dice: no lo hay	This one says there is none
Este dice: ¿Que haremos?	This one asks "What shall we do?"
Esta dice: ¡Lo robaremos!	This one says "We'll rob some"
Esta dice: ¡No, no, que nos castigara nuestro mamá!	This one says "No, no, our mother will punish us!"

Hallando un Huevo   *Finding an Egg*

(Count on the fingers for each "Este." Look for water with the fingers, at the elbow, and then at the shoulder. End with a tickle under the arm.)

Este nini halló un huevo;	This little boy found an egg
Este lo coció;	This one cooked it;
Este lo peló;	This one peeled it;
Este le hechó la sal;	This one salted it;
Este gordo chaparrito se la comió.	This fat little one ate it.

Le dio sed,	He became thirsty,
Y se fue a buscar agua . . .	And he went to look for water . . .
Buscó y buscó . . .	He looked and looked . . .
¡Y aqui halló!	And here he found it!
Y tomó y tomó y tomó . . .	And drank and drank and drank . . .

Rima De Chocolate	*Chocolate Rhyme*

(Count with the fingers)

Uno, dos, tres, cho-	One, two, three, cho-
Uno, dos, tres, -co-	One, two, three, -co-
Uno, dos, tres, -la-	One, two, three, -la-
Uno, dos, tres, -te-	One, two, three, -te-
Bate, Bate chocolate	Chocolate, chocolate, beat the chocolate.

Tortillitas	*Tortillas*

"Tortillitas" is a Spanish equivalent of "patty-cake."
(Pat hands, alternating directions of fingers like a tortilla-maker.)

Tortillitas para Mamá	Tortillas for Mother
Tortillitas para Papá	Tortillas for Father
Las quemaditas para Mamá	The burnt ones for Mother
Las bonitas para Papá.	The good ones for Father
Tortillitas, tortillitas,	Tortillas, tortillas,
Tortillitas para Mamá	Tortillas for Mother
Tortillitas para Papá	Tortillas for Father
Tortillitas de salvado	Leftover tortillas
para Papá cuando está enojado	for Father when he's angry
Tortillitas de manteca	Tortillas of butter
para Mamá que está contenta.	so Mother is happy.

Tengo Una Vela	*Jack Be Nimble*

Children enjoy jumping over a small object—it doesn't have to be a candlestick—while saying this rhyme together.

Tengo una vela	Jack be nimble
en un candelero	Jack be quick
la pongo en el suelo	Jack jump over the
y la brinco ligero.	Candlestick.

Sana, Sana	*Get Well, Get Well*

Sana, sana,	Get well, get well,
colita de rana,	little frogs tail,
Si no sanas hoy,	If you don't get better today,
Sanarás mañana.	You'll be better tomorrow.

El Gato	*The Cat*
Cuatro patas tiene un gato, Uno, dos, tres, cuatro.	Four paws has a cat, One, two, three, four.
Este Niño Tiene Sueño	*This Little Child Is Sleepy*
Este niño tiene sueño, tiene ganas de dormir, tiene une ojito cerrado, y el otro no lo puede abrir.	This little child is sleepy, she wants to go to sleep, she has one eye closed, and she can't keep the other open.
Naranja Dulce	*Sweet Orange*
Naranja dulce, Limón partido. Dame un abrazo Que yo te pido	Sweet orange, Lemon slice. Give me the hug That I ask you for.
Si fueron falso Mis juramentos, En poco tiempo Se olvidarán.	If my oaths Were false, In a short time They will be forgotten.
Toca la marcha, mi pecho llora, adios señora, yo yo me voy.	Play a march, my chest cries, goodbye my lady, I'm going away.
Un Ratón	*Three Blind Mice*
(A song)	

Un ratón, un ratón,
Corriendo por aqui,
   corriendo por alli,
Comiendo queso,
   comiendo pan,
Al fin, los gatos lo agarrarán.
	One mouse, one mouse,
	Running here, running there,
	
	Eating cheese, eating bread,
	
	In the end, the cats will kill him
	   dead.

Al ratoncito se comerán, ¡Qué caray! ¡Qué caray!	They'll eat him whole. What a pity! What a pity!

Storytime Themes for Preschool Programs

There are many options for presenting bilingual books in preschool story-times. The books recommended here have different levels of Spanish. Some books have Spanish words and phrases sprinkled throughout, but are not truly bilingual in the sense that the complete text is presented both in Spanish and English. Of course, there are many bilingual books in which this is the case: Spanish and English texts are presented side by side, or one below the other. The third scenario focuses on books that were originally published in one language, but have subsequently been made available in a translated edition. This means that you have both Spanish and English available, but they are in separate volumes. Obviously, your ability to present these books will be dependent on how comfortable you are with Spanish. However, there are a number of techniques to present a storytime bilingually. Many librarians use a team approach, where English- and Spanish-speaking librarians team up and read a story in both languages. They can go back and forth, with one librarian reading a page in English, and the second person repeating it in Spanish. This can work with both bilingual books, or with the librarians reading from separate English and Spanish translations. Of course, you might also choose to read the book all the way through in each language, if you feel you can do so without losing the attention of the children.

Here is an example of a typical storytime, courtesy of Lucía Gonzales of the Broward County Library. Lucía's outline, found in her article, "Developing Culturally Integrated Children's Programs," provides a good sense of the elements that should be the basis of a bilingual storytime.

1. Opening routine
   Use an opening rhyme or song. Lucía suggests "Cancion de los elefantes" (Song of the elephants) which can be found in Lulu Delacre's book *Arroz con leche*.
2. Book
   Lucía suggests *Loz zapaticos de Rosa* by Jose Marti.
3. Rhymes or riddles
   Parents can participate by sharing rhymes they remember from their childhoods.
4. Oral story
   Try a story that you can tell without a book. Lucía suggests one of the Tio Conejo, or Uncle Rabbit, stories such as "The Day Tio Conejo fooled Tio Zorro."
5. Book
   Try *La ratita presumida*, mentioned in the bibliography.
6. Closing routine

Lucía always ends her programs with A-la-rueda-rueda, which is the Spanish version of "Ring-Around-the-Roses" and the game Lobo (Wolf). A-la-rueda-rueda can be found in Alma Flor Ada's book *¡Pio Peep!*.

STORYTIME SUGGESTIONS

Storytime 1: Fairy Tales
Elya, Susan Middleton. **Fairy Trails: A Story told in English and Spanish**.
Salinas, Bobbi. **The Three Pigs/Los tres cerdos: Nacho, Tito and Miguel**.

Any of the fairy tales in Spanish mentioned in the core collection highlight can be used here. Pick your favorite!

Storytime 2: Conozcandote/Getting to Know You
Reiser, Lynn. **Margaret and Margarita/Margarita y Margaret**.

This is a perfect storytime for the librarian who is uncomfortable with her ability to speak Spanish. The Spanish required for this story is minimal. The themes of these stories are Spanish and non Spanish-speaking children working together and getting to know each other. In *Margaret and Margarita*, Margaret speaks only English and Margarita speaks only Spanish. They find a way to communicate when they meet in a park. You can add most any other bilingual story you like to this theme.

Los Diez Perritos (Song)

This is a favorite song. You can have children hold up ten fingers as you begin the song, and then put a finger down as you begin losing dogs.

Yo tenía diez perritos, y uno se cayó en la nieve
ya no más me quedan nueve, nueve, nueve, nueve, nueve.

De los nueve que tenía, uno se comió un bizcocho,
ya no más me quedan ocho, ocho, ocho, ocho, ocho.

De los ocho que tenía, uno se golpeo su frente,
ya no más me quedan siete, siete, siete, siete, siete.

De los siete que tenía, uno se quemó los pies,
ya no más me quedan seis, seis, seis, seis, seis.

De los seis que tenía, uno se escapó de un brinco,
ya no más me quedan cinco, cinco, cinco, cinco, cinco.

De los cinco que tenía, uno se metió en un teatro,
ya no más me quedan cuatro, cuatro, cuatro, cuatro, cuatro.

De los cuatro que tenía, uno se cayó al reves,
ya no más me quedan tres, tres, tres, tres, tres.

De los tres que tenía, uno sufrió de un tos,
ya no más me quedan dos, dos, dos, dos, dos.

De los dos que tenía, uno se murió de ayuno,
ya no más me queda uno, uno, uno, uno, uno.

Ten Puppies

I had ten puppies, one fell in the snow,
now I only have nine, nine, nine, nine, nine.

Of the nine that were left, one ate a biscuit
now I only have eight, eight, eight, eight, eight.

Of the eight that were left, one banged his forehead,
now I only have seven, seven, seven, seven, seven.

Of the seven that were left, one burned his feet,
now I only have six, six, six, six, six.

Of the six that were left, one ran away,
now I only have five, five, five, five, five.

Of the five that were left, one went into a theater
now I only have four, four, four, four, four.

Of the four that were left, one fell backwards,
now I only have three, three, three, three, three.

Of the three that were left, one caught a cold,
now I only have two, two, two, two, two.

Of the two that were left, one died of fasting,
now I only have one, one, one, one, one.

The tune for this song can be found in **A Fiesta of Folk Songs from Spain and Latin America**, by Henrietta Yurchenko. Illustrated by Jules Maidoff. New York: Putnam, 1967.

Storytime 3: Los libros y la biblioteca/Books and the Library
Mora, Pat. **Tomás and the Library Lady**.
Nizri, Vicki. **Un asalto mayusculo**.
Robles Boza, Eduardo. **Cuatro Letras Se Escaparon**.
Niera, Maria, and Anna Wennberg. **Mamá Oca y las vocals**.

Cuatro Letras Se Escaparon by Eduardo Robles Boza

As it appears to have gone out of print, here the Spanish text and the English translation for *Cuatro Letras Se Escaparon.*

De un libro de muchas páginas, cuatro letras se escaparon.

From a book with many pages, four letters escaped.

Dando saltos y maromas llegaron a un cuaderno de rayas muy derechitas. Por poco tropiezan con la goma y el lapis que descansaban sobre la hoja.

Doing jumps and loops, they arrived at a notebook that had very straight lines. Shortly they encountered an eraser and a pencil that rested on top of the page.

¡Estaban felices! La *P* correteaba a la gordinflona *O*, la *E* jugaba a ponerse de cabeza, mientras la escandalosa *R* ejecutaba un salto verdaderamente complicado.

They were happy! The *P* pursued the fat little *O*, the *E* played at standing on its head, while the scandalous *R* executed a very complicated jump.

Les sobraba imaginación, así que decidieron tomar una raya de la hoja del cuaderno para brincar a la cuerda. La *O* hacía grandes esfuerzos para no caer.

Their imagination was overflowing, so they decided to take one of the lines from the page in the notebook to play jump rope. The *O* made a great effort not to fall.

De pronto dijo la *E*: "¡Vamos a formar palabras!" Y las cuatro amigas lo intentaron.

Shortly, the *E* said, "Let's form some words!" And so the four friends tried to do just that.

Pero eran palabras extrañas. Se cambiaban de lugar y seguían siendo raras . . . porque escribían en inglés.

But they were strange words. (In the illustrations, the four letters form the word *OPRE*, then *EROP*, and then finally *ROPE*). They changed places and the words continued to be strange . . . because they were writing in English.

Abandonaron la última palabra y reanudaron el juego. ¡Como se divertía la *E* pantinando en el cuaderno!

They abandoned that last work and began to play again. The *E* had a wonderful time skating on the notebook!

—¡Ya he encontrado la palabra!—dijo la *O*, emocionada—. La *P* primero, después la *E*, luego la *R* y al final yo. Espero que la hayan visto, por que la palabra es . . . *PERO* (translation: BUT).

"I've found a word!, said the *O*, excitedly. The *P* first, then the *E*, then the *R*, and finally me. I hope that you have seen it, because the word is . . . *PERO*.

—¡Es muy prostestona!

—¡Siempre se mete en problemas!

—¡Es muy concflictiva!

Y la palabra, por fea, desaparació de cuaderno.

"It's very negative!

"It always gets itself into problems!"

"It's very conflicting!"

And the word disappeared from the notebook.

Nuevemente intentaron construir algo major. Eran persistentes, insistían y no se daban por vencidas, así que la encontraron, pero resultó . . . *PEOR* (WORSE).

Again they tried to construct a better word. They were persistent, insistent, and didn't give up, and so they came up with a new word, but the word was . . . *PEOR*.

¡No sirive!—exclamó la *R*. Tenían razon. Eran buenas amigas, pero solo formaban palabras conflictivas, así que aprovecharon que el viento soplaba y se dejaron llevar de regreso al libro.

"This won't do!" exclaimed the *R*. He was right. They were good friends, but they were only able to form conflicting words, so they made use of the wind that was blowing and they let it take them back to the book.

Las cuatro traviesas se metieron en sus páginas y se acuurucaron para dormir. Temblaban como gelatina, pero no de frío, sino por el miedo de que las regañaran las demás letras del abecedario.

The four mischevious letters went back in to the pages, and tucked themselves to sleep. They trembled like gelatin, but not because of the cold, but rather because of the fear that the other letters of the alphabet would make fun of them.

Al día siguiente fueron recibidas por sus compañeras como heroínas, por valientes. Habían regresados sanas y salvas al diccionario, donde hacían tanta falta.

The next day they were received by their companions as heroines for their valor. They had returned safe and sound to the dictionary, where they had been missed a great deal.

A la *A* y *A* la *Z*, la primera y la última letras de abecedario, les contaron su pena: "No sabemos como formar buenas palabras. Ésa es nuestra disgracia."

To the *A* and the *Z*, the first and last letters of the alphabet, they explained their sorrow: "We don't know how to form good words. This is our shame."

—Pero retornaron sin un rasguño y eso es una hazaña—dijo la *Z*.

—Nosotras dos queremos unirnos a ustedes para darles un significado—exclamó la *A*, emocionada.

Y así lo hicieron, mientras las demás letras de abecedario, en coro, advirtieron;—*PERO* es una objeción y escribirla da pereza, pero *PEOR* es peor y en cambio hazaña es . . .

"But they returned without a scratch and that is a feat," the Z said. "We two want to join with you to help you make a word," exclaimed the A, moved. And that's what they did, while the other letters of the alphabet, in chorus, exclaimed "*BUT* is an objection and writing it makes you lazy, but *WORSE* is worse, however, you can change it into . . . *PROEZA.*"

Cuenta la leyen que así nació esta palabra.

And legend has it that this is how the word *PROEZA* was born.

The illustration shows the definition of Proeza, which is spirited action, an act of valor. Spanish text © 1986 Editorial Trillas S. A. de C. V.

Activity: For the story *Cuatro Letras Se Escaparon*, make small signs, one with each of the letters *P, R, O, E, Z,* and *A*. Child volunteers can hold these letters and move around spelling the different words created by the escaped letters as the story progresses.

Poem: "Las palabras son pájaros/Words are Birds" from **Laughing Tomatoes and Other Spring Poems/Jitomates risueños y otros poemas de primavera**, by Francisco X. Alarcon. Illustrated by Maya Christina Gonzalez. Children's Book Press, 1997.

Storytime 4: Ratones, Ranas y Peces/Mice, Frogs and Fishes

Books:

Lionni, Leo. **Nadrarin.**
———. **Frederick.**
Mistral, Gabriela. **Crickets and Frogs: A Fable.**
Sastrías, Marta. **El sapo que no quería comer.**

Note: Tell "Un Cuento de Sapos."

Poems

Los Pescaditos	*The Little Fish*
Los pescaditos andan en el agua	The little fish swim in the water
nadan, nadan, nadan	Swim, swim, swim
Vuelan, vuelan, vuelan	They fly, fly, fly
Son chiquititos, son chiquititos	They are little, they are little
Vuelan, vuelan, vuelan	They fly, fly, fly
Nadan, nadan, nadan	They swim, swim, swim.

La Ranita Soy Yo	*I am the Frog*
La ranita soy yo	I am the frog
glo, glo, glo	glo, glo, glo
El sapito eres tú	You are the toad
glu, glu, glu	glu, glu, glu
Cantemos así	We sing like this
gli, gli, gli	gli, gli, gli
Que la lluvia se fué	The rain went away
gle, gle, gle	gle, gle, gle
Y la ronda se vá	And the round goes on
gla, gla, gla	gla, gla, gla

A FROG STORY

Synopsis: A long time ago there lived Mr. and Mrs. Frog. Mr. Frog liked to stay out late with his friends, and would not come home for dinner, which made Mrs. Frog angry.

One day he arrives home, expecting food, but finds a note from Mrs. Frog saying "I've already eaten and left. Don't wait up." He goes out to find something to eat and does not come home till even later than usual. He finds Mrs. Frog knitting in the living room. She asks him where dinner is. Mr. Frog replies that he's the one who's hungry. Mrs. Frog, of course, just wants to get his goat and has already eaten, so she replies:

"I'm not."

"I am," replies Mr. Frog.

"I'm not."

"I am."

They go back and forth like that all night long and into the morning. Their racket catches the attention of Noah, who tries to get them to shut up without success. (This was, you see, just after all the animals had descended from the ark.) Noah enlists the aid of St. Peter and together they decide to punish the frogs, so that from then on they would only be able to say those two stupid words. And that is why to this day, frogs say, "Ribbit, Ribbit."

UN CUENTO DE SAPOS

Resulta que hace muchos años vivía un matrimonio de sapos que se querían grandemente y lo pasaban bien a la orilla de una charca. Las casa era de dos pisos, con terraza y todo, y en el verano salían de excursión en un bote hecho con una table y un pedazo de lona vieja. Y eran muy felices con sus trajes de seda verde y sus pecheras blancas y sus ojos que parecían bolitas negras que se les fueran a salir de la cara.

Por la única cosa que a veces peleaban era porque al señor Sapo le gustabe quedarse conversando con sus amingos de la gran ciudad Anfibia, y llegaba a lamorzar a las mil y tantas, y entonces la señora Sapa se enojaba mucho y discutían mucho más aún, y a veces las cosas se ponían harto feas.

Un día llegó el señor Sapo con las manos metidas en los bosillos del chaleco, silbando una canción de moda, muy contento. Y ya habían dado las tres de la tarde. ¡En verdad, no era hora para llegar a almorzar!

Como nadie saliera a recibirlo, en señor Sapo dijo, llamando:

—Sapita Cuacua . . . Sapita Cuacua . . .

Pero la señora Sapita Cuacua no apareció. Volvió a llamarla y volvió a obtener el silencio por respuesta. La fue a buscar el comedor, al salón, al dormitorio, al baño, a la cocina, al prepostero. Hasta se asomó a la terraza. Pero en ninguna parte estaba su mujercita vestida de verde.

De repente, el señor Sapo vio sobre una mesa del salón un papel que decía: ALMORCE Y SALI. NO ME ESPERES EN TODA LA TARDE.

Al señor Sapo le pareció pésima la noticia, ya que no tendria quein le siriviera el almuerzo. Se fue entonces a la concina; pero vio que las ollas estaban todas vacías, limias y colgando de sus soportes. Se fue al repostero y encontró todos los cajones y estantes con llave.

El señor sapo comprendió que todo aquello lo había hecho la señora Sapita Cuacua para darle una lección. Y sin mayores aspavientos, se tovo que ir a donde la señora Rana, que tenía un despacho cerca del sauce de la esquina, a comprarle un pedazo de arrollado y unos pequenes para matar el hambre.

Pero como este señor Sapo era muy porfiado y no entendía lecciones, en ve de llegar esa noche a come a las nueve, como era lo habitual, llegó nada menos que un cuarto para las diez.

La señora Sapita Cuacua estaba tejiendo en el salón, y sin saludarlo siquiera, le dijo de muy mal modo:

—No hay comida.

—Tengo hambre—contestó el señor Sapo de igual mal humor.

—Yo, no.

—Yo, sí.

—Yo, no.

—Yo, sí.

Y como eran un par de porfiados y ninguno de ellos quería dar su brazo a torcer—como vulgarmente se dice—, a medianoche estaban todavía repitiendo:

—Yo, no.

—Yo, sí.

—Yo, no.

—Yo, sí.

Y cuando apareció el sol por sobre las montes, el matrimonio de los señores Sapos seguía empecinado, diciendo:

—Yo, no.

—Yo, sí.

—Yo, no.

—Yo, sí.

Y todo eso pasabe poco después que Noe echó a los animales del Arca, porque el diluvio había terminado. Ese día Noe había salido muy temprano a ver sus viñedos, y al pasar cerca de la charca oyó la discusión y movió la cabeza en señal de disgusto, porque le gustaba muy poco que los animales se pelearan. Y cuando por tarde pasó de regreso a su casa, le llegaron de nuevo las mismas palabras:

—Yo, no.

—Yo, sí.

—Yo, no.

—Yo, sí.

A Noe ya le dio un poco de fastidio, y acercándose a la puerta de las casa de los señores Sapos, les dijo:

—Quieren hacer el favor de callarse?

Pero los señores Sapos, sin oirlo, siguieron diciendo:

—Yo, no.

—Yo, sí.

—Yo, no.

—Yo, sí.

Entonces a Noe le dio rabia de veras, y les gritó, enojado:

—Se quieren callar los bochincheros?

Y San Pedro—que estaba asomado a una de las ventanas del cielo tomando el aire—le dijo a Noe, también medio enojado, porque hasta allá arriba llegaban las voces de los discutidores porfiados.

—Los vamos a castigar, y desde ahora, cuando quieran hablar, sólo podrán decir esas dos palabras estúpidas.

Y ya saben ustedes, mis queridos niños, por qué los Sapos de todas las charcas del mundo sólo pueden deci a toda hora y a propósito de toda cosa:

—Yo, no.

—Yo, sí.

—Yo, no.

—Yo, sí.

Source: Marta Brunet, in Carmen Bravo-Villasante's, **Historia y antología de la literatura infantil iberoamericana**, vol. 1., pp. 185–187.

Storytime 5: Comida/Food

Bertrand, Diane Gonzalez. **Sip, Slurp, Soup/Caldo, caldo caldo**.

Hayes, Joe. **The Day It Snowed Tortillas**.

Paulsen, Gary. **La Tortilleria/The Tortilla Factory**.
Sastrías, Marta. **El sapo que no quería comer**.
Soto, Gary. **Chato's Kitchen**.

Poems

Tortillitas	*Tortillas*

(Pat hands, alternating directions of fingers like a tortilla-maker).

Tortillitas para Mamá,	Tortillas for mother
Tortillitas para Papá,	Tortillas for father
Las quemaditas para Mamá	The burnt ones for mother
Las bonitas para Papá	The good ones for father
Tortillitas, tortillitas,	Tortillas, tortillas,
tortillitas para Mamá;	Tortillas for mother,
tortillitas para Papá.	Tortillas for father,
Tortillitas de salvado	Leftover tortillas
para Papa cuando está enojado;	for father when he's angry;
tortillitas de manteca	Tortillas of butter
para Mamá que está contenta.	So mother is happy.

Arroz Con Leche	*Rice With Milk*
Arroz con leche,	Rice with milk
me quiero casar	I want to marry
con un mexicano	a Mexican
que sepa cantar.	who knows how to sing.
El hijo del rey,	The son of the king
me manda un papel,	sent me a letter
me manda decir,	to ask
que me case con él.	if I would marry him.
Con éste no,	With this one, no,
con éste sí,	With this one, yes,
con éste niño	With this child
me caso yo.	I will be married.

Note: This can also be a tortilla storytime by omitting *Chato's Kitchen*.

Storytime 6: Pollitos/Chickens
Ada, Alma Flor. **Mediopollito/Half Chicken**.

Barbot, Daniel. **Rosaura en bicicleta/A Bicycle for Rosaura.**
Delacre, Lulu. **The Bossy Gallito/El gallo de bodas.**

Poems

Doña Pata	*Mrs. Duck*

Detrás de Doña Pata (point behind)
corren los patitos (make running motion with fingers)
por allí, por allá, (point to left and right)

cuá, cuá, cuá	
Detrás de Doña Gallina	Behind Mrs. Duck
siguen los pollitos	run the ducklings
por allí, por allá,	over here, over there . . .
pío, pío, pa	Behind Mrs. Hen
Detrás de Doña Cabra	follow the little chicks
van las cabritos	over here, over there . . .
por allí, por allá,	Behind Mrs. Goat
baa, baa, baa	come the baby goats
	over here, over there . . .

Cinco Pollitos	*Five Baby Chicks*
Cinco pollitos	My aunt has
tiene mi tía;	five baby chicks,
uno le canta,	one sings,
otro le pía	one goes "peep"
y tres le tocan la symphonia	and three play the symphony.

Fingerplays:

La Gallinita Napolitana	*The Napolitan Hen*
La gallinita napolitana	The Napolitan hen
Pone un huevo cada semana	Lays one egg a week
pone dos,	Lays two
pone tres,	Lays three
pone cuatro,	Lays four
pone cinco,	Lays five
pone seis,	Lays six
¡Pone siete a la semana!	Lays seven in the week!
pone ocho,	Lays eight
pone nueve,	Lays nine
pone diez,	Lays ten
la gallinita, ya lo ves,	The hen, now you see,
quiere que escondas tus pies	Wants you to hide your feet.

Song

Los Pollitos	*The Baby Chicks*
Los pollitos dicen	Baby chicks are singing
"Pio, pio, pio,"	"Pio, pio, pio,"
Cuando tienen hambre,	"Mamma we are hungry
Cuando tienen frio.	"Mamma we are cold."
La gallina busca	Mamma looks for wheat,
El maíz y el trigo,	Mamma looks for corn,
Les da la comida	Mamma feeds them dinner,
Y les presta abrigo.	Mamma keeps them warm.
Bajo sus dos alas	Under mamma's wings
Acurrucaditas	Sleeping in the hay
Hasta el otro día	Baby chicks all huddle
Duermen los pollitos.	Until the next day.

The tune for this song can be found in **De Colores: and Other Latin-American Folk Songs for Children**, by José-Luis Orozco. Illustrated by Elisa Kleven. New York: Dutton, 1994, p. 32.

Variations: You could use **El sancocho del sábado** by Torres.

Storytime 7: Abuelos/Grandparents
Dorros, Arthur. **Isla**.
——. **Abuela**.
Leon, Georgina Lazaro. **El flamboyan amarillo**.
Mora, Pat. **Pablo's Tree**.
Delgado, María Isabel. **Chave's Memories/Los recuerdos de Chave**.
Reiser, Lynn. **Tortillas and Lullabies/Tortillas y cancioncitas**.

Activity: Have the children draw a picture of themselves with their grandparents, doing whatever they like to do best together. If grandparents are there, have them draw a picture, too.

Note: These books can serve for an intergenerational program. Invite the grandparents to be there with the children.

Storytime 8: Bodas y Familias/Weddings and Families
Moreton, Daniel. **La cucaracha Martina: A Carribean Folktale**.
Orihuela, Luz, adap. **La ratita presumida**.
Belpré, Pura. **Perez y Martina** (if available).
Soto, Gary. **Snapshots from the Wedding**.
Van Laan, Nancy. **La Boda: A Mexican Wedding Celebration**.

Storytime 9: El sol y la luna / The Sun and the Moon
Aardema, Verna. **Borrguita and the Coyote**.
Ada, Alma Flor. **The Lizard and the Sun/La lagartija y el sol**.
Ehlert, Lois. **Moon Rope/Un lazo a la luna**.
Johnston, Tony. **The Tale of Rabbit and Coyote**.

Poem

El Dia Que Tu Naciste	*The Day You Were Born*
El día que tú naciste	The day you were born
nacieron las cosas bellas	All the beautiful things were born
nació el sol, nació la luna	The sun was born, the moon was born
y nacieron las estrellas	And the stars were born.

Activity: Both the Aardema and Johnston books retell the folktale where Coyote is tricked into thinking that the reflection of the moon on the water is a cheese. Use whichever you prefer. Either of these stories provide excellent opportunities for creative dramatization. A great art project to go along with this storytime would be to have the children draw and color an Aztec-style sun, complete with a face. All you need are crayons and paper.

Storytime 10: Pesadillas/Nightmares
Hayes, Joe. **El terible tragadabas/The Terrible Tragadabas**.
Sanromán, Susana. **Señora Regañona: A Mexican Bedtime Story**.

Activity: *The Terrible Tragadabas* can be told effectively without the book. After reading *The Terrible Tragadabas* and *Señora Regañona,* have the children draw a picture of what they think these characters might look like.

Storytime 11: Birthday Party
Guy, Ginger Fogelsong. **¡Fiesta!**
Isol. **Un regalo sorpresa**.
Ryan, Pam Muñoz. **Mice and Beans**.

Activity: This would be the perfect program at which to break a piñata, or to serve birthday cake.

Storytime 12: Art
Pellicer Lopez, Carlos. **Julieta y su caja de colores**.
Winter, Jeanette. **Diego**.
————. **Josefina**.

Activity: After these stories, spread a piece of butcher paper over a table. Have the children gather around it. Have plenty of crayons. Have them illustrate a scene from their own life and sign their name. The resulting mural can be hung on a library bulletin board.

Storytime 13: Lucha Libre
Garza, Xavier. **Lucha Libre: The Man in the Silver Mask**.

Activity: Lucha Libre is the Mexican version of pro-wrestling. You can have the children make their own masks with paper plates, using a template to make eyes, ear and mouth holes in the mask. They can color it and even make it glittery.

Note: This idea was shared by Francisco Vargas of the Phoenix Library. This would be appropriate for an all ages storytime. The book is long enough so that it can support the program along with the mask project.

Storytime 14: Music
Brown, Monica. **My Name is Celia: The Life of Celia Cruz/Me llamo Celia: La vida de Celia Cruz**.

Music: This book absolutely cries out for music. Get a Celia Cruz CD and let the children hear her sing.

Storytime 15: *Dichos*/Proverbs
Anzaldua, Gloria. **Friends from the Other Side/Amigos del otro lado**.
Gonzalez, Rafka, and Ana Ruiz. **Mi primer libro de dichos/My First Book of Proverbs**.

Activity: Make a book of *dichos* or proverbs. Have kids write down their own proverbs in a book they make themselves. You can create your own books with cardstock for the front and back covers. Punch two holes and use a rubber band to go through the holes, and fasten the rubber band to a plastic coffee stirrer.

Note: This idea was shared by Francisco Vargas of the Phoenix Public Library.

Storytime 16: César Chávez
Book
    Krull, Kathleen. **Harvesting Hope: The Story of César Chávez**.
Poem
    Ada, Alma Flor. **Gathering the Sun: An Alphabet in Spanish and English**.

Oralia Garza de Cortés has an excellent plan for a storytime celebrating not only Chávez, but also heroes in general. She includes craft projects and Web connections as well as suggestions for poetry to use. The document can be found at: http://www.reforma.org/CYASCSchool-ageSpanishandbilingual program.doc

Storytime 17: The Migrant Experience: A Search for Home
Books
> Altman, Linda Jacobs. **El camino de Amelia** (*Amelia's Road*).
> Mora, Pat. **Tomás and the Library Lady**.
> Anzaldúa, Gloria. **Friends from the Other Side/Amigos del otro lado**.
> Herrera, Juan Felipe. **Calling the Doves/El canto de las palomas**.

Poems
> Delacre, Lulu. **Arrorró, mi niño: Latino Lullabies and Gentle Games**.

Storytime 18: Tall Tales and Folk Tales
Montes, Marisa. **Juan Bobo Goes to Work: A Puerto Rican Folk Tale**.
Mora, Pat. **Doña Flor: A Tall Tale About a Giant Woman with a Great
> Big Heart**.
Ryan, Pam Muñoz. **Nacho and Lolita**.

Storytime 19: Desert
Mora, Pat. **Listen to the Desert/Oye al desierto**.

Storytime 20: Magic and Dreams
Pellicer Lopez, Carlos. **Juan y sus zapatos** (*Juan and His Shoes*).
————. **Julieta y su caja de colores** (*Julieta and Her Box of Paints*).

ELEMENTARY PROGRAMS

Booktalks

BOOKTALK: BECOMING NAOMI LEÓN BY PAM MUÑOZ RYAN.

Naomi León's full name is Naomi Soledad León Outlaw. She lives in a trailer
park with her brother Owen and Gram, who is really her great-grandmother.
Her life is happy until her mother Skyla shows up after an absence of seven
years. Skyla wants to be part of Naomi's life, but Naomi is suspicious of her
motives. The only way for that not to happen is to find Naomi's father, who
is a carver somewhere in the state of Oaxaca, Mexico. Naomi and Owen and
Gram literally pick up and drive the motor home they have been living in to
Mexico. Will they find Naomi's father? Will she have to go with her mother
and her mother's slimy new boyfriend? This book is truly an adventure.

BOOKTALK: ESPERANZA RISING BY PAM MUÑOZ RYAN.

Esperanza is happily preparing for her thirteenth birthday celebration when
she discovers that her father has been murdered by bandits. And this is just the
beginning of her trials. Esperanza's evil uncles try to force Esperanza's mother
to marry one of them. To force her hand, they burn down Esperanza's beloved

ranch. The family is forced to flee in secret to America where they end up as migrant farmworkers. Esperanza is especially sad that her beloved grandmother was not able to accompany them, and hopes to bring her to America.

A sense of the power of this story can be conveyed through a personal story. On a driving trip, my wife and I were listening to the audio book of *Esperanza Rising*. It was late at night, and we thought that our then four-year-old daughter was asleep is the back. When the story reached the point where the family ranch is burned to the ground, we heard sobs coming from the back of the car. We asked our daughter what was the matter, and she replied, "This is a SAD story!" We pulled over to the side of the road and stopped the car. My wife cradled our daughter in her arms and discussed the story. Our daughter wanted to continue listening—she wanted to know what happened next.

Booktalk: My Name Is María Isabel by Alma Flor Ada.

On her first day of school in the United States, María is told that since there are already two Marías in her class, that she will be called Mary Lopez. María Isabel does not recognize herself in this "strange new name" (12). She has always loved her name because she was named for her father's mother and for her Puerto Rican grandmother. María has to write a theme for her teacher on the subject of "My Greatest Wish":

> ". . . I think my greatest wish is to be called María Isabel Salazar López. When that was my name, I felt proud of being named María like my papá's mother, and Isabel like my Grandmother Chabela. She is saving money so that I can study and not have to spend my whole life in a kitchen like her. I was Salazar like my papá and my Grandpa Antonio, and López, like my Grandfather Manuel. I never knew him but he could really tell stories. I know because my mother told me.
>
> "If I was called María Isabel Salazar López, I could listen better in class because it's easier to hear than Mary López." (49–51)

Activity: Have children ask their parents the background of their name. Were they named after a relative? Children can share the meaning of their name.

Theme Programs

Program: Animal Folktales

Ehlert, Lois. **Cuckoo/Cucu.**
———. **Moon Rope/Un lazo a la luna**.
Kouzel, Daisy. **Cuckoo's Reward/El premio del Cucu.**

Activity: Compare and contrast the Ehlert and Kouzel versions of the Cuckoo legend. Note that the two Lois Ehlert books are connected by the fact that the character of mole appears in both.

PROGRAM: PEDRO DE URDEMALAS TALES

Aardema, Verna. **Pedro and the Padre**.
Brusca, María Cristina, and Tona Wilson. **The Blacksmith and the Devils**.

Video program—Gary Soto

Use one or both of the following Gary Soto videos:

No Guitar Blues. New York: Pheonix/BFA, 1991. 27 min.

A video of a story taken from *Baseball in April*. Fausto gets ridden with guilt over the dishonest way he obtains money to buy the guitar he wants. Later he receives a present of a bass guitarrón, which has been in the family.

The Pool Party. 1993. 29 min.

A video based on Soto's book of the same name. Rudy Herrera gets invited to Tiffany Perez's pool party. Tiffany is one of the richest kids in school. His family tries to help him get ready and select a gift. Winner of the Andrew Carnegie Medal for Excellence in Children's Video.

Holiday Programs

PROGRAM 1: EL DÍA DE LOS MUERTOS/DAY OF THE DEAD

Books
Anaya, Rudolfo. **Maya's Children: The Story of La Llorona**.
Ancona, George. **Pablo recuerda/Pablo Remembers**.
Anzaldúa, Gloria. **Prietita and the Ghost Woman/Prietita y la llorona**.
Kimmel, Eric. **The Witch's Face: A Mexican Tale**.
Levy, Janice. **The Spirit of Tío Fernando/El espíritu de tío Fernando**.
Johnston, Tony. **Day of the Dead**.

Poems

Calavera I   *Skull I*

Calaveras (skulls) can be spooky poems or songs for the Day of the Dead

Por aquí pasa la Muerte	Here passes Death
con su aguja y su dedal	with his needle and his thimble
remendando sus naguas	mending his petticoat
para el día del carnaval.	for carnival day.

Calavera II	*Skull II*

This calavera is a skull made of sugar candy, colorfully decorated with the child's name on it.

Ahí viene el agua	There comes the water
por la ladera	down the slope
y se me moja	and my calavera got wet.
mi calavera	

Chumba La Cachumba

If you wish, you can use the illustrated version of this poem published by Ediciones Ekaré.

Cuando el reloj marca la una, (When the clock strikes one,)
los esqueletos salen de la tumba. (the skeletons leave their tomb.)
¡Chumba la cachumba
la cachumbambá!

Cuando el reloj marca las dos, (When the clock strikes two,)
los esqueletos cantan a una voz. (the skeletons sing in one voice.)
¡Chumba la cachumba
la cachumbambá!

Cuando el reloj marca las tres, (When the clock strikes three,)
los esqueletos mueven los pies. (the skeletons move their feet.)
¡Chumba la cachumba
la cachumbambá!

Cuando el reloj marca las cuatro, (When the clock strikes four,)
los esqueletos juegan al teatro. (the skeletons play at theater.)
¡Chumba la cachumba
la cachumbambá!

Cuando el reloj marca las cinco, (When the clock strikes five,)
los esqueletos pegan un brinco. (The skeletons jump.)
¡Chumba la cachumba
la cachumbambá!

Cuando el reloj marca las seis, (When the clock strikes six,)
los esqueletos nombran al rey. (The skeletons name a king.)
¡Chumba la cachumba
la cachumbambá!

Cuando el reloj marca las siete, (When the clock strikes seven,)
los esqueletos lanzan un cohete. (the skeletons launch a rocket.)

¡Chumba la cachumba
la cachumbambá!

Cuando el reloj marca las ocho, (When the clock strikes eight,)
los esqueletos comen bizcocho. (the skeletons eat biscuits.)
¡Chumba la cachumba
la cachumbambá!

Cuando el reloj marca las nueve, (When the clock strikes nine,)
los esqueletos ven como llueve (the skeletons look like rain.)
¡Chumba la cachumba
la cachumbambá!

Cuando el reloj marca las diez, (When the clock strikes ten,)
los esqueletos corren una res (the skeletons chase a cow.)
¡Chumba la cachumba
la cachumbambá!

Cuando el reloj marca las once, (When the clock strikes eleven,)
los esqueletos tocan los bronces. (the skeletons play the cymbals.)
¡Chumba la cachumba
la cachumbambá!

Cuando el reloj marca las doce, (When the clock strikes twelve,)
los esqueletos se ponen en pose. (the skeletons strike a pose.)
¡Chumba la cachumba
la cachumbambá!

Cuando el reloj marca la una, (When the clock strikes one,)
los esqueletos van a la luna. (the skeletons go to the moon.)
¡Chumba la cachumba
la cachumbambá!

STORY: DELACRE, LULU. "THE LAUGHING SKULL" FROM GOLDEN TALES

Activities:

1. Have the children draw a skeleton. Use chalk on black paper.
2. Make a Day of the Dead altar. Read about the altar in Ancona's book and then have children make objects to place on an altar. For this activity you could bring out all your miscellaneous craft materials.
3. Decorate sugar candy caleveras. They can be decorated with colorful icing, and then placed on the altar.

PROGRAM 2: CINCO DE MAYO/5TH OF MAY

Books

Beherns, June. ¡**Fiesta!**

Marcos, Subcomandante. **The Story of Colors**.

Poems

"Las palabras son pájaros/Words are Birds" and "Cinco de Mayo" from **Laughing Tomatoes and Other Spring Poems/Jitomates risueños y otros poemas de primavera**, by Francisco X. Alarcon. Illustrated by Maya Christina González. Children's Book Press, 1997.

PROGRAM 3: MEXICAN INDEPENDENCE DAY SEPTEMBER 16

A good source for craft ideas to celebrate this day is **25 Latino Craft Projects**, by Ana-Elba Pavon and Diana Borrego.

PROGRAM 4: LAS NAVIDADES/CHRISTMAS

Anaya, Rudolfo. **The Farolitos of Christmas**.

Ciavonne, Jean. **Carlos, Light the Farolito**.

Soto, Gary. **Too Many Tamales**.

Song

Las Navidades by Lulu Delacre.

Refreshments: Serve tamales or *buñuelos*, fried tortillas sprinkled with cinnamon.

TEEN PROGRAMS

Booktalks

BOOKTALK: THE LEGEND OF THE WANDERING KING BY LAURA GALLEGO GARCÍA

An incredible story of redemption. Prince Walid has organized a poetry contest and is shamed when he loses to a carpet weaver named Hammad. In retribution, he gives Hammad some impossible tasks that Hammad manages to complete, but which drive him to his death. One of the tasks Walid gave Hammad was to weave a carpet that shows the future of the human resources. Walid is consumed by guilt, and when the carpet is stolen, he tries to find redemption by embarking on an epic journey to find it.

This book can be used to discuss important moral issues, such as whether revenge is ever justified, and what it takes to redeem oneself, and how one overcomes significant character flaws.

BOOKTALK: THE TEQUILA WORM BY VIOLA CANALES

This is a story that displays the warmth of an extended Latino family. Canales is able to weave together a series of episodes that celebrate Latino culture and family life with the thread of a daughter's love for a father, and universal fear of what happens when you leave your family. Sofia is the daughter who is faced with the choice of leaving her family for a boarding school, where she can pursue her dreams.

This book can be used to launch discussions of how families celebrate their culture, and also what children would do if placed in a similar situation to that of Sofia.

PARENT AND CAREGIVER PROGRAMS

I have two favorite stories to use in programs where I am introducing parents or caregivers to the importance of reading, and the types of books they can share with their children. I like to use *Un regalo sorpresa* by Isol. In the story Nino discovers his wrapped birthday present in the closet and tries to figure out what it is. I take a box with a ribbon, and put a book inside it. I tell the story, and use the box as a prop. When Nino wonders if the present is a soccer ball, I pretend to kick it. At the end of the story, I open the box, and just like Nino, find a book inside.

The other story that has worked well for me is the one I saw performed by the Spanish puppeteer at the book fair in Guadalajara. It is "El ratón muy alto y el ratón muy bajo" (The Very Tall Mouse and the Very Short Mouse) from *Historias de ratones* (*Mouse Tales*) by Arnold Lobel. As the tall mouse and the short mouse walk together, the tall mouse says hello to things that are up high, and the short mouse greets things down low. At the end of the story the tall mouse holds the short mouse up to the window so that they can both say hello to a rainbow after a rainstorm. To do this, get two mouse puppets. Hold one up high at full arm's length. The other can be down at waist level.

INTERGENERATIONAL PROGRAMS

Since the family unit is so integral in Hispanic culture, many schools and libraries have found success in programs that bring parents or grandparents and children together. This programming goes beyond traditional storytimes to bring families together. There are many examples of successful programs, but the one thread they have in common is parent and children involvement. At the most basic level, bilingual or Spanish storytime should be done at a time when children and parents can attend together. Building from this foundation, more instructional programs can be held for parents, teaching them how to read to their children, and how to model a reading habit. Librarians or teachers can demonstrate how to read a book with a child, and suggest activities to be used with particular books.

One format that has worked for me is to involve at least two people, and to have a meeting with parents in one area of the library, while a storytime is being held for the children in another. At the end of the program, parents and children are brought back together. Obviously, this requires two staff people for it to work. It can be done based on staff or volunteer availability. You can also seek out guest speakers, such as Latino artists or storytellers from the community. This sort of programming can be organized as a one-time only program or as a series of workshops. If you were doing a one-time only program, you could choose any children's storytime mentioned here for the children. You might want to have some additional craft activities so that you do not have to fill up all the time with stories. Prepare a story, such as Eduardo Robles Boza's *Cuatro Letras Se Escaparon* that children could present to their parents.

A possible agenda for the adult part of the program could include the following:

- Welcome (from library manager or other person in charge).
- Introduction to Library Services.
- Discussion of the types of children's literature available in Spanish, and different ways they can be shared. Discuss the importance of reading to children, focusing on the educational aspect.
- Bring children back in and have them help tell a story to their parents.
- Have a book display and printed booklist to give out of books in your collection. Serve refreshments afterwards, and offer parents a tour of the library.

The primary key to making a program like this work is getting parent involvement, and the key to that is reaching the parents in a way that will make them want to participate. Some libraries have used variations on the "Born to Read" format: reaching pregnant women before babies are born, giving them instruction and materials. When the women apply for library cards, they are provided with incentives such as "Born to Read" T-shirts or rompers for their children. Library programs are held in which librarians can model interaction with books to children.

Outreach to Latinos

Another type of outreach can be found in a program done by the Bensenville, Illinois, public library: "A Community of Readers." This grant-funded program sent librarians to Latino homes, where a program was done with a family. Families received a bag containing books, a puppet or fingerplay, and library publicity materials. Staff would talk to the parents about the importance of reading themselves and of reading to their children (Rodriguez 332.) This led to increased literacy and use of the library.

Participation in Library Programs

The next step was bringing these people to programs in the library. Programs were initiated for the families contacted through the "Community of Readers" program but were open to all. A program called "Stories and Songs for Babies" was created for infants. This was a program designed for parent and toddler interaction. Some of the suggested storytimes in this chapter could be used in programs of this sort. "Stories and Songs With Grands" was a program designed for grandparents and preschoolers.

Another excellent model for an intergenerational program is "Gente y Cuentos" or People and Stories developed by Sarah Hirschman, which is a program where young adults and senior citizens meet to read and discuss short stories and poetry that have significant cultural content. The simple idea of reading stories and then discussing them can be adapted to work in many different group situations. The following is a list of stories and books which work well when read aloud in a group setting. They are a bit longer, but not too long to be read in one session. They could serve as the basis for programs with any mix of older children and/or families or other adults. They are all great catalysts for discussion. The full bibliographic information for the books can be found in the bibliography.

El caballito que quería volar by Marta Osorio.
A beautiful story about a wooden carousel horse who wants to become a bird so that he can fly. He finally gets his wish. He is a different sort of horse from the beginning—he is the only horse on the carousel who is different. When he was made, he came from the carpenters' last piece of tree trunk, which had a large open gash. Two church bells overhear him and dispatch an owl to work some magic.

"Yo quiero volar—dijo más arriba aún de donde pueden ver mis ojos, cantar libremente y vivir en los jardines y en los parques, aunque existen el frío y el hambre, el calor y la sed . . ." ("I want to fly. I want to fly higher than even my eyes can see, sing freely and live in the gardens and in the parks, even though I may be cold and hungry, or hot and thirsty . . .")

La calle es libre by Kurusa.
English edition: **The Streets Are Free**.
The true story of a group of kids who, with support from the neighborhood

librarian, take matters into their own hands when the government will not supply them with a park to play in instead of the streets.

"The Circuit" by Francisco Jiménez from **Leaving Home**. Edited by Hazel Rochman and Darlene Z. McCampbell. New York: HarperCollins, 1997.

This story is an unflinching look at the lives of migrant farmworkers. Just as the narrator finds a sympathetic teacher who will help him to learn to play the trumpet, he goes home to find that his family is packed and ready to move away to the next field.

Elena by Diane Stanley.

In this story based on tales passed down through her family, Stanley writes in the voice of a young Mexican-American girl who recalls how her mother was forced to take their family to the United States because of the Mexican Revolution.

"Tuesday Siesta" by Gabriel Garcia Marquez from **Collected Stories**. Translated by Gregory Rabassa and J. S. Bernstein. New York: Harper-Collins, 1984, 1991, pp. 99–106.

A mother and daughter take a train ride into a town that has shut down for the afternoon siesta. They find the priest, and ask to see the grave of a thief who was killed in that town. The woman is revealed to be the mother of the thief. This story is notable for what is *not* said, and can spark discussion of many aspects of Latin culture.

"La United Fruit Company," poem by Pablo Neruda from **Canto general** (General Song). Translated by Jack Schmitt. Berkeley: University of California Press, 1991.

This poem, which details how Jehovah divided the earth between Coca Cola Inc., Ford Motors and other entities, as well as the United Fruit Company, will spark discussion of how Latin America has been affected by American industry.

Any of Gary Soto's books of poetry would also be effective in this type of setting. Both parents and young adults could write poems or recollections about their own neighborhood or growing up, using Soto's poems and essays as inspiration. The point is that ultimately, the most successful programming done with Latinos will be that which focuses on and involves families.

A Basic Programming Collection

Ada, Alma Flor, and F. Isabel Campoy. **Mamá Goose: A Latino Nursery Treasury/Un tesoro de rimas infantiles**. Illustrated by Maribel Suárez. New York: Hyperion, 2004. ISBN: 0786819357 (picture book anthology).

An anthology of Nursery Rhymes, lullabies, songs, riddles and other treasures presented bilingually with appealing illustrations.

Delacre, Lulu. **Arroz con leche: Popular Songs and Rhymes from Latin America** (Rice with Milk). New York: Scholastic, 1984. ISBN: 0590418874 (music).

The Spanish and English lyrics to these songs are enhanced by Delacre's lovely illustrations. The music is included at the back of the book. Includes: "Aserrín, asserán."

————. **Golden Tales: Myths, Legends, and Folktales from Latin America**. New York: Scholastic, 1996. ISBN: 059048186X (short story collection 7–11).

Spanish edition: **De oro y esmeraldas: Mitos, leyendas y cuentos populares de Latinoamérica**. ISBN: 0590676830.

These stories are from 13 Latin American countries as well as indigenous cultures. Delacre demonstrates the breadth of her research by including maps as well as source and background notes. Out of print, but look for used copies.

————. **Las Navidades: Popular Christmas Songs from Latin America**. New York: Scholastic, 1990. ISBN: 0590435485 (music).

Selected and illustrated by Lulu Delacre. English lyrics by Elena Paz. Musical arrangements by Ana-María Rosado.

González, Lucia M. **Señor Cat's Romance and Other Stories from Latin America**. Illustrated by Lulu Delacre. New York: Scholastic, 1997. ISBN: 0439278635 (short story collection, for ages 7–11).

This is one of my favorite all-time collections, which is sadly out of print. It includes the following stories: "Little Half Chicken," "Juan Bobo and the Three-Legged Pot," "Martina, the Little Cockroach," "The Billy Goat and the Vegetable Garden," "How Uncle Rabbit Tricked Uncle Tiger," and "Señor Cat's Romance."

Longo, Adriana. **Adivinanzas: ¿Qué tiene el rey en la panza?** (Riddles: What Does the King Have in His Belly?). Illustrated by Daniel Chaskielberg. New York: Scholastic (Ediciones Kumquat), 2004. ISBN: 043968370X.

The answer to the title riddle is the king's bellybutton, of course. This is a simple spinner-rack style book with riddles and bold stylized illustrations that will delight very young children.

————. **Aserrín, aserrán: Las canciones de la abuela** (Aserrín, aserrán: Songs of Grandmother). Illustrated by Clara Harrington Villaverdde.
New York: Scholastic (Ediciones Kumquat), 2004. ISBN: 0439637767.

A companion to Adivinanzas, this includes the words to a number of well-known Latin nursery rhymes. No music is included, however.

Orozco, José-Luis. **De Colores and Other Latin-American Folk
Songs for Children**. Illustrated by Elisa Kleven. New York: Dutton,
1994. ISBN: 0525452605 (music).

Selected, arranged and translated by José-Luis Orozco. Orozco provides background on the origins of the songs as well as some related games.

Songs include: "El chocolate," "La araña pequeñita"/"The Eensy, Weensy Spider," and "Los Pollitos."

Reviejo, Carlos, and Eduardo Soler. **Canto y cuento: Antología poet-
ica para niños** (Song and Story: A Poetry Anthology for Children).
Madrid, Spain: SM, 1997. ISBN: 8434856646 (poetry for ages 7–11).

An excellent poetry anthology that is a must for all collections. A sequel is Carlos Reviejo and Eduardo Soler, **Cantares y decires: antología de fo-
clore infantil** (Songs and Sayings: Anthology of Juvenile Folklore). Madrid,
Spain: SM, 1998. ISBN: 843486293X (poetry for ages 7–11).

Both of these are out of print, but are worth tracking down.

Rockwell, Ann. **El toro pinto and Other Songs in Spanish**. New York:
Macmillan, 1971. ISBN: 0689718802 (music).

Music and guitar chords are included for songs from all over Latin America. The country of origin of each song is noted, and English translations are included. Includes "Señor Don Gato" and "Cielito Lindo." Out of print, but worth finding.

Syverson-Stork, Jill, and Nancy Abraham Hall. **Los pollitos dicen/The
Baby Chicks Sing: Juegos, rimas y canciónes infantiles de países
de habla hispana/Traditional Games, Nursery Rhymes and
Songs from Spanish-Speaking Countries**. Illustrated by Kay
Chorao. Boston: Little Brown, 1994. ISBN: 0316338524 (picture book an-
thology).

Traditional songs, rhymes and games presented in a bilingual format. Includes "A la víbora de la mar."

RESOURCES

Dígame un cuento/Tell me a Story: Bilingual Library Programs for Children
http://www.tsl.state.tx.us/ld/pubs/bilingual/index.html
Bilingual Storytime Clip Art
http://www.tsl.state.tx.us/ld/pubs/bilingual/clipart/index.html

WORKS CITED

Gonzalez, Lucia M. "Developing Culturally Integrated Children's Programs." *Library Services to Youth of Hispanic Heritage.* Edited by Barbara Immroth and Kathleen de la Pena McCook. North Carolina: McFarland and Company, 2000. 19–23.

Rodriguez, Jill, and Maria Tejeda. "Serving Hispanics through Family Literacy: One Family at a Time." *Illinois Libraries* 75(5): 331–335.

Chapter 5

Strategic Marketing
of the Core Collection

OUTREACH AND PUBLICITY

A lesson, which I learned early in my career, was that you should never market something that you cannot deliver. This is absolutely relevant to marketing a collection of Spanish-language materials. You cannot begin getting people excited about something and then not have it available when they arrive at your library. So, the first step in marketing a collection is obtaining a collection, which has been the focus of this manual. Once a basic core collection is in place, you need to begin to let your customers know about it.

As you begin the process of reaching out, it is important to assess what marketing is to help understand the need to market. Marketing is a process to inform people of products and services available that they may need or enjoy. It is a powerful tool to help organizations advance their mission and fulfill goals set out in their strategic plans. Marketing should give you answers about your customers, their needs and desires as it relates to information and library materials. Most importantly, marketing can create a demand for your services. The demand may already be there, and you may just be scrambling to meet it. Or you may create demand by providing services that your clients did not know existed, but that once they see them, they will realize they want them.

Whether you are working in a school or a library, outreach is something that should be second-nature when working with Latinos. Since there is no tradition of public library service in Mexico and other Latin American countries, often a Latino immigrant will have no practical experience with a library and its standard services such as story-hour programs. There should never be any question as to whether outreach in the Latino community is necessary. It should just be done. Children will not come to programs unless their parents bring them. Simply putting up signs advertising a program cannot do the outreach I am talking about. Parents must be reached on a more personal basis. This can be accomplished during monthly PTA meetings or when there are parent-teacher conferences. For the public library it can be a little more difficult. Librarians can visit PTA meetings. Many schools have special educational programs that involve parents and children together. Seek these groups out. I have visited with groups of parents with younger children who met in a school cafeteria. Other groups have brought parents and children into the library. Usually these groups are stay-at-home moms with preschoolers. Libraries can be a great resource for these types of groups. One school year, we sponsored meetings for the HIPPY program, which teaches parenting skills to young Latino mothers, while providing enrichment activities for their infants and toddlers. A kindergarten teacher, on his own initiative, took the time out to invite all the parents of the children in his class to a tour of the library. The people in this group had never been to the library before. Encourage this sort of thing—otherwise many of these parents and children might never visit the library. It's a good idea to visit or, even better, sponsor English as a second language and citizenship classes.

The Latino media are also a great place to reach your audience and publicize your programs. If you live in an area where there are Latino media outlets such as newspapers, radio, or TV stations, this is one of the best ways to promote the school or library. Arrange for an interview on radio or TV. Make sure your news gets sent to all of these outlets.

Press releases should include the following information

Event:

Date:

Time:

Place:

Who Is Sponsoring the Event:

Who Can Participate:

How Many are Expected:

Purpose of Event:

Deadline for Reservations (if applicable):

What Else Do People Need To Know About Your Event:

Phone Number That Can Be Publicized for Event Information:

Name and Phone Number of Contact Person:

The information regarding the contact person should be in the upper left or right hand corner of the news release. A news release should have a specific date of release, or the words "For Immediate Release" at the top. The first paragraph should summarize in one or two sentences what the release is about, using the five point method: "who, what, when, where and why." After the first paragraph, continue to develop your story in more detail. Use the "inverted pyramid" structure, moving from general information to more detail. Limit the release to one page whenever possible. If you must use more than one page, put "more" at the bottom of each page but the last. Use the ### symbol at the very bottom of your release. The release should be double-spaced with wide margins on letter-sized paper. Use short sentences with action verbs. Keep it simple. Check for correct spelling and grammar. Know and meet any deadlines set by media outlets. Do not write a headline for your release. All abbreviations must be understood, so write things out. Spell out numbers from one to ten. Use numerals for numbers from 11 up.

BASIC STEPS

It is important to go about marketing in a systematic way. There are several basic steps to follow:

- Needs Assessment
- Planning
- Implementation
- Evaluation

Needs Assessment

Libraries are customer-focused institutions, and no plan can begin without establishing a need. It is assumed that if you are developing a collection of Spanish-language and bilingual books, there is a need for them. But how do you determine that? On the front lines, serving the public, it is pretty easy to say what customers are requesting, and you might very well establish a need for more Spanish materials based on strictly anecdotal evidence from people using the library. However, it is important that you not base a plan on that evidence alone. A good marketing program begins with a clearly established need that is based on hard data and evidence. Based on the customers you see in the library, you know that your Latino population is growing. You can back that up with census data, or other demographic statistics. Schools can provide excellent statistics on numbers of Latino children enrolled. You know that you do not have enough books to meet the needs of the parents coming into the library. You can back that up with statistics about your collection: the number of volumes in Spanish, circulation figures for those volumes, and a comparison with your population figures.

The flip side to this is that your Spanish-speaking population may largely consist of non-users. You can base your needs assessment on those you see in the library, but you should also take into account those not seen. In a small rural farming community here in Arizona where the county has a branch library, our branch manager noticed that mothers were waiting outside while their children went into the library. They felt that somehow the library was only for their children, and not for them. At the manager's request, I did a workshop with some of these mothers in a Head Start program. I talked with them about the library and about reading to their children, and I shared some stories. The branch manager later told me that some of these mothers came into the library for the first time after this presentation. I had given them permission to come into the library. Many of these same mothers later enthusiastically joined a Motheread program where they practiced their skills. What this means for marketing is that you need to go outside of the library as well.

The basic rule that applies here is that you should never assume what a community's needs are. You should let the community tell you. Ways of doing this include doing surveys in PTA meetings, going to Head Start and other parent-child programs, talking in churches, or any other place in your community where people gather. Based on what you find, you can then begin developing a plan to meet those needs. In this case we shall assume that the need is clearly more materials for children, and that you have also ascertained through talking with both adults and children the sorts of Spanish and bilingual materials they would like to see in the library.

Planning

Armed with your needs assessment data, you can begin planning how you will do your marketing. The plan may include the acquisition of materials based on your needs assessment, but that should not be the primary focus. The focus for marketing is how you will use and publicize the collection. Let us assume that you have obtained a core collection and are ready to market it. The two basic steps of planning a public relations campaign are, first, to set goals and then to set measurable and quantifiable objectives based on those goals. Examples of simple goals might be to increase circulation of the collection or to increase the number of library card holders. It is important that your goals are clearly defined and that you ask yourself if and how they directly relate to the needs you have identified. You should be able to flow point by point from your identified needs, through to the goals, and ultimately to the evaluation of your program.

Once you have established the goals of your marketing efforts, the next step is to express the results that you would like to see in the form of measurable objectives. Measurable objectives mean ones that can be quantified. Ask yourself the following questions about what you want to achieve: how much and by when? So to return to the examples in the previous section, if the goal is to increase circulation or library card holders, then the objective might be to increase circulation or library card holders by a specific percentage over a specific time frame. The measures you set should be reasonable. Do not set unachievable objectives. Do not set yourself up for failure, but do challenge yourself. Hopefully, if you do your marketing right, your expectations will be exceeded.

Implementation

Implementation begins with good planning. It is always wise to look at the steps you need to take to go from step one to the conclusion of a successful marketing effort. Another lesson to be learned is that of setting a timeline. Your measurable objectives should be time sensitive, so the timeline should reflect the steps you need to take to get from point A to point B in the timeframe you have specified. With a clear idea of your plan and deadlines in place, you can start to make your vision happen. Do not, however, expect that everything will go perfectly as you have planned. You can expect unexpected hurdles along the way. For example, you have planned some programming to market your new Spanish collection on a certain date. Your plan has allowed for enough lead time to order and process the materials to have them in place prior to that date. But your materials vendor experiences some problems, and the books are not there, and your program is already advertised. Certainly any timeline should take into account contingencies, but even then you cannot control everything. One lesson I have learned is to always have a backup plan. Think through what you will do if something happens. What *are* your contingencies?

The successful implementation of your effort should bring the satisfaction of reaching your objectives, and through them your bigger goals. And that should mean that your collection is being used, and hopefully making a difference for the customers for whom it was selected.

Evaluation

If all of the steps above have been completed, then the evaluation of your marketing strategies should be easy. You should be able to look at your initial objectives and then the actual results based on the statistical measures you have chosen and tracked through the implementation phase. You will not always meet all your objectives, but that is also part of the evaluation. Besides the statistics, you should be able to evaluate in general terms what went well and what did not. What were you able to learn from the experience? What would you do differently next time? In terms of collection building for a specific audience such as we are focusing on here, the marketing process should be ongoing, with continual acquisition and promotion of new materials, along with expanding the audience for those materials.

CREATING A WRITTEN MARKETING PLAN

Using the steps outlined above, you can develop a written marketing plan that will be the guide for your promotional efforts and that you may also need to present to your administrators or supervisors. Writing the steps out in a formal way can help you think through the entire process. As you go through this process, be a devil's advocate, and ask yourself the hard questions. What do you really want to achieve? Is what you are planning related to what you want to achieve? Remember that a marketing plan should be customer-focused and customer driven. In developing marketing strategies, listen to your customers. We should be obsessed about our customers and provide them with great service and selection. That is what this core collection is about. We need to think creatively and devise ways to accommodate the information needs of our customers. Based on contact with our customers, we can personalize our services to them.

The following is a sample marketing plan based on one developed for my Library District. The Library District's overall marketing plan was developed by a marketing team on which I participated, and which was led by our Development and Marketing Coordinator, Audrey Brownell. This marketing plan includes some good questions you can ask yourself as you think through how you want to market your collection. You will notice that those questions refer to the product you are marketing. Just as if you were in a retail environment, you can think of your collection as the product you have to sell (or loan for free in this case).

Model Written Marketing Plan for a Spanish-Language and Bilingual Book Collection

Goal: Learn demographics and customers' needs and interests to discover the size of the Latino population served by the library.

Goal: Based on this information, develop and market a collection to meet those expressed needs and interests.

Goal: Through consistent delivery of materials and programs, establish your niche in the community as the place to find Spanish materials.

OBJECTIVES

- Conduct focus groups with Latinos in all locations by (insert date).
- Based on customer input, prepare a selection plan by (insert date). This will include evaluations of existing branch collections.
- Core collections of Spanish-language, bilingual and other culturally appropriate materials will be available for circulation by (insert date).
- Increase the use of Spanish-language; bilingual and other culturally appropriate materials for children that address the leisure and learning needs of the children and parents in the Latino community by 15 percent annually.
- Increase the number of and participation in literature-based, cultural enrichment and educational programs for children by 15 percent annually.
- Each branch will update its own community profile twice a year to keep up with ongoing demographic trends.

Goal: Strengthen employee ownership and understanding of the marketing plan for the Spanish-language and bilingual collection.

OBJECTIVES

- Conduct a workshop to introduce staff to the plan by (insert date).
- After workshops are completed, e-mail staff monthly with updates on new materials and what is being promoted, so that they can tell customers, answer questions and get customers responses/suggestions.

Goal: Nurture relationships with the Latino community.

OBJECTIVE

- Each branch will form partnerships with at least four new agencies by (insert date).

UTILIZING THE SIX Ps OF MARKETING

Marketing professionals have identified six areas of focus, known as the six Ps to look at when developing a marketing plan.

1. Product
2. Publics
3. Price
4. Place
5. Production
6. Promotion

The idea is that you have to know what your product is and who is the audience for that product. From there you must think about the cost to the customer, about where the customer can obtain the product, and, finally, about producing and promoting the product. In the context of a library collection, you can ask yourself the following questions related to these six areas of focus:

1. What is the product?
   The product is a collection of Spanish-language and bilingual books that are culturally relevant for children.
2. To whom will the product be marketed?
   It will be marketed to the primary publics who value particular benefits of the product.
3. Who are the primary publics?
   Primary publics are Latino children and their parents and caregivers, including both those who are bilingual and Spanish speakers. A secondary public is people learning Spanish.
4. What are the benefits of the product?
   It will provide Spanish-speaking and bilingual children with materials in their native language and through which they can see themselves and better understand their culture.
   It will provide support for Spanish-speaking parents.
   It will help parents support children's growth and development.
   It will help develop a respect for cultures.
   Books in Spanish not easily available in bookstores, and the library can provide a wider variety of choices in Spanish and selection of materials that may not be available elsewhere.
5. What is the price at which this product is available to the customer?
   Free.
6. Where is the product available?
   Available at this (these) library location(s):
   Branch Libraries
   Locations visited by bookmobiles
7. How will we effectively meet the demand we hope to create?
   To effectively meet demand we will develop, implement, and monitor customer satisfaction surveys and track customer reserves.
   Based on this we will implement ongoing collection maintenance.
8. What are the major features of the collection that we can promote?
   Availability.
   No cost.
   Breadth, size and variety of the collection.
9. What will be our basic approach to promotion?

Our basic approach to promotion will be to create a 12–18-month schedule of specific books and topics from the collection to promote and highlight through advertising, displays, and programming. This will be the centerpiece of the marketing campaign.

Promotional Ideas
Promote Spanish titles on Web site.
Children's Spanish book of the month.
Promote books in calendar of events.
E-mail announcements to customers.
Create brochures with booklists.
Put booklists on Web site.
Displays.
Posters, flyers and bookmarks.
Use ALA "Lea" posters.
Special events.
Newspaper ads in Spanish-language papers.
Talk shows/TV and radio. Have Spanish-speaking staff member go on the radio to market the collection.
Word of mouth.
Use stickers or buttons with a message promoting the Spanish collection for staff to wear such as "Tenemos libros en español" (We have books in Spanish).
Display of books on topics being done in programming. Have books in areas where programs are being done.
Promote books in a major way through print pieces that show what's new; include reviews.
Hire a full time outreach librarian who speaks Spanish to promote the collection in the community.

MARKETING IN THE CLASSROOM

Teacher librarians and teachers have a much easier job of marketing than do public libraries, because they have a captive audience. It is not too hard to define a school's public! However, the same basic marketing principles that we discussed still apply. Also, within a school classroom setting, the most important things that will market Spanish-language and bilingual books are also the simplest things to do: read the books to the class and have the books displayed in the classroom. If the teacher does not speak Spanish, perhaps students can read out loud. When using bilingual books, one person can read the Spanish, the other the English. The most important thing is to convey a personal enthusiasm about the books. Talk about the books with your class in such a way that they know you are excited about them. Similarly, in a school library setting, teacher librarians can display books and promote books through reading out loud and booktalks when classes come into the library. They can also promote them during the times for announcements.

Part II. Planning Programs for Bilingual and Spanish-Speaking Children

Chapter 6

Programming with Latino Folktales and Folklore

Latino children's literature begins with folklore. Folktales, many of which have been passed down through oral tradition, are the foundation of any collection of Latino materials, and of any programming with Latino children. They represent the basic cultural touchstones every child should know. In this chapter, I would like to focus first on some important types of Latino folktales, then on folklore more generally, and specific ways of using folktales and folklore in the classrooms and libraries. While Latino children are familiar with much of the world's folklore in translation, here I wish to focus on the most common Latino folktales. There are several major stories that seem to be common, and I will list the various retellings available that are appropriate to share with children. I realize that some of these retellings are out of print, and may be difficult to acquire, but I retain them here to provide as complete a list of possible of the retellings that have been available, with the hope that they are still available in many library collections.

FOLKTALES

Latino folktales can be grouped into four main types. First, there are animal stories such as Tío Conejo (Uncle Rabbit). Second, there are traditional fairy tales, some of which show European or Spanish influences. The Catholic faith brought to Latin America by the Spaniards has also been an important influence, and many folktales have distinctly religious content. This can present a problem in public schools and libraries where mention of religion is taboo. Religion is so deeply interwoven in these tales, however, that it cannot be separated. When sharing them with a Latino audience, it is generally not a problem because the religious element is quite deep-rooted in the culture and generally accepted. In both animal and traditional fairy tales, you will find many trickster characters. The clever animal or person who is able to outwit the supposedly smarter animal or person is a popular motif. The third major category is ghost stories. Finally, there are stories from the Indian oral tradition. I'll explore the most common tales from each of these types.

Animal Tales

"Perez and Martina"

Top of the list of Latino tales which every child should know is "Perez and Martina." Originating in Cuba, it tells the story of a little cockroach who rejects all her suitors except the gentlemanly mouse Perez. As each suitor approaches Martina, who is fanning herself on her porch or balcony, they propose marriage. To each in turn, Martina coyly says: "Perhaps, but tell me how you will speak to me in the future." Each suitor in turn is turned down because their way of speaking is not to her liking. The beautiful voice of Perez enchants her, however. They are married in a lavish ceremony, but then later, when Martina is cooking a soup, Perez becomes too curious, and falls into the pot and is boiled to death. Martina mourns the loss of her beloved. In a number of versions of this tale, Perez is miraculously restored to health. In some versions, Martina is a butterfly or an ant instead of a cockroach. This tale is notable because it is the earliest Latino folktale to come to prominence in this country through the version written by Pura Belpré. Her version and others are listed below.

> Belpré, Pura. **Perez and Martina: A Puerto Rican Folktale**. Illustrated by Carlos Sanchez. New York: Viking, 1960 and 1991.
> The classic original retelling complete with the tragic ending.

> González, Lucia M. "Martina the Little Cockroach" from **Señor Cat's Romance: And Other Favorite Stories from Latin America**. Illustrated by Lulu Delacre. New York: Scholastic, 1997.
> In this version, doctors bring Perez back to life, and all ends happily ever after.

> Hayes, Joe. **Mariposa, Mariposa**. Illustrated by Lucy Jelinek. Santa Fe, NM: Trails West, 1988.
> A variation on "Perez and Martina." Mariposa finds some money and gets a beautiful dress (her wings). She asks various animals who want to marry her how they will talk when they are married. She likes the mouse. Mouse gets

eaten by cat. Friends brought flowers; she likes them so much that she flies from flower to flower to this day.

Herrmann, Marjorie E. **Perez and Martina/Perez y Martina: Fables in English and Spanish/Fábulas bilingües**. Lincolnwood, IL: National Textbook Company, 1988.

A controlled vocabulary version of the story for children to read on their own.

Moreton, Daniel. **La cucaracha Martina: A Carribean Folktale**. New York: Turtle Books, 1997.

A hip version of the "Perez and Martina" story. In this version, Martina marries a cricket instead of the ratoncito Perez.

Orihuela, Luz, adaptation. **La ratita presumida** (The Conceited Little Mouse). Illustrated by Rosa M. Curto. Barcelona, Spain: Combel Editorial, 2003.

ISBN: 8478647635 (picture book)

In this version, the little rat receives marriage proposals from a number of animals, and finally accepts the cat's proposal. The cat promptly eats her. This is actually a lot of fun and the illustrations are charming.

Soler, Carola. **El pájaro de nieve y otras lecturas para niños** (The Snow Bird and Other Texts for Children). Madrid: Aguilar, 1967.

Includes "El ratón pelado," a version of "Perez and Martina." Martina is an ant, and it includes an exchange between the ant and her beau, which is nicely poetic:

> Ratón: ¡Hormiguita, qué guapa estás! (Little Ant, how beautiful you are!)
> Hormiga: Hago bien, que tu no me lo das. (I'm doing well, no thanks to you.)
> Ratón: ¿Te quieres casar conmigo? (Will you marry me?)
> Hormiga: ¿Cómo vas a arrullar al niño? (How will you sing the baby to sleep?)
> Ratón: Con amor y cariño. (With love and caring.)
> Hormiga: Bueno, me casaré contigo. (Then yes, I will marry you.)

"ROOSTER AND THE WEDDING"

This cumulative tale is known by many different titles. It is a classic folktale form: Rooster is on his way to his Uncle Parrot's wedding when he sees a kernel of corn in the mud. He eats it, dirtying his beak. Not presentable to go to his uncle's wedding, he asks the grass to clean his beak. The grass refuses, and so Rooster petitions the goat to eat the grass to make it clean his beak. The goat, too, refuses. This chain of events continues until it reaches Rooster's friend, the sun. This is a wonderful tale to use to introduce children to Latino folklore. The preferred version is the bilingual Lucia González retelling with illustrations by Lulu Delacre. An effective way to share this story is to have a colleague read either the English or Spanish, after you have read it in the other language. Going back and forth between the two languages heightens the fun of this story. This is perfect to use in mixed-language groups and in programs where you are introducing the library to Latino users. The most readily available versions of this tale are listed below.

> Ada, Alma Flor. **The Rooster Who Went To His Uncle's Wedding: A Latin American Folktale**. Illustrated by Kathleen Kuchera. New York: Whitebird (Putnam), 1993.
>
> González, Lucía. **The Bossy Gallito/El gallo de bodas: A Traditional Cuban Folktale**. New York: Scholastic, 1997.
>
> Purá Belpre honor book for writing and illustration, 1996.

(This retelling can also be found, with illustrations by Molly Bang and titled "El Gallo de Bodas: The Rooster on the Way to the Wedding" in Amy L. Cohn, compilation **From Sea to Shining Sea: A Treasury of American Folklore and Folksongs**. New York: Scholastic, 1993.

> Hayes, Joe. **No Way, José!/¡De ninguna manera José!** Illustrated by Lucy Jelinek. Santa Fe, NM: Trails West, 1986.

If you use this version, you can get everyone to call out "No way, José" as you tell the story. Due to the format of the book, this version is probably more appropriate for telling.

TRICKSTERS: COYOTE AND TÍO CONEJO

Among the most popular of folktales with Latino children, the stories of Tío Conejo (Uncle Rabbit) show how the smallest and weakest of the animals can defeat the strongest, and that cleverness can win out over brute force. Tío Conejo can be a rogue, but he is very creative and even wise. He is a figure with whom children can identify, which explains his popularity with Latino children. Tío Tigre (Uncle Tiger) is often a character in these stories, and usually is the object of Tío Conejo's tricks. Full of humor, these stories come from the African tradition, but have become uniquely part of the Latino culture as they have been retold and passed down from one generation to the next.

> Belpré, Pura. **The Tiger and the Rabbit and Other Tales**. New York: Lippincott, 1965. ISBN: 0397315910

This retelling was the basis for Lucía Gonzáles's book, listed below. Lucía recommends it as a good source for storytelling and puppet shows. At this writing, it is available inexpensively on Amazon.com

González, Lucía M. "How Uncle Rabbit Tricked Uncle Tiger" from **Señor Cat's Romance: And Other Favorite Stories from Latin America**. Illustrated by Lulu Delacre. New York: Scholastic, 1997.

Tío Conejo tricks Tío Tigre and ties his tale into a knot. Then after a few days, he puts honey all over himself and then covers himself with leaves. Tío Tigre has been waiting at the watering hole, but doesn't recognize this little leafy animal. Tío Conejo has the last laugh again as he reveals himself to Tío Tigre.

Johnston, Tony. **The Tale of Rabbit and Coyote**. Illustrated by Tomie DePaola. New York: Putnam, 1994.

Coyote is tricked again and again by Rabbit. Johnston says this tale comes from the state of Oaxaca, Mexico. In a scene reminiscent of "Brer Rabbit," Rabbit gets stuck to a wax image a farmer has placed in his field because Rabbit has been stealing his chiles. But despite this setback, Rabbit is able to get the better of Coyote—first by duping him into taking his place in a stew pot. In another familiar episode, Rabbit tricks Coyote into drinking a lake to reach the "cheese" that is actually the reflection of the moon in the water. The ending explains why Coyotes howl at the moon: This is where Rabbit has taken refuge.

Traditional Folk Tales

PEDRO DE ORDIMALAS TALES

Pedro de Ordimalas is known by many different names, but the stories are found throughout Latin America. Some of the variants I have seen include the following:

Pedro, el de Malas (Wicked Peter)
Pedro Remales
Pedro Malasartes (Peter Evilarts)
Pedro de Urdemales/Juan de Urdemalas (Peter or John Evilschemer)
Pedro Animales
Pedro Tecomate (Peter Gourd)

Regardless of what name he masquerades under, Pedro descends from the Spanish picaresque tradition of Don Quixote, a roguish hero going out on adventures. In fact, Cervantes wrote a play in which Pedro appears. In some stories Pedro is a hero trying to correct injustices. In others he is much more of a trickster. Some of Pedro's stories are also shared by other protagonists such as Tío Conejo and Juan Bobo. Pedro is trying to get rich or to get out of having to do work. He loves to trick the mostly foolish and greedy people with whom he comes in contact. He can make bandits believe that money grows on trees. He can even win a battle of wits with the Devil himself, and gets Saint Peter to let him into heaven.

VERSIONS OF PEDRO DE ORDIMALAS

Brusca, María Cristina, and Tona Wilson. **El Herrero y el diablo** (The Blacksmith and the Devils). Illustrated by María Cristina Brusca. New York: Holt, 1992.

This version closely follows the basic version of the story with the main character now called Juan Pobreza, or John the Poor One. The illustrations in this version are particularly delightful, especially the ones showing the rich, young, Juan partying, riding elephants and showering people with money from his airplane.

Brusca, María Cristina, and Tona Wilson. **Pedro Fools the Gringo and Other Tales of a Latin-American Trickster**. Illustrated by Maria Cristina Brusca. New York: Redfeather (Holt), 1995.
Includes the following stories:

"Clever Little Pedro." Pedro fools the priest into believing that he has read books in the library to teach him how to steal the priest's cheese. In reality, Pedro has simply stacked the books so he can climb up on them. He also convinces the priest that there are one-legged chickens.

"Painted Horses." Pedro paints horses in order to pass them off as something they are not, but the paint washes off in the rain.

"Golden Partridge." A sure gross-out. Pedro does his business by the side of the road, then covers it up with a hat when two men ride up. He convinces them that there's a valuable golden partridge under the hat.

"Magic Pot" and "Money Tree." These two stories are also Juan Bobo tales. Pedro tricks the same men who thought he had a golden partridge into thinking that he has all the things mentioned. Their greediness makes them easy targets.

"Pig Tails in the Swamp." Pedro's master asks him to sell some pigs at market. Pedro pockets the money, cuts off the pigs tails, and makes his master think they drowned in the swamp.

"Helper Rabbit." Pedro fools a man into thinking a rabbit can deliver messages.

"Burro Gold." Another gross-out sure to get a response. Pedro feeds his burro gold coins, and cons a man into giving him everything he owns in return for the gold-producing burro.

"Pedro and the Devil." This is a Latin American version of the story which is known as "Tops and Bottoms." Pedro cheats the devil out of his crops.

"Pedro Fools the Gringo." Pedro fools a gringo into thinking that a squash is actually a mare's egg, which will produce a racing colt.

"Good-bye to Your Machetes." Pedro escapes from his captors by putting their whips, machetes, pistols and knives in a sack while they are sleeping. He then heaves it over the side of a cliff.

"Pedro Goes to Heaven." Pedro fools his way through the pearly gates.

Griego y Maestas, Jose, and Rudolfo A. Anaya. "Pedro de Ordimalas." **Cuentos: Tales from the Hispanic Southwest**. Santa Fe: Museum of New Mexico Press, 1980. 160–171.

Juan Bobo Tales

Juan Bobo tales are sometimes indistinguishable from those about Pedre de Ordimalas. "Bobo" means "stupid" or "dunderhead." And as this name indicates, his stories are more characterized by stupidity than by cleverness, as with Pedro de Ordimalas. If Juan triumphs, it is generally by mistake. Children love Juan Bobo stories because they see that they are smarter than he is. Here are some children's versions of his stories:

Belpré, Pura. **Juan Bobo and the Queen's Necklace: A Puerto Rican Folktale**. Illustrated by Christine Price. New York: Warne, 1962.

When the Queen's pearl necklace is stolen, Juan Bobo tells his mother that he wants to get the reward. He is accepted at the palace even though he is a Bobo because no one else has been able to find the necklace. While staying in one of the rooms of the palace, he is waited on by three maids who believe that he has discovered that they stole the necklace, because of a nonsense song he sings to nightingales flying by as he looks out the window. They confess to him, and he saves their skins by making it appear that the necklace was eaten by a goose, which is cooked for dinner.

Bernier-Grand, Carmen T. **Juan Bobo: Four Folktales from Puerto Rico**. Illustrated by Ernesto Ramos Nieves. New York: Harper, 1994.

"The Best Way to Carry Water." Juan Bobo tries to carry water to his mother, using a wicker basket. He thinks he is strong because the basket is so light, but of course all the water has seeped out.

"A Pig in Sunday Clothes." Juan Bobo dresses up the family pig in his mother's clothes in order to take it to church. It promptly rolls in the mud.

"Do Not Sneeze, Do Not Scratch, Do Not Eat." Literally following his mother's instructions about good manners, Juan Bobo doesn't get anything to eat.

"A Dime a Jug." Juan Bobo ends up selling his jugs to flies.

Ferré, Rosario. **Los cuentos de Juan Bobo** (The Stories of Juan Bobo). Río Piedras, PR: Ediciones Huracán, 1981.

Five Juan Bobo stories. They include a story about Juan and young ladies from Manto Prieto, Juan going to mass, Juan making a fool of himself dining in a wealthy home, and Juan journeying to the capital city.

González, Lucía M. "Juan Bobo and the Buñuelos." In Amy L. Cohn, compilation. **From Sea to Shining Sea: A Treasury of American Folklore and Folksongs**. New York: Scholastic, 1993.

Juan Bobo's wife comes to the rescue when Juan finds gold hidden by robbers. Juan Bobo's wife has him bring home the ingredients to make a mountain of buñuelos, and makes him think that it has rained buñuelos. She also makes it appear that the family donkey is eating with its tail. When the robbers arrive, looking for the gold, Juan tells his wife to bring out the gold that he found the day before it rained buñuelos and the donkey ate with its tail. The robbers, thinking that Juan Bobo is crazy, depart and leave the gold safe with Juan and his wife.

González, Lucía M. "Juan Bobo and the Three-Legged Pot." In **Señor Cat's Romance: And Other Favorite Stories from Latin America**. Illustrated by Lulu Delacre. New York: Scholastic, 1997.

Montes, Marisa. **Juan Bobo Goes to Work: A Puerto Rican Folk Tale**. Illustrated by Joe Cepeda. New York: HarperCollins, 2000. ISBN: 0525675752 (picture book). Pura Belpré Illustrator Honor Book, 2002.

Retellings of traditional Puerto Rican folktales starring the classic folklore character, Juan Bobo.

Pitre, Felix. **Juan Bobo and the Pig: A Puerto Rican Folktale**. New York: Lodestar (Dutton), 1993.

Another version of the story in which Juan Bobo dresses the pig to send it to church.

Ghost Stories

La Llorona

Most Latino children have grown up being told the story of La Llorona (the weeping woman) by their parents. In most cases it is used as a motivational tool to promote good behavior. La Llorona is said to haunt "rivers, lakes and lonely roads" (*Maya's Children*). It is said that she appears at night and is searching for her own lost children. In the original version, La Llorona has taken her children's lives, and this is the reason for her ghostly apparition. This story is found in many Latin American countries. Children are told that unless they are good, La Llorona will come and take them away.

Anaya, Rudolfo. **The Legend of La Llorona**. TQS Publications, 1984.
A straightforward retelling of the original legend.

Anaya, Rudolfo. **Maya's Children: The Story of La Llorona**. Illustrated by Maria Baca. New York: Hyperion, 1997.
Some may balk at this version in which a villain, Señor Tiempo (The God of Time), steals Maya's children, instead of her killing them, causing her to become La Llorona. Maya is born with a mark that is known as a sign of immortality. Señor Tiempo becomes crazy with jealousy over this usurpation of his powers, and so robs Maya of her dearest treasure, her children.

Anzaldua, Gloria. **Prietita and the Ghost Woman/Prietita y La Llorona**. Illustrated by Maya Christina Gonzalez. San Francisco, CA: Children's Book Press, 1996.
Prietita searches for an herb, rue, and meets La Llorona.

Hayes, Joe. **La Llorona/The Weeping Woman**. Illustrated by Vicki Trego-Hill. Cinco Puntos Press, 1986.
This version is the best for storytelling because it is basically a transcription of the version Hayes uses when he tells the story out loud. (Hayes's version can also be found in Amy L. Cohn, **From Sea to Shining Sea: A Treasury of American Folklore and Folk Songs**. New York: Scholastic, 1993.

MARÍA ANGULA

Librarian, author and storyteller Lucía M. González says this is her favorite story to tell around Halloween. It comes from the oral traditions of Ecuador, but is a story similar to that of the more well-known "Tailypo." When María is married, her husband asks her to make various special dishes for him, and she has never done much to learn how to cook. After a major cooking disaster, María goes to the house of her neighbor, Doña Mercedes, for advice. When Mercedes tells María how to prepare the dish her husband requested, she replies flippantly, "If that is all there is to making that dish, *I knew that.*" María repeatedly returns to Doña Mercedes for help, and each time gives the same reply, that she already knew how to make the dish in question. Finally, Doña Mercedes becomes annoyed, and when María asks her about a dish that includes tripe, Mercedes tells her to obtain the ingredient, and others from a fresh corpse in the cemetery. María does so, but that same night, the spirit whose entrails María took, comes to ask for them back. When her husband wakes, his wife has disappeared, never to be seen again.

"María Angula." **Cuentos de espantos y aparecidos** (Stories of Ghosts and Apparitions). Edited by Veronica Uribe. Sao Paulo, Brazil: Editorial Atica, Coedición Latinoamericana, 1984, pp. 33–40.

Tales from the Indian Oral Tradition

MACARIO

One of my favorite stories that arises out of the Indian oral tradition is "Macario." This story appeared as a major Mexican feature film based on the adult novel by the mysterious B. Traven. Macario is a young peasant who cannot provide for his family and becomes despondent. On the Day of the Dead, he meets Death himself, who comes disguised as a peasant like Macario. Death trades the power to cure for a portion of turkey that Macario has. Macario soon becomes famous for his magical skill. That is, until he disobeys Death's instructions. An interesting version of the story can be found in the book *Cuentos*.

Griego y Maestas, Jose, and Rudolfo A. Anaya. "La comadre Sebastiana/Doña Sebastiana." **Cuentos: Tales from the Hispanic Southwest**. Santa Fe: Museum of New Mexico Press, 1980, pp. 14–21.

In this version the poor woodcutter goes nameless. He denies help to the Lord and the Virgin Mary before meeting Death, who is portrayed as a woman, Doña Sebastiana. When the man disobeys Death's direction to never cure a person if he saw Death at the head of the bed, Death takes the woodcutter to a room with two candles, representing life. The woodcutter's candle goes out: "At that moment the flame of the short candle went out, and the curandero's soul was added to Doña Sebastiana's cart as it slowly made its way into eternity."

Macario. Directed by Roberto Gavaldon. Mexico, 1958. 91 Minutes. Available from Facets Video.

The appearance of death as a character is common in Latino folklore, and one of the common motifs is tricking death. This motif appears in some of the Pedro de Ordimalas tales. Another good folktale where death is tricked is from storyteller Olga Loya:

Loya, Olga. "Tía Miseria" (Aunt Misery) from Amy L. Cohn, **From Sea to Shining Sea: A Treasury of American Folklore and Folk Songs**. New York: Scholastic, 1993.

Aunt Misery is tired of the boys that climb her pear tree and taunt her. When she takes in a magician, he repays her by granting her wish that anyone who climbs her tree will not be able to come down until she says some magic words. This wish comes in handy when Death comes calling.

OUR LADY OF GUADALUPE

The story of Our Lady of Guadelupe is one cherished by all Mexicans. The Virgin Mary appears to a poor man named Juan Diego, and tells him that she wishes a church to be built on the site where they are standing, and instructs him to go to the bishop. This is a miracle accepted as truth by most Catholic Latinos, and cherished because it shows how marvelous events happen to ordinary people. Two versions of this tale are retold for children.

dePaola, Tomie. **The Lady of Guadelupe**. New York: Holiday House, 1980. Spanish Translation: **Nuestra Señora de Guadelupe**. Translated by Pura Belpré.

This retelling of the story of the appearance of the Virgin Mary to the peasant Juan Diego is enhanced by dePaola's simple and respectful illustrations.

Parish, Helen Rand. **Our Lady of Guadalupe**. Illustrated by Jean Charlot. New York: Viking, 1955.

An older version of the story most appropriate for providing material for the storyteller, who is going to tell the tale of Juan Diego and the Virgin Mary.

POINSETTIA

Another legend involves that of the poinsettia flower, the traditional flower during the holiday season.

dePaola, Tomie. **The Legend of the Poinsettia**. New York: Putnam, 1994.

Lucinda helps her mother weave a blanket to be used for the Baby Jesus in a Christmas procession. When her mother gets sick, Lucinda tries to finish the blanket but only ends up tangling the yarn. Lucinda fears that she has ruined the celebrations until an old woman appears to her and tells her that the Baby Jesus will accept any gift she gives because it comes from the heart.

Mora, Pat, and Charles Ramãirez Berg. **The Gift of the Poinsettia/El regalo de la flor de nochebuena**. Illustrated by Daniel Lechhãon. Houston: Piñata (Arte Público), 1995.

In this story it is a little boy participating in the Las Posadas festivities who worries what gift he can bring to the Baby Jesus.

FOLKLORE

Storytelling and Folklore

The tales that I have mentioned in this chapter all lend themselves to oral telling without using a book. Stories like "Perez and Martina" and "The Bossy

Gallito" have a cumulative structure that make them easy to tell. Find the version or combination of versions that you like best. Make the story your own, adding your own flourishes or style. Sometimes this happens over repeated tellings. You can adapt them to your level of proficiency in Spanish from using only a few Spanish words throughout to being able to tell the entire tale in Spanish. I find that with cumulative tales it is easier to begin with a 3 × 5 inch card used as a "cheat sheet" with the salient points. For example, if telling "The Bossy Gallito," you could simply list each of the animals or things the Gallito encounters (i.e. the grass, the fire) to jog your memory.

Puppet Shows from Folklore

Puppet shows are always an excellent way to present the folklore of any culture. Most of the Latino folktales I've mentioned adapt themselves easily for theatrical presentation. If you don't feel comfortable with writing your own adaptation, just use the dialogue as it comes from your source material. You can make adaptations to fit the puppets you have on hand if necessary. There are many folktales that can be adapted for puppet shows. One of the best models for this comes from Lucía González, Associate Director for Youth Services with the Broward County Library.

Lucia's idea was to provide puppet shows and other programs that celebrated Latino heritage to smaller and medium-sized libraries in her system. To do this, she put together a group of both Latino and non-Latino librarians who called themselves Colorin-Colorado. This group concentrated on adapting Latino folktales as puppet shows. Colorin-Colorado has adapted and performed Lucia's own retellings of "Juan Bobo and the Bunuelos" and "How Uncle Rabbit Tricked Uncle Tiger" as puppet shows, as well as "Martina: The Little Cockroach," "Ote," and "The Tiger and the Rabbit" all by Pura Belpré. Additionally, they have done "Menique" from a story by Jose Marti, "The Three Feathers," a Venezuelan folktale and a humorous adaptation of Don Quixote.

Two of the following puppet shows, "Señor Conejo, Señor Coyote, y el Espantapajaros" (Mr. Rabbit, Mr. Coyote and the Scarecrow) and "Perez and Martina" were adapted by Mary Alice Cortez and Sandra McLean of the Dallas Public Library Children's Center. They are reprinted here with their permission. A third show, "Marinerito Juan Trombón" (Little Sailor John Trombone) adapted from a show by Elsa Lira Gaiero of Uruguay was anthologized in Carmen Bravo-Villasante's *Historia y antologia de la literatura infantil Iberoamericana,* volume 2. All of these can be duplicated for the purpose of presentation in a school or library, where admission is not charged. In addition to the three scripts, here are some other stories which could work well as puppet shows:

"The Rooster Who Went to His Uncle's Wedding." Source: **The Rooster Who Went to His Uncle's Wedding: A Latin American Folktale**. Illustrated by Kathleen Kuchera. New York: Whitebird (Putnam), 1993.

This story makes an excellent puppet show, as well as being ideal to tell aloud. Simple stick puppets will work just fine. Use red and orange tissue paper for fire and blue cellophane for water.

"La cesta magica" (The Magic Basket). Source: Angeles Gasset, "La cesta magica." In Carmen Bravo-Villasante, **Antologia de la literatura infantil en lengua espanola**, vol. 2. Madrid: Doncel, 1973, pp. 439–449.

In this more ambitions puppet show, a gentleman with a feather in his hat finds a magic basket full of money. When you pull out a bill, another appears in its place. Pelos takes the basket for Panchita, his wife, who wants a basket for shopping. The gentleman then schemes to get the basket back.

"Coyote Rings the Wrong Bell." Source: Francisco X. Mora, **Coyote Rings the Wrong Bell: A Mexican Folktale**. Chicago: Children's Press, 1991.

Coyote gets tricked by rabbit. Rabbit avoids being eaten by Coyote by telling him that he can have all the tender juicy young rabbits he wants by ringing a bell in a tree. When he shakes the tree in an attempt to ring the bell, he is attacked by a swarm of bees.

"La Gran fiesta de la primavera" (The Great Spring Festival). Source: Francisco X. Mora, **La gran fiesta**. Fort Atkinson, WI: Highsmith Press, 1993.

Crow shows his bird friends how to celebrate spring by decorating a tree. This show can be adapted to take place during winter as well.

"The Hummingbirds' Gift." Source: **The Hummingbirds' Gift**. Illustrated by Stefan Czernecki; straw weavings by Juliana Reyes de Silva and Juan Hilario Silva. New York: Hyperion, 1994.

Consuelo saves the hummingbirds' lives, they teach her to save her family from the drought. This is a possibility for a Día de los Muertos program because of the fact that Consuelo is inspired to sell her woven figures for that holiday.

Señor Conejo Señor Coyotey el Espantapajaros
(Mr. Rabbit, Mr. Coyote and the Scarecrow)

Cast

Coyote w/velcro

Rabbit w/velcro

Farmer
Mono (Scarecrow w/velcro)
Sun/Moon
Narrator (Beau, the crow)

Props
Corn plant
Rake
Hoe
Watering can
Slip whistle
Music
Turkey baster w/water
Blue backdrop
The End/El Fin sign

NARRATOR: (Welcomes audience.) In Mexican folktales the conejo (rabbit) and the coyote are favorite characters. Señor Conejo is known as the trickster who lives by his wits and Señor Coyote is always very greedy and hungry. So please join us for (give title of show).

FARMER (enters whistling, holding a rake/watering can): Oh what a beautiful day for gardening! I think I'll plant some corn.

(Scratches around w/rake and whistles; uses watering can.)
There, I'm finished; now we'll let mother nature take her course.
(Farmer exits; play music and pass moon/sun overhead a few times; use slide whistle and push corn plant up slowly.)

FARMER: Oh look at the beautiful corn; I think I'll let it ripen one more day and then come back and pick it for my dinner.

(Farmer exits.)

RABBIT: Hola! What a beautiful garden and I'm hungry. (Looks around and hams it up; eventually steals corn plant and gleefully leaves; pass moon/sun once.)

FARMER (enters whistling): How is my corn today? My mouth is watering for a corn on the cob dinner. Mmmmmm (sees corn is missing and has a fit; looks everywhere; asks audience if they saw anyone). What should I do? I think I will replant it and put a mono by it to protect it. (Sets to work. First he hoes, then he waters. For a good effect at this point squirt audience with turkey baster. He then sets out the mono and leaves; Turn on music and pass moon/sun over set several times. Then use slip whistle and slowly bring up the corn.)

RABBIT: Boy am I hungry I'd like some more of that corn! (Bumps into mono.)

Hey, get out of my way! (Mono doesn't move.) Didn't you hear me? Let me pass! (Mono doesn't move; Rabbit pushes doll with paw and gets stuck.) Aiee, let go of me! (Gets other paw stuck; milk this for all it is worth: ask audience for help.)

FARMER (enters whistling): Hm! What do we have here? Mmm a tasty rabbit. I think I'll go home and start the pot of water boiling for my favorite dish, corn and rabbit stew.

(Exits.)

RABBIT (pleads with audience): Help me get unstuck; do you think the farmer will really boil me into a stew? (Pass moon/sun over the stage once.)

Next day . . .

COYOTE (whispers to audience): Hmm, what do we have here? Tasty young rabbit for my dinner. (TO RABBIT) Señor Rabbit, what are you doing stuck up there?

RABBIT: Señor Coyote, I stole some corn from the farmer and for my punishment he tied me to this mono so that I would not run away. He said he is coming back to take me down and put me in his chicken house. He wants to lock me in there with all of those chickens. I hate chickens.

COYOTE (to audience): Hmmm! Did you say chicken house? I love juicy little chickens, slurp, drool, etc. Señor Conejo, I am always ready to do a favor for a friend. Let me change places with you.

RABBIT: Are you sure you wouldn't mind? It's hot and noisy and crowded in that chicken house.

COYOTE: Anything for a friend. Here, let me help you down. (Unsnap velcro.)

RABBIT: Thank you; I am most grateful. Here, let me help you up. (Snap velcro.) There, are you alright?

COYOTE: Couldn't be better.

RABBIT (runs off chanting): Nyah, nyah, nyah, nyah, nyah.

FARMER: My cooking pot is boiling and I'm ready to fix that corn and rabbit stew. Mm Mm Mm, I'm hungry.

RABBIT (Peeaks up from behind the curtain and repeats): Nyah, nyah, nyah, nyah, nyah!

(Hold up The End/El Fin sign)

Perezy Martina

The following adaptation of Perez and Martina is very versatile. You can adapt the show by using whatever animal puppets you have on hand as Martina's suitors.

Characters

Martina, a cockroach
Perez, the mouse
Señor borrega (Sheep)
Señor abeja (Bee)
Señor pato (Duck)
Señor sapo (Frog)

Props

Broom
Cooking pot
Sun
Moon
Black/white mantilla/scarf
Powder puff
Music/wedding & flamenco
Chair
Roses
Confetti
Peseta

Scene 1

(Blue backdrop/roses/chair. Martina enters with broom/scarf over her head.)

MARTINA: —Que hermoso día! Me encanta tener my casita y jardín en orden y limpio. Hm! ¿Que es esto? Una peseta brillosa. Debe ser mi día con suerte. Que haré, la guardo o la gasto? Ya, ya me ejite. Gasto la peseta, si, iré a comprar polvo y una mantilla.

(Martina exits play flamenco music/she reenters wearing black mantilla and poofing herself with powder puff/she dances to the music.)

Mmmm ahora con esta fragancia y la mantilla nueva, me siento hermosa(sigh). Cuando vendrá el guapisimo Señor Perez, el Ratón?

(Martina sits in the white chair/off music.)

BORREGA: —Good day Senorita Martina. You're so pretty.
MARTINA: —Gracias, Señor Borrega.
BORREGA: —Will you ma-a-a-arry me?
MARTINA: —Oh, quizás, si me dices como me hablarás en el futuro.
BORREGA: —Así: Baaaaaaaaaaaaaaa!
MARTINA: —No, no, Basta! ¿Ha visto al Señor Perez, el Ratoncito? El es un caballero.

(Señor Borrega leaves crying and whining:

Music on/martina dances until snake enters/off music.)

ABEJA: —Good day, Señorita Martina.

MARTINA: —Buenos días, Señor Abeja.

ABEJA: —ZZZZZZZZZZZZZZZZZZ Will you marry me? ZZZZZZZZZZZZ

MARTINA: —Oh, quizás, si me dices como me hablarás en el futuro.

ABEJA: —zzzzzzzzzzzzzzzzzzzzzzzzzzzzzzzzzzzzzzzzzzzzzzzzzzz

MARTINA: —Basta, basta! No, Señor Abeja. Lárgate de aquí.

(Bee buzzes off.)

MARTINA: —Nadie, nadie se compara al gran galán, Señor Perez.

MARTINA: —Aye, aye, aye, aye (To the tune of "Cielito Lindo") ¿Donde esta el
   guapisimo Señor Perez y cuando vendrá a visitarme?

(Señor Sapo hops in noisily.)

SAPO: —Y yo? Will you marry me?

MARTINA: —Tal vez si me dices como me hablarás en el futuro.

SAPO: —Borom, borom, borom . . . (and hops all over the place).

MARTINA: —No, no, no me casaré con usted. No me gusta su voz, y ademas, he
   oido decir que ustedes, los sapos, hablan constantemente día y noche.

(Señor sapo hops away loud and fast.)

MARTINA: —¡O mi estimado Perez, cuando vendrá? Se hace tarde, tal vez es
   mejor ir a la cocina y preparar una sopa para la cena. (Martina begins to
   exit just as singing is heard offstage.) Aye, parece que escucho al Señor
   Perez, vale ir a ponerme chevere. (Martina rushes off and returns with the
   powder puff.) Uuu, uuu, debo verme hermosa para mi guapisimo, Señor
   Perez. (Turns to the audience) ¿Me miro bonita?

(Perez enters singing a tune)

PEREZ: —Un ratoncito soy. A handsome mouse am I.

MARTINA: —Oh, Señor Perez, su canción mueve mi corazón.

PEREZ: —Gracias, Señorita Martina! For sometime now, I've wanted to ask you
   something. Will you marry me?

MARTINA: —Oh quizás si me dice como me hablarás en el futuro.

PEREZ: —Certainly, I shall read to you, and sing like this: Chui, Chui, Chui,
   Chui, . . .

MARTINA: —¡Ay que lindo! Suena como música, si, si, Señor Perez, me casaré
   con usted. Debo ir a preparar para la boda. (Martina departs.)

PEREZ (sings a reprise of above song): —Yes, my darling, and do not forget the reception. We shall serve the best we have to offer our guests. Pastries, food, and drink.

MARTINA: —Si, si, la comida para la boda con pasteles, pan de polvo, carne guisada, arroz frijoles y refrescos. Hasta luego, mi caballero, Señior Perez.

(The bluebird flys in singing. Martina enters to the wedding march and the couple parades back and forth on the stage. Throw confetti out into the audience. Perez and Martina dance together.)

PEREZ: —Chui, chui, chui

PEREZ AND MARTINA: —¡Vamos a la recepcion! To the reception! (Puppeteers say or hold up sign saying "and they lived happily ever after/Viveron feliz para siempre." El Fin.)

Marinerito Juan Trombon
Adapted from the puppet show by Elsa Lira Gaiero

Characters
    Juan Trombón
    Captain Tornado

Props
    Broom
    Captain's Cap

JUAN: —(Appears singing and dancing)
Juan Trombón,
Juan Trombón,
Marinerito,
Juan Trombón,
I sail the seven seas
In my little cardboard boat.
CAPTAIN (from inside): —¡Juan Trombón!
JUAN: —Presente, Capitán Tornado.
CAPTAIN: —What were you doing, Juan Trombón?
JUAN: —Cantaba, Capitán Tornado.
CAPTAIN: —You weren't cleaning the boat as I ordered you?
JUAN: —No, Capitán Tornado.
CAPTAIN (furious): —And what were you waiting for?
JUAN (trembling): —Que usted me viera, Capitán Tornado.
CAPTAIN: —You don't need to wait for me. Now get to it. ¡Pues, rápido! Scrub down the deck! Sweep, wash, dust, clean pronto!, ¡pronto!

(While the Captain shouts, Juan Trombón runs around like a madman doing everything the Captain orders. Finally, when the Captain finishes his tirade, Juan leans over the side of the puppet stage breathing heavily.)

CAPTAIN: —¡Juan Trombón!

JUAN (back up at attention): —¡Presente, Capitán Tornado!

CAPTAIN: —¡Rápido! ¡Siga lavando, fregando, barriendo! (Juan Trombón begins to clean again, but after a moment falls over the side of the stage, heaving). ¡Juan Trombón!

JUAN (trying to catch his breath): —¡Presente, Capitán Tornado!

CAPTAIN: —Scrub the deck, clean the windows, fold the sails, raise the anchor, recoja las cuerdas, sweep the cabin, cook the food, mend the clothes. (Juan runs about again, doing everything the Captain orders, then leans over the side of the stage, exhausted).

CAPTAIN: —Es usted un desobediente, Juan Trombón, I will punish you as you deserve . . . (the furious Captain drops his cap, which he has been holding. Juan Trombón picks it up).

CAPTAIN: —Give me back my cap, Juan Trombón!

JUAN: —Pues, no, señor, ahora soy yo el capitán y puedo mandar.

CAPTAIN (crying): —Tiene razón. Whoever has the cap is captain of the ship. !Ay mi gorra! Now I am no longer captain. ¡Ay, ay!

JUAN: —¡Marinero Juan Tornado!

CAPTAIN: —Presente, Capitán Trombón.

JUAN: —Más firme, Marinero Tornado. !Más derecho! Lift up your head, straighten those shoulders, suck in that gut. March now. Uno dos, uno dos, uno dos, left, right, left, right, left, right. (The captain marches back and forth). Now scrub the deck, clean the windows, fold the sails, raise the anchor, recoja las cuerdas, sweep the cabin, cook the food, mend the clothes! (While the captain is working, Juan Trombón begins to sing as he did in the beginning.)

Juan Trombón,
Juan Trombón
Marinerito,
Juan Trombón
nevega por los mares
en su barco de cartón.

Creative Dramatization of Folklore

One of the most effective ways of sharing folktales is through creative dramatization. Any of the tales I have mentioned would probably lend themselves well to dramatic treatment. Children can enjoy being Martina and her suitors, or the Rooster. In an after-school program I shared a number of tales with a group of middle school students who had newly immigrated to this country. I asked them to choose their favorite to dramatize. They picked Pedro. Together, we wrote a script and put on the production, complete with costumes, for an appreciative audience of parents and friends. Here is the script we used, in both languages. If having enough time to memorize lines is a problem, have children carry the scripts. We did our production twice, once in Spanish, and then again in English. Since these children knew little English, it was a challenge, but one that they enjoyed.

Pedro de Ordimalas

Escena 1

NARRATOR: —Había una vez hace mucho tiempo, tanto tiempo que casi olvido que vivía un hombre llamado Pedro de Ordimalas.

PEDRO: —Voy al casino. Tal vez hoy gane suficiente dinero para traer algo de comida a casa para ti y el bebé

ESPOSA DE PEDRO: —¡Oh!, Pedro. Tu me tratas bien, mejor de lo normal, aunque los juegos en el casino son tu único vicio. Pareces un bribón. ¿Porque no podemos vivir honestamente? Teníamos dinero, pero ya no. Lo has perdido todo.

PEDRO: —Dame una oportunidad. Estoy seguro que hoy será me día de suerte.

NARRATOR: —En Éste día El Señor y San Pedro decidieron disfrazarse y venir a la tierra a ver que tan caritativa y bondadosa es la gente.

SEÑOR: —Apiádense de Éste pordiosero. ¿Buen hombre, una limosna por favor?

PEDRO: —No tengo dinero, pero espérame aquí y consigueré algo para ti.

NARRATOR: —Pedro corrió hacia el casino y pidió a sus amigos que le prestaran cincuenta centavos. Ellos no le querían prestar nada, porque pensaron que el los utilizaría para darlos de limosna. Pedro insistió hasta convencerlos que no sería así, y prometió que se los devolvería tan pronto como pudiera. Entonces Pedro corrió hacia los dos pordioseros y les dio el dinero.

SEÑOR: —Pedro, por haberte apiadado de los pobres he decidido gratificarte concediéndote un deseo.

PEDRO: —Todo lo que quiero es mi cincuenta centavos. De otra manera mis amigos no confiarán nunca mas en mi.

SEÑOR (En tono sarcástico): —No, eso no es suficiente para alguien tan bondadoso y de buen corazón como tú, quien ha tenido que pedir a sus amigos algo para ayudar a los pobres. Pide algo más.

PEDRO: —Bien. Una cosa que me gustaría mucho es que cuando vaya a un lugar y no quiero dejarlo, ni siguiera Dios todo poderoso puede hacerme abandonarlo.

SEÑOR: —Eso no es suficiente. ¿No deseas algo mas?

PEDRO: —Bien . . . (sus ojos brillaron). ¿Me podrías dar un paquete de cartas mágicas?

SEÑOR: —Muy bien, pide algo mas.

PEDRO: —Biiiieeeen . . . Hmmmm . . . algo que siempre he querido es un tambor. Pero no un tambor común y corriente sino uno mágico. En el cual que se siente a tocar éste tambor no puede pararse sin mi permiso. Y de la misma forma, ¿Porque no te haces cargo de toda mi familia, ellos no tienen porque sufrir nunca más. Ahora que soy tan pobre no puedo soportarlos como se les merecen.

SEÑOR: —¿Algo más, Pedro? A pesar de tu renuencia creo que tienes anhelos en la vida.

PEDRO: —Está bien. Cuando yo muera, prométeme que tomarás mi cuerpo y mi alma. ¡De esta forma no moriré!

SEÑOR: —Te concederé todo cuanto has pedido. (A un lado a San Pedro). Hay que ver como el granuja de Pedro hace uso de sus nuevos dones.

NARRATOR: —Desde entonces, Pedro siempre ganó con sus cartas mágicas. Creció rico pero desatendió a su familia, quienes eventualmente crecieron enfermos y murieron. Pedro estaba solo, aunque no realmente. Tenia caudales de dinero para mantenerse acompañado.

PEDRO: —Tengo tanto dinero. No se que hacer, ya que no tengo familia.

Escena 2

NARRATOR: —Una noche, después de haber transcurrido varios años, Pedro escucho pasos de alguien que se acercaba y entonces tocó a la puerta.

PEDRO: —¿Quien es?

LA MUERTE 1: —La muerte, he venido a llevarte conmigo.

PEDRO: —Si iré, pero primero me gustaría que te sentaras aquí a tocar mi tambor. Cuando la gente pobre lo escuche vendrá, y entonces les daré toda mi riqueza. Después me podrás llevar.

NARRATOR: —Una vez que La Muerte se sentó a tocar el tambor, descubrió que no se podía parar.

MUERTE 1: —¡Me has engañado, no me puedo parar!

PEDRO: —Me voy al casino.

NARRATOR: —Pedro regresó ocho días mas tarde.

MUERTE 1: —¿Pedro, que vas a hacer conmigo?

PEDRO: —Te dejaré ir, solo si prometes darme el doble de años de vida que me quedan.

MUERTE 1: —Te concederé el deseo, todo lo que quiero es liberarme de éste tambor mágico.

NARRATOR: —La Muerte fue a reportar lo que sucedido al Señor.

MUERTE 1: —Es imposible traer a Pedro.

SEÑOR: —Enviare a la Muerte que carga la guadaña.

NARRATOR: —Otra vez una noche, Pedro escucho pasos acercarse y de pronto a alguien que tocaba a la puerta.

PEDRO: —¿Quien es?

MUERTE 2: —Soy la Muerte que carga una guadaña. He venido a llevarte conmigo.

PEDRO: —Si iré, pero primero me gustaría que te sentaras aquí a tocar mi tambor. Cuando la gente pobre lo escuche vendrá y entonces les daré toda mi riqueza. Después tu podrás llevarme.

NARRATOR: —Una vez que La Muerte que carga la guadaña se sentó a tocar el tambor, descubrió que no se podía parar.

MUERTE 2: —¡Me has engañado, no me puedo parar!

PEDRO: —Ahora me voy al casino.

NARRATOR: —Pedro regresó ocho días mas tarde.

MUERTE 2: —¿Pedro, que vas a hacer conmigo?

PEDRO: —Te dejaré ir solo si prometes darme el doble de años de vida que me quedan.

MUERTE 2: —Te concederé el deseo, todo lo que quiero es liberarme de éste tambor mágico.

NARRATOR: —La Muerte que carga la guadaña fue a reportar lo sucedido al Señor.

MUERTE 1: —Es imposible traer a Muerte 2.

Señor: —Como te pudo hacer tonto, igual que la Muerte 1. Enviare a La Muerte del carruaje que lleva un arco y una flecha.

NARRATOR: —Esta vez era mediodía. Pedro no solo escucho pasos, sino también el terrible galopar de los caballos tirando el carruaje de la muerte, Pedro salió a recibirla.

MUERTE 3: —Yo soy la Muerte del carruaje que carga un arco y una flecha. He venido a llevarte conmigo. Cierra tus ojos.

NARRATOR: —Pedro cerró los ojos sin pensarlo, y antes de que los pudiera abrir fue muy tarde. Sintió que la flecha de la muerte lo atravesó, y enfrente del dijo las llamas del infierno. La muerte finalmente se llevó a Pedro de Ordimalas.

Escena 3

NARRATOR: —Pedro llego al infierno en vísperas de la celebración de la fiesta anual. Los diablos del infierno le encomendaron cuidar de la leña. Mientras éste la juntó, Pedro también recolectó un tarro de goma de árbol. El día de la fiesta lo enviaron a arreglar las sillas, y conforme las acomodaba les ponía goma. Los diablos llegaron y se sentaron, y justo cuando se preparaban a comer Pedro dijo . . .

PEDRO: —Momento, no podemos empezar a comer sin antes dar gracias a Dios.

DIABLOS: —¡No! ¡No menciones ese nombre!

PEDRO: —Santo, Santo, Santo es el Señor Dios.

NARRATOR: —Aquellas palabras infundieron pánico en el infierno. Los diablos aterrorizados intentaron correr pero ellos estaban pegados a sus sillas. Se tropezaban unos con otros en su afán por liberarse. La puerta estaba cerrada de tal manera que algunos aun pegados a sus sillas lograron saltar por la ventana. Entre mas fuerte cantaba Pedro mas consternación y pánico causaba.

PEDRO: —Santa María, ¡Madre de Dios!

NARRATOR: —Finalmente, uno de los diablos se escapó y fue a quejarse con San Pedro.

DIABLO: —Pedro nos esta volviendo locos a todos allá en el infierno. Porque no te lo traes?

SAN PEDRO: —Lo reportaré. (Y Éste fue al Señor.) Los diablos en el infierno no pueden soportar a Pedro de Ordimalas.

SEÑOR: —Ya sabía de él, y he tenido suficiente de ese bribón.

NARRATOR: —De tal forma que San Pedro, escoltando a Pedro lo trajo ante la presencia del Señor.

SEÑOR: —Quizás si te enviamos lejos a cuidar ovejas ya no te meterás en tantos líos.

PEDRO: —Pero Señor, no me iré. Recuerdas que uno de los deseos que me concediste consiste en que si yo no quiero abandonar un lugar ni siquiera Dios Padre pueda obligarme.

SEÑOR: —Engañaste a dos de mis mejores muertes. Burlaste a los diablos mas diablos del infierno. Pero no conseguirás burlarte de mi.

Permanecerás en la gloria pero lo harás en forma de piedra.

PEDRO: —Si, Señor, pero al menos seré una roca con ojos.

Pedro de Ordimalas

Scene 1

NARRATOR: A long time ago, so long that it has almost been lost in the memory, there lived a man named Pedro de Ordimalas.

PEDRO: I'm going to the casino. Perhaps today I will win enough to bring some food home for you and the baby.

PEDRO'S WIFE: Oh, Pedro. You treat me well, better than most, but the casino is your one vice. You are something of a rascal when it comes to that. Why is it that we cannot eat honestly? There used to be money but now there is none; you have squandered it all away.

PEDRO: Give me a chance, I'm sure today will be my lucky day.

NARRATOR: That very day the Lord and Saint Peter disguised themselves and came to earth to see who the charitable people were.

LORD: Alms for a poor crippled man. Good sir, can you spare any money?

PEDRO: I have none, but wait right here and I'll get something for you.

NARRATOR: Pedro ran back to the casino and asked his friends for fifty cents. They did not want to give it to him, because they thought he would give it to charity. He managed to convince them that he would not, and promised that he would return quickly. Pedro ran to the two beggars and gave his money to them.

LORD: Pedro, for having felt sorry for the poor, I am prepared to grant you any wish.

PEDRO: All I want is my fifty cents back. Otherwise my friends won't believe me.

LORD (with a hint of sarcasm): No, that is certainly not enough for someone as kind and bighearted as you, who would borrow from his friends in order to give to the poor. Ask for something more.

PEDRO: Well, one thing I would like a lot is that if I am in a place and I don't want to leave, not even God almighty could make me go.

LORD: That is nothing. Don't you want anything more?

PEDRO: Well . . . (His eyes brighten). Could I have a magical deck of cards?

LORD: Very well, ask for more.

PEDRO: Weeelll . . . Uh . . . Something I've always wanted is a drum. Not just an ordinary drum, but a magical drum. Whoever sits down to play this drum won't be able to get up without my permission. And, by the way, why don't you take all my family. They don't need to suffer anymore. Now that I'm so poor, I haven't been able to support them very well.

LORD: Anything else, Pedro? Despite your reluctance, you appear to have no lack of desires.

PEDRO: Okay. When I die, promise that you will take both my body and my soul. That way I won't die!

LORD: I will give you all that you have requested. (Aside to Saint Peter) We shall see just how this rascal Pedro makes use of his new found riches.

NARRATOR: From then on, Pedro always won with his new deck of cards. He grew rich, but neglected his family, who all eventually grew sick and died. Pedro was alone, but not really. He had plenty of money to keep him company.

PEDRO: I have too much money. I don't know what to do with it all, now that I have no family.

Scene 2

NARRATOR: One night, many years later, Pedro heard footsteps, and then a knock at the door.

PEDRO: Who is it?

DEATH 1: Death. I have come to take you with me.

PEDRO: I will come, but first I would like you to sit here and play my drum. When the poor people hear it, they will come and I will give them all my wealth. Then you may take me.

NARRATOR: When Death sat down at the drum, she discovered that she couldn't move.

DEATH 1: You've tricked me, I can't move.

PEDRO: I'm off to the casino.

NARRATOR: Eight days later, Pedro returned.

DEATH 1: Pedro, what are you going to do with me?

PEDRO: I will only let you go if you promise to double the years of life left to me.

DEATH 1: I will grant your wish; all I want is to be free of this magic drum.

NARRATOR: Death went back to the Lord to make a report.

DEATH 1: It is impossible to bring Pedro.

LORD: I will send the Death that carries the scythe.

NARRATOR: Again one night, Pedro heard footsteps, and then a knock at the door.

PEDRO: Who is it?

DEATH 2: I am the Death who carries a scythe. I have come to take you with me.

PEDRO: I will come, but first I would like you to sit here and play my drum. When the poor people hear it, they will come and I will give them all my wealth. Then you may take me.

NARRATOR: When the Death who carries a scythe sat down at the drum, she discovered that she couldn't move.

DEATH 2: You've tricked me, I can't move!

PEDRO: I'm off to the casino.

NARRATOR: Eight days later, Pedro returned.

DEATH 2: Pedro, what are you going to do with me?

PEDRO: I will only let you go if you promise to double the years of life left to me.

DEATH 2: I will grant your wish; all I want is to be free of this magic drum.

NARRATOR: The Death who carries a scythe went back to the Lord to make a report.

DEATH 2: It is impossible to bring Pedro.

LORD: How could you let yourself be fooled just like the first death? I will send the Death that rides a cart and carries a bow and arrow.

NARRATOR: This time it was midday. Pedro not only heard footsteps, but also the terrible creaking of Death's cart. Instead of waiting for her to knock, he went out to greet her.

DEATH 3: I am the Death who rides a cart and carries a bow and arrow. I have come to take you with me. Close your eyes.

NARRATOR: Pedro closed his eyes without thinking, and before he could open them it was too late. He felt the arrow of death pass through him, and in front of him he saw the flames of hell. Death had finally gotten the best of Pedro de Ordimalas.

Scene 3

NARRATOR: Pedro arrived in hell just in time for the annual *fiesta*. The devils put him in charge of the firewood. As he gathered it, he also collected a jar full of sticky pitch. On the day of the party they sent him to arrange the chairs. As he set each chair, he put a lump of pitch on the seat. The devils came and took their places, and were just about ready to eat when Pedro said . . .

PEDRO: We can't eat until we've said grace.

DEVILS: NO! Don't say his name!

PEDRO: Holy, holy, holy is the Lord God.

NARRATOR: The words spread panic throughout hell. The devils tried to jump up to escape but they were stuck to their chairs. They bumped and stumbled into each other in their mad dash to get out. The door was locked so some jumped out the windows. The more consternation and panic Pedro caused, the louder he sang.

PEDRO: Holy Mary, Mother of God!

NARRATOR: Finally, one devil escaped and went to complain to Saint Peter.

DEVIL: Pedro is driving us all crazy down there. Why don't you take him?

SAINT PETER: I will report it. (He goes to the Lord) The devils in hell can't stand Pedro de Ordimalas.

LORD: Have him brought before me. I have had enough of that rascal.

NARRATOR: So, Saint Peter had Pedro escorted into the presence of the Lord.

LORD: Perhaps if we sent you far away to tend sheep, you would not get into so much trouble.

PEDRO: But Lord, I will not leave. Don't you remember that one of the gifts you gave me clearly states that if I don't want to leave a place, not even God the Father can make me.

LORD: You got the best of two of my deaths. You got the best of the devils in hell. But you will not get the best of me. You will remain in the glory, but you will do so as a rock.

PEDRO: Yes, Lord, but at least I will be a rock with eyes.

Chapter 7

Programming with Latino Folk Rhymes, Riddles, and Fingerplays

There is a wealth of Latino children's poetry that rivals Mother Goose for the delightful way the language sounds when read out loud. These rhymes are meant to be shared with children. A literal translation of many of the rhymes is provided so that the person who does not speak Spanish can understand their meaning. Note that when a translation is not provided it means that the rhyme is made up of primarily nonsense words that do not have much meaning beyond the sound of the language itself. In this chapter, I have tried to cover some of the most common and important rhymes as well as some favorites I have enjoyed using in programs over the years.

RHYMES

The heritage of folk rhymes in Spanish is one that must be preserved for all children. Reading these rhymes aloud gives a new appreciation of the beauty of the Spanish language. Some of these rhymes are virtually untranslatable, because they depend so much on the sound of the Spanish cadences and rhymes. Some of them have English Mother Goose equivalents, such as "This little piggy went to market," which in Spanish becomes "Éste niño compró un huevito" (This child bought a little egg). Others are completely original. All of these rhymes provide an excellent way to remind Latino children who are becoming more and more English dominant of the sounds of their mother tongue. Some of these have even been collected from Latino library patrons. As you do programs with Latino families you can be your own folklorist and gather new rhymes and riddles from your adult patrons that they may have learned as children. I've divided the rhymes into categories. First are rhymes that are used to begin a story, then rhymes to end a story. Following these are fingerplays, Mother Goose rhymes in Spanish, songs and games, nonsense and miscellaneous rhymes, goodnight rhymes, tongue twisters, and finally riddles.

To Begin a Story

El Cuento

¿Quieres que te cuente un
    cuento?
Dime que sí
y te lo contaré.
dime que no
y no te lo diré.

The Story

Do you want me to tell you
    a story?
Say yes
And I'll tell you one.
Say no
And I won't.

Otro Cuento

¿Quieres que te cuente un
    cuento?
El burro está contento.
¿Quieres que te cuente otra vez?

El burro está al revés.

Another Story

Do you want me to tell you
    a story?
The burro is contented.
Do you want me to tell it to
    you again?
The burro is backwards.

Esto Es Verdad

Esto es verdad
y no me miento.
como me lo contaron
te lo cuento.

It's the Truth

It's the truth
And I'm not lying.
As it was told to me
I am telling it to you.

To End a Story

Voy por un Caminito

Y voy por un caminito,
y voy por otro,
y si éste cuento les gusto

mañana les cuento otro.

I Go On One Path

I go on one path
and go on another,
And if you liked this
    story
Tomorrow I'll tell you
    another.

El fin del Cuento

Se acabo el cuento
Y se lo llevó el viento
Se fué . . . por el mar adentro.

The Story Is Over

The story is over
The wind carried it away
It's gone beneath the ocean.

Colorin Colorado

Y colorín colorado
Éste cuento se ha acabado
y pasó por un zapato roto
para que mañana te cuente otro.

Colorin Colorado

Colorín colorado
This story is over
It passed by a broken shoe
So that tomorrow I can tell
you another.

El Cuento Se Acabo

Y el cuento se acabó
cuando lo vuelva
a encontrar
se lo volvaré a contar.

The Story Is Over

And the story is over
When I meet you again
I'll tell it to you again.

FINGERPLAYS

The following are Spanish takes on "This little piggy went to market."

Hallando un Huevo

Éste niño halló un huevo; (hold up
    little finger)
Éste lo coció; (hold up ring finger)
Éste lo peló; (hold up middle finger)
Éste le hecho la sal; (hold up index
    finger)
Éste gordo chaparrito se lo comió.
    (hold up thumb)

Le dio sed,
Y se fué a buscar agua . . .

Buscó y buscó . . . (Use fingers
    to look for water at elbow, then
    shoulder)

Finding an Egg

This little boy found an
    egg;
This one cooked it;
This one peeled it;
This one salted it;

This fat little one ate it.

It made him thirsty,
And he went to look for
    water . . .
He looked and looked . . .

¡Y aquí halló!   And here he found it!
Y tomó y tomó y tomó . . .   And drank and drank and
  (Tickle under the arm)   drank . . .

Los Niños Traviesos   *The Mischievous Children*

Éste pide pan (hold up thumb)   This one asks for bread.
Éste dice: no lo hay (hold up   This one says there is none
  index finger)
Éste dice: ¿Que haremos? (hold   This one asks, "What shall
  up middle finger)   we do?"
Éste dice: ¡Lo robaremos! (hold   This one says, "We'll rob
  up ring finger)   some"
Éste dice: ¡No, no, que   This one says, "No, no, our
  nos castigara nuestro   mother will punish us!"
  mamá! (hold up little
  finger)

Este, Chiquitito y Bonito   *This One Pretty and Small*

Este, chiquito y bonito, (hold   This one, pretty and small
  up little finger)
éste, el rey de los anillitos,   This one, king of the rings
  (hold up ring finger)
éste, tonto y loco, (hold up   This one, silly and foolish
  middle finger)
éste, se marcha a la escuela,   This one, goes to school
  (hold up index finger)
y éste, se lo come todo. (hold   And this one, eats everything up.
  up thumb)

Here are some other fingerplays:

Con los Manos   *With My Hands*

Con los manos (hold up both   With my hands
  hands)
aplaudo, aplaudo, aplaudo   I clap, clap, clap
  (clap three times)
Y ahora las pongo   And now I put them
En mi repaso. (put both hands   In my lap.
  in your lap)

La Hormiguita

Andaba la hormiguita (walk
    fingers up and down arm)
juntando su comidita
le coge un aguacerito
¡Que corre pa' su casita!
    (run fingers quickly
    down to hand)
y se metió en su covachita.
    (cup one hand around
    the other)

The Ant

The little ant walked

Carrying her food
She gets caught in a rainstorm
How she runs to her little house!

And goes into her little hole.

El Ratoncito

Poy ahí viene un ratoncito
que le cayó un aguacerito
y corriendo, corriendito (run
    fingers up arm)
se metió en un agujerito. (end
    in the ear)

The Little Mouse

There comes a little mouse
Caught by the rain
And runs

Into a hole.

Cinco Lobitos

Cinco lobitos (hold up five
    fingers)
tiene la loba,
cinco lobitos

detrás de la escoba. (make a
    sweeping motion with
    the hand)
A los cinco los parió
y a los cinco los crió
y a los cinco lobitos
leche les dio.

Five Baby Wolves

Five baby wolves

Have their mother
Five baby wolves behind the
    broom
To the five she gave birth,

She raised them
And gave them milk to drink.

Los Lobitos

Cinco lobitos, (hold up five
    fingers to represent the
    five little wolves)

The Baby Wolves

Five baby wolves

tiene la loba,	have their mother.
blancos y negros	They are black and white
detrás de la toba	behind the tuba.
Uno le canta (hold up one finger)	One sings
todo el día	all day,
y otros le tocan (hold up four fingers)	And the others play
la sinfonía.	a symphony.

Chocolate   *Chocolate*

Chocolate	Chocolate
molinillo, (move hand in a circle as if you are grinding chocolate.)	grinder,
corre, corre, (move hand as if it is running away.)	run, run
que te pillo. (wag finger of your other hand at the "bad" hand.)	you are naughty.

Rima de Chocolate   *Chocolate Rhyme*

Uno, dos, tres,–cho–(count with the fingers for each line)	One, two, three,–cho–
Uno, dos, tres,–co–	One, two three,–co–
Uno, dos, tres,–la–	One, two three,–la–
Uno, dos, tres,–te–	One, two, three,–te–
Bate, bate chocolate. (use one arm to make a big bowl, and use the other hand to beat the chocolate)	Beat the, beat the, beat the chocolate.

La Gallinita Napolitana   *The Neapolitan Hen*

La gallinita napolitana	The Napolitan hen
Pone un huevo cada semana (hold up one finger)	Lays one egg a week
pone dos, (hold up two fingers)	Lays two
pone tres, (hold up three fingers)	Lays three

pone cuatro, (hold up four fingers)	Lays four
pone cinco, (hold up five fingers)	Lays five
pone seis, (hold up six fingers).	Lays six
¡Pone siete a la semana! (hold up seven fingers)	Lays seven in the week!
pone ocho, (hold up eight fingers)	Lays eight
pone nueve, (hold up nine fingers)	Lays nine
pone diez, (hold up ten fingers)	Lays ten
la gallinita, ya lo ves,	The hen, now you see,
quiere que escondas tus pies. (cover your feet with your hands)	Wants you to hide your feet.

Una Gallina En Un Arado	*The Hen on a Plow*
Una gallina en un arado	The hen on a plow
puso un huevo colorado	laid a colored egg,
puso 1 (hold up one finger)	laid one, (hold up one finger)
puso 2 (hold up two fingers)	laid two, (hold up two fingers)
puso 3 (hold up three fingers)	laid three, (hold up three fingers)
puso 4 (hold up four fingers)	laid four, (hold up four fingers)
puso 5 (hold up five fingers)	laid five, (hold up five fingers)
puso 6 (hold up six fingers)	laid six, (hold up six fingers)
puso 7 (hold up seven fingers)	laid seven, (hold up seven fingers)
puso 8 (hold up eight fingers)	laid eight, (hold up eight fingers)
puso 9 (hold up nine fingers)	laid nine, (hold up nine fingers)
puso 10 (hold up ten fingers)	laid ten, (hold up ten fingers)
puso Puaff! (close hands, then open them quickly)	laid Puaff! (close hands, then open quickly)
La Luna.	The Moon.

Cinco Pollitos	*Five Chicks*
Cinco pollitos (hold up five fingers)	Five chicks

tiene mi tía

uno le canta, (hold up one
  finger)

otro le pía (hold up two
  fingers)

y tres le tocan la chirimía.
  (hold up three fingers)

has my aunt

one sings,

another cries

and another plays the flute.

Pingüino

Penguin

Pin-uno, pin-dos, pin-tres
  (hold up fingers for
  each number)
pin-cuatro, pin-cinco, pin-seis,
pin-siete, pin-ocho, pingüino!
  (wiggle all eight fingers on
  "pingüino")

Pin-one, pin-two, pin-three

pin-four, pin-five, pin-six,
pin-seven, pin-eight, penguin!

Los Pescaditos

The Little Fish

Los pescaditos andan en el
  agua,
nadan, nadan, nadan. (move
  hands apart in a slow
  swimming motion)
Vuelan, vuelan, vuelan,
  (stretch out arms on
  either side, and make
  a flying motion)
Son chiquititos, son chiquititos
  (put thumb and finger close
  together to indicate
  something small)
Vuelan, vuelan, vuelan
  (swimming motion
  again)
Nadan, nadan, nadan. (flying
  motion again)

The little fish swim in the water,

They swim, swim, swim.

They fly, fly, fly.

They are little, they are little.

They fly, fly, fly.

They swim, swim, swim.

Papas y Papas

Potatoes and Potatoes

Papas y papas para Papá,
papas y papas para Mamá.

Potatoes and potatoes for father
potatoes and potatoes for mother

Las quemaditas para Papá;
las calientitas para Mamá.

The burnt ones for father
The hot ones for mother.

La Araña

La araña pirulina
por la pared se subió (make
    climbing motions with
    fingers)
y mi Tía, Catalina,
con la escoba se barrió. (make
    sweeping motions with
    hands)

The Spider

The spider
climbed up the wall

and my Aunt Catalina
brushed it away with a broom.

Tengo

Tengo, tengo, tengo (point
    to self)
Tu no tienes nada (point to
    someone else)
Tengo tres ovejas en mi
    manada (hold up three
    fingers)
Una me da leche (point to
    first finger)
una me da lana (point to
    second finger)
y otra mantequilla (point to
    third finger)
para la semana.

I Have

I have, I have, I have

You don't have anything

I have three sheep in my flock

One gives me milk

One gives me wool

And the other butter

for the week.

Éste y Éste

En la casa de éste y éste (hold
    up one finger each time
    you say "éste")
condivadan a éste con éste

y dicen éste y éste
que sino va éste con éste

no irá éste sin éste.

This One and This One

To the house of this one and
    this one

They invite this one with this
    one
And this one and this one say
That if this one doesn't go with
    this one
This one will not go with this
    one.

Los Animalitos	*The Little Animals*
Detrás de Doña Pata (point behind)	Behind Mrs. Duck
corren los patitos (make running motion with fingers)	run the ducklings
por allí, por allá, (point to left and right)	over here, over there . . .
cuá, cuá, cuá.	quack, quack, quack.
Detrás de Doña Gallina (point behind)	Behind Mrs. Hen
siguen los pollitos (make running motion with fingers)	follow the little chicks
por allí, por allá, (point to left and right)	over here, over there . . .
pío, pío, pa.	cheep, cheep, cheep.
Detrás de Doña Cabra (point behind)	Behind Mrs. Goat
van las cabritos (make running motion with fingers)	come the the baby goats
por allí, por allá, (point to left and right)	over here, over there . . .
baa, baa, baa.	baa, baa, baa.

Abranlas, Ciérrenlas	*Open Them, Close Them*
Abranlas, ciérrenlas, (open hands, close hands)	Open them, close them,
Abranlas, ciérrenlas, (open hands, close hands)	Open them, close them,
Pla, pla, pla, pla, pla,	Pla, pla, pla, pla, pla,
Abranlas, ciérrenlas, (open hands, close hands)	Open them, close them,
Abranlas, ciérrenlas, (open hands, close hands)	Open them, close them,
Pónglanlas acá. (put hands in lap)	Put them here.

A, e, i, o, u

A, e, i, o u, arbolito de pirú
(point to different children)
dime cuantos años tienes tú.
(the person you land on
tells his or her age)
A, e, i, o u, arbolito de pirú
(point to different children)
dime el nombre que llevas tú.
(the person you land on
tells his or her name)

A, e, i, o, u

A, e, i, o u, little tree of Piru

Tell me your age.

A, e, i, o u, little tree of Piru

Tell me your name.

El Pollito Asadito

El pollito asadito (curve fingers
of left hand to look like a
chicken)
con su sal y su mojito. (cound
fingers, raising them one
by one)
¡Por aquí pasó el pollito!
(surprise children by making
chicken fly to your other
hand and tickle it)

The Roasted Hen

The roasted hen

with its salt and its little cake.

The little chick went this way!

Contando y Cantando

Uno, dos, tres, cuatro y cinco,
(hold up each finger on
one hand)
Seis, siete, ocho, nueve, y diez.
(hold up each finger on
other hand)
Con esta mano cuento cinco
(hold up first hand)
Y con la otra hasta diez. (hold
up other hand)

Counting and Singing

One, two, three, four and five,

six, seven, eight, nine, and ten.

With this hand I count five

With the other up to ten.

Al Subir Una Montaña

Al subir una montaña
(make climbing motions
with arms)

While Climbing a Mountain

While climbing a mountain

una pulga me picó; (pinch arm)	A flea bit me
la cogí de las narices (pinch tip of nose)	I caught it by the nose
y se me escapó. (make flying motion with fingers)	and it escaped.
Botín, botero, y salió	boot, boot-maker, and left (nonsense)
rosa, clavel, y botón.	rose, carnation, button. (nonsense)

Cinco Centavos Cafés	*Five Brown Pennies*
Cinco centavos cafés en mi bolsa. (hold up five fingers)	I have five cents in my purse.
Éste es para el chicle; (point to thumb)	This one is for gum;
Éste es para un anillo; (point to index finger)	This one is for a ring;
Éste es para un tambor; (point to middle finger)	This one is for a drum;
Éstos los guardaré en mi bolsa (point to ring finger)	And these I'll keep in my purse
Para otra cosa. (point to little finger)	For something else.

¿Cuantos Dedos Son?	*How Many Fingers Are There?*
¿Cuantos dedos tengo aquí? (hold up nine fingers).	How many fingers do I have here?
(Children count)	(Children count)
¡Nueve!	Nine!
La colita se mueve. (wiggle the little finger)	The tail wags.

Mother Goose Rhymes

Children enjoy jumping over a small object, it doesn't have to be a candle-stick, while saying this rhyme together.

Tengo Una Vela	*Jack Be Nimble*
Tengo una vela en un candelero	Jack be nimble, Jack be quick,

la pongo en el suelo
y la brinco ligero.

Humpty Dumpty

Jack jump over the
Candlestick.

Humpty Dumpty

This little miracle translates exactly as the English rhyme, except for changing the references to all the king's horses and all the king's men.

Humpty Dumpty se sentó en
    un muro
Humpty Dumpty se cayó muy
    duro
Ni la guardia civil (Neither the
    civil guard)
Ni la caballería (Nor the cavalry)
Supieron como se incorporaría.

Humpty Dumpty sat on a
    wall
Humpty Dumpty had a great
    fall.
All the king's horses,

And all the king's men
Couldn't put Humpty
    together again.

Un Ratón

Un ratón, un ratón,
corriendo por aquí, corriendo
    por allí,
comiendo queso, comiendo pan
al fin los gatos lo agarrarán,

al ratoncito se comerán
¡qué caray! ¡qué caray!

Three Blind Mice

One mouse, one mouse
Running here, running there

Eating cheese, eating bread
In the end the cats will kill him
    dead
They'll eat him whole
What a pity! What a pity!

SONGS AND GAMES

This song tells the story of Don Gato (Mr. Cat) who is engaged to be married, but then falls off a roof and is thought to be dead. In some versions of the song he calls for a doctor, in other versions a priest. Some versions give more details about his injuries, such as a broken head, spine and ribs. When his funeral procession goes through the street where fish are sold, the odor revives him. In some versions of the song, this resurrection does not occur.

Estando El Señor Don Gato

Estando el señor Don Gato
sentadito en su tejado,

There was Mr. Cat

There was Mr. Cat
Sitting on his roof

marramamiau, miau, miau,	Meow, meow, meow,
sentadito en su tejado.	Sitting on his roof.
Ha recibido una carta	He had received a letter
que si quiere ser casado,	Asking him if he wanted to be married
marramamiau, miau, miau,	Meow, meow, meow,
que si quiere ser casado.	Asking him if he wanted to be married.
Con una gatita blanca,	To a white cat
hija de un gato pardo,	Daughter of a brown cat
marramamiau, miau, miau,	Meow, meow, meow,
hija de un gato pardo.	Daughter of a brown cat.
Don Gato por ir a verla	Mr. Cat going to see her
se ha caído del tejado,	Has fallen from his roof,
marramamiau, miau, miau,	Meow, meow, meow,
se ha caído del tejado.	Has fallen from his roof.
Se ha roto siete costillas,	He has broken seven ribs
es espinazo y el rabo,	His spine and his tail,
marramamiau, miau, miau,	Meow, meow, meow,
el espianzo y el rabo.	His spine and his tail.
Vengan, vengan pronto	Come, come quick
médicos y cirujanos,	Doctors and nurses,
marramamiau, miau, miau,	Meow, meow, meow,
médicos y cirujanos.	Doctors and nurses.
Mátenle gallinas negras	Kill some black hens
y denle tazas de caldo,	And give him spoonfuls of soup,
marramamiau, miau, miau,	Meow, meow, meow,
y denle tazas de caldo.	And give him spoonfuls of soup.
Y que haga testamento	And make a will
de todo lo que ha robado,	Of everything that has been taken,
marramamiau, miau, miau,	Meow, meow, meow,
de todo lo que ha robado.	Of everything that has been taken.
Ya lo llevan a enterrar	Now they're taking him to be buried
por la calle del Pescado,	Along Fish Street,
marramamiau, miau, miau,	Meow, meow, meow,
por la calle del Pescado.	Along Fish Street.

Al olor de las sardinas el gato ha resucitado, marramamiau, miau, miau, el gato ha resucitado.	When he smells the sardines, The cat wakes up, Meow, meow, meow, The cat wakes up.
Por eso dice la gente: siete vidas tiene un gato marramamiau, miau, miau, siete vidas tiene un gato.	Because of this the people say A cat has seven lives, Meow, meow, meow, A cat has seven lives.
Y aquí se acaba la copla de Don Gato enamorado, marramamiau, miau, miau, de Don Gato enamorado.	And this is how the ballad ends Of Mr. Cat in love, Meow, meow, meow, Of Mr. Cat in love.

Si me Dan Pasteles	*If you Give Me Pies*
Si me dan pasteles . . . démelos calientes,	If you give me pies, give them to me hot,
Que pasteles fríos . . . empachan la gente.	Because cold pies people don't like.
Si me dan pasteles no me den cuchara,	If you give me pies don't give me a fork,
Que mamá me dijo que se los llevara.	Because my mama told me to carry them.

Los Diez Perritos	*I Had Ten Puppies*

This is a favorite song. You can have children hold up ten fingers as you begin the song, and then put a finger down as you begin losing dogs.

Yo tenía diez perritos, y uno
    se cayó en la nieve
ya no más me quedan nueve,
    nueve, nueve, nueve, nueve.
	I had ten puppies, one fell in the
	    snow,
	now I only have nine, nine, nine,
	    nine, nine.

De los nueve que tenía, uno
    se comió un bizcocho,
ya no más me quedan ocho,
    ocho, ocho, ocho, ocho.
	Of the nine that were left, one ate
	    a biscuit
	now I only have eight, eight,
	    eight, eight, eight.

De los ocho que tenía, uno
    se golpeo su frente,
	Of the eight that were left, one
	    banged his forehead,

ya no más me quedan siete,
siete, siete, siete, siete.

De los siete que tenía, uno
se quemó los pies,
ya no más me quedan seis,
seis, seis, seis, seis.

De los seis que tenía, uno se
escapó de un brinco,
ya no más me quedan cinco,
cinco, cinco, cinco, cinco.

De los cinco que tenía, uno
se metió en un teatro.
ya no más me quedan
cuatro, cuatro, cuatro,
cuatro, cuatro.

De los cuatro que tenía, uno
se cayó al revés,
ya no más me quedan tres,
tres, tres, tres, tres.

De los tres que tenía, uno
sufrió de un tos,
ya no más me quedan dos,
dos, dos, dos, dos.

De los dos que tenía, uno se
murió de ayuno,
ya no más me queda uno,
uno, uno, uno, uno.

now I only have seven, seven,
seven, seven, seven.

Of the seven that were left, one
burned his feet,
now I only have six, six, six, six,
six.

Of the six that were left, one ran
away,
now I only have five, five, five, five,
five.

Of the five that were left, one went
into a theater,
now I only have four, four, four,
four, four.

Of the four that were left, one fell
backwards,
now I only have three, three, three,
three, three.

Of the three that were left, one
caught a cold,
now I only have two, two, two,
two, two.

Of the two that were left, one died
of fasting,
now I only have one, one, one, one,
one.

Los Pollitos

Los pollitos dicen
"Pió, pió, pió,"
Cuando tienen hambre,
Cuando tienen frío.

La gallina busca
El maíz y el trigo,
Les da la comida,
Y les presta abrigo.

Baby Chicks

Baby chicks are singing
"cheep, cheep, cheep,"
When they are hungry,
When they are cold.

Mamma looks for wheat,
Mamma looks for corn,
Mamma feeds them dinner,
Mamma keeps them warm.

Bajo sus dos alas	Under Mamma's wings
Acurrucaditas	Sleeping in the hay
Hasta el otro día	Baby chicks all huddle
Duermen los pollitos.	Until the next day.

Víbora De La Mar	*To The Serpent*

This game is played everywhere. It is similar to "London Bridge Is Falling Down." Two children each choose a different fruit to be. They then form an arch. Everyone gets in a line and holds on to the waist of the person in front of them. Everyone moves under the arch. The person who happens to be under the arch when the song is completed is captured. The captured person chooses which side he or she wish to be on and gets behind the chosen side. When everyone has been captured, you have two long lines of kids facing each other, and they play tug of war. In the version given here, the two fruits (sides) chosen are melón and sandía (cantaloupe and watermelon).

A la víbora, víbora	To the serpent, the serpent
de la mar, de la mar	Of the sea, of the sea,
por aquí puede pasar.	It can pass here.
Los de adelante corren mucho,	Those in front run fast,
los de atrás se quedarán	Those behind will stay
tras, tras, tras, tras.	Behind, behind, behind, behind.
Una mexicana	A Mexican girl
de fruta vendida,	A fruit seller,
ciruela, chavacan,	Plum, apricot,
melón o sandia.	Cantaloupe or watermelon.
Será melón, será sandía,	It will be cantaloupe, it will be watermelon,
será la vieja del otro día.	It will be the old woman of the other day.
(Spoken) ¿Con quien te vas, con melón o sandia?	(Spoken) Who will you go with? Cantaloupe or watermelon?
After everyone has chosen sides they pull apart as they say:	After everyone has chosen sides they pull apart as they say,
El puente es de oro,	The bridge is made of gold,
el puente es de plata,	The bridge is made of silver,

el puente es de papel,	The bridge is made of paper,
el puente es de cáscara de plátano.	The bridge is made from a banana peel.

Que Llueva, Que Llueva	*It's Raining*

A game similar to "Ring Around the Rosie"

Que llueva, que llueva,	It's raining, it's raining
la Virgen de la Cueva,	The Virgin of the cave
los pajaritos cantan,	The birds sing
las nubes se levantan,	The clouds raise
que sí, que no,	Yes? No?
que caiga el chaparrón,	The rain pours
que toquen los tambores	The drums pound
porro, porrón pon pon,	porro, porron pon pon (nonsense)
que rompan tus cristales	it breaks your glass
y los míos no.	and not mine.

Nonsense and Miscellaneous Rhymes

The following are versions of a rhyme that goes back to the seventeenth century. A game can be played as you say it. Since the words "aserrín, aserrán" connote a sawing sound and motion, two people can sit facing each other. They hold hands and as they say the rhyme they rock back and forth. The object is to stretch as far back as possible without breaking the handclasp. If it is broken, it is permitted to tickle the other person.

A Remar	*Row*
¡A remar, a remar,	Row, row,
marineros de San Juan!	sailors of San Juan!
¡A los chicos darles leche,	Give the little ones milk,
a los grandes darles pan!	and the big ones bread.

Los Maderos de San Juan	*The Loggers of San Juan*
Aserrín, aserrán,	Saw, saw,
los maderos de San Juan;	the loggers of San Juan
piden pan y no les dan,	ask for bread and don't get it,
piden queso, les dan hueso,	ask for cheese and get bones,

piden ají
¡eso sí!

ask for chili pepper
That yes!

Aserrín, Aserrán

Aserrín, aserrán,
los maderos de San Juan;
piden queso,
piden pan.
Los de Rique alfeñique,

los de Roque alfandoque.
Los de Trique,
triqui tran
triqui, triqui, triqui tran
triqui, triqui, triqui, tran.

Saw, Saw

Saw, saw,
the loggers of San Juan;
they ask for cheese,
they ask for bread.
Los de Rique alfeñique, (the rest
   of the rhyme is all nonsense)
los de Roque alfandoque.
Los de Trique,
triqui tran
triqui, triqui, triqui tran
triqui, triqui, triqui, tran.

Asserín, Asserán

Aserrín, aserrán
las sierras aquí están
las del rey, sierran bien,
las de la reina también,
las del duque
truque truque truque,
y las mías sierran en el río,
aunque hace frío.

Aserrín, aserrán,
sierran todas las sierras
los piños de San Juan.

Saw, Saw

Saw, saw
the saws are here,
the king's saws saw well
the queen's saw well as well
the duke's saws
truque truque truque (nonsense)
and my saws saw in the river
even though it's cold.

Saw, saw,
all the saws saw
the pines of San Juan.

¿Que Te Dijo El Calderon?

Dique, dique,
dique don,
que te dijo el calderón
que comieras y bebieras
y en tu casa estuvieras
arrimadita en un rincón
Que dedo tienes en el
   corazón

What did the Cauldron Say?

Dique, dique, (nonsense)
dique don, (nonsense)
What did the cauldron tell you?
that you should eat and drink
and stay in your house
curled up in a corner.
What finger do you have in your
   heart,

el chiquito o el mayor	the little one or the big one?
El chiquito.	The little one.
Si hubieras dicho el mayor	If you had said the big one,
no pasarías tanto dolor.	You wouldn't have been in such pain.
Dique, dique,	Dique, dique, (nonsense)
dique, don.	dique, don. (nonsense)

Las Campanas De Montalban	*The Bells of Montalban*
Las campanas de Montalban,	The bells of Montalban
unas vienen y otras van;	some come and some go,
las que no tienen badajo	those that do not sound
van abajo, abajo, abajo!	go down, down, down.
Tente, chiquito,	The little one,
tente, bonito,	the beautiful one,
que te vas a tierra,	are going to the earth,
a tierra, a tierra!	to the earth, to the earth.

Tin Marín De Dos

Here's a series of nonsense rhymes based on the words "Tin marín" or "Pin marín." These are used for choosing sides, or as counting out rhymes for circle games. The gist of the rhyme is that "It wasn't me, it was someone else. Hit them."

Tin marín de dos
quien fué.
Cucara macara
títere fue.

Tin Marín De Dos Pingüe

Tin marín de dos pingüe,
cucara macara titiri fué.
Yo no fui, fue Teta
pégale, pégale que ella fue.

Al Subir Por La Escalera	*While Going up the Stairs*

Another rhyme for choosing sides:

Al subir por la escalera	While going up the stairs,
una mosca me pico.	a fly bit me.

La agarre por las orejas,	I took her by the ears
la tire por el balcón.	And threw her over the
	balcony.
Taco, taco,	Taco, taco,
al que le toque	the one who's picked
el numero cuatro	is number four.
Una, dos, tres y cuatro.	One, two, three and four.

Pin, Pin, San Agustin

This rhyme combines part of the "Neapolitan Hen" with the nonsense words about a king passing by.

Pin, pin, San Agustin,
la meca, la seca, la tortoleca,
el hijo del rey paso por aquí
comiendo maní
a todos les dio menos a mi
la gallina encluecada
puso un huevo en la granada
puso uno, puso dos,
puso tres, puso cuatro,
puso cinco, puso seis,
puso siete, puso ocho,
pan y bizcocho para el burro mocho,
palos con palos para los caballos,
tuturutu para que salgas tu.

Por Aquí Viene Un Gallo	*Here Comes the Rooster*

Here are some fun animal rhymes:

Por aquí viene un gallo,	Here comes the rooster,
por aquí viene una gallina	here comes the hen
cada uno se meta en	each one will end up in my
su cocina.	kitchen.

Los Pollitos	*The Chickens*

Cinco pollitos tiene mi tía;	My aunt has five chickens,
uno le salta, otro le pía	one jumps, one clucks,
y otra le canta la sinfonía.	and the other one sings the
	symphony.

Tengo Un Gato

Tengo un gato en mi cocina
que me dice la mentira.
Tengo un gato en mi corral
Que me dice la verdad.

I Have a Cat

I have a cat in my kitchen
that tells me lies.
I have a cat in my corral
That tells me the truth.

Perico Tuvo Un Gato

Perico tenia un gato,
lo mando a por tobacco,
le compro una corbata
que le llegaba hasta las patas,
una, dos y tres.

Parrot Had a Cat

Parrot had a cat,
he sent it to get some tobacco,
the cat bought a tie instead
that went down to his paws,
one, two and three.

Chango, Gorila

Chango, gorila,
¿Quien te hizo el pelo?
¡Ramón!
¿Cuanto costo?
¡Tostón!
¿Como te quedo?
¡Chueco!

Hey, Gorilla

Hey, gorilla,
who did your hair?
Ramón!
How much did it cost?
A lot!
How does it look on you?
Crooked!

Nadaban Los Patos

Nadaban, nadaban
nadaban los patos.
nadaban, nadaban
y no se mojaban.

The Ducks Swam

The ducks swam,
swam, swam.
They swam, swam
and didn't get wet.

La Ranita Soy Yo

La ranita soy yo
glo, glo, glo.
El sapito eres tú
glu, glu, glu.
Cantemos así
gli, gli, gli.
Que la lluvia se fué
gle, gle, gle.
Y la ronda se va
gla, gla, gla.

I Am the Frog

I am the frog,
glo, glo, glo. (nonsense)
You are the toad,
glu, glu, glu. (nonsense)
We sing like this,
gli, gli, gli. (nonsense)
The rain went away,
gle, gle, gle. (nonsense)
And the round goes on,
gla, gla, gla. (nonsense)

Un Barco Chiquito	*The Small Boat*

These rhymes are like "The Song that Doesn't End."

Había una vez un barco chiquito,	Once upon a time there was a small boat,
que no podía, que no podía navegar,	that couldn't, couldn't navigate,
pasaron 1, 2, 3, 4, 5, 6, 7, semanas	1, 2, 3, 4, 5, 6, 7, weeks passed,
y el barquito, y el barquito no podía navegar,	and the little boat, the little boat still couldn't navigate
y si la historia no les parece larga,	and if this story doesn't seem long,
y si la historia no les parece larga,	and if this story doesn't seem long,
y si la historia no les parece larga,	and if this story doesn't seem long,
volveremos, volveremos, volveremos a empezar.	we'll go back, go back, go back to the beginning.
Había una vez . . .	Once upon a time . . .

Una Hormiguita	*Little Ant*

Esta era una hormiguita	This was a little ant
que salió de un hormiguero,	who left his anthill,
se robó un granito	he robbed a seed,
y volvió a su hormiguero.	and returned to his anthill
Y vino otra hormiguita	There came another little ant
del mismo hormiguero	from the same anthill
se robó un granito	he robbed a seed,
y volvió al hormiguero	and returned to his anthill
Y vino otra hormiguita . . .	There came another little ant . . .

Una, Dola

This is a nonsense counting rhyme:

Una, dola,
trela, cuatrola,
quina, quinete,

estaba la reina
en su gabinete.
Vino Gil,
apago el candil
candil, candilon,
cuenta las veinte
que las veinte son.

| *Cuando Me Recorta El Pelo* | *When I Get a Haircut* |

This wonderful rhyme uses nonsense words to create the sound of scissors cutting hair.

Cuando me recorta el pelo	When I get a haircut
la tijera de mama	Mama's scissors
va diciendo en su revuelo:	Say in their flight
chiqui–chiqui–chiqui–cha . . .	chiqui–chiqui–chiqui–cha . . .
aletea,	aletea,
viene y va,	viene y va,
y a mi oido cuchichea,	y a mi oido cuchichea,
chiqui-chiqui-chiqui-cha.	chiqui-chiqui-chiqui-cha.
Cuando el pelo me recorta	When I get a haircut
la tijera de mama	Mama's scissors
charla mas de lo que corta:	Sing more than they cut:
chiqui–chiqui–chiqui–cha.	chiqui–chiqui–chiqui–cha.
—By *German Berdiales*	

Rhymes about Home and Family

Palmas, Palmitas	*Palm, Little Palm*
Palmas, palmitas	Palm, Little Palm,
que viene papá	Papa's coming
y trae un perrito	with a dog
que dice quá, quá.	that says quá, quá.

Papa, Mama	*Father, Mother*
Papá, mamá	Father, Mother,
me quiero casar	I'd like to marry
con un pajarito	A beautiful bird
que sepa bailar.	Who can dance like a fairy.

Colita De Rana

Frog's Tail

This is a rhyme a mother will say if her child is ill.

Sana, sana, colita de rana
Si no sanas ahora,
Sanarás mañana.

Get well, get well little frog's tail
If you don't get better today
You'll get better tomorrow.

Azota Manitas

Hammer It Handyman

Azota manitas,
que viene papá
azótalas bien,
que pronto vendrá.

Hammer it handyman,
because father is coming
Hammer it well
because he'll be here soon.

Mi Buena Mamita

My Good Mommy

Mi buena mamita
Me lleva a la mesa
me da la sopita
y luego me besa.

My good mommy
Brings me to the table
She gives me soup
And then she kisses me.

Arroz Con Leche

Rice With Milk

Arroz con leche,
me quiero casar,
con una señorita
de Éste lugar.
Que sepa escribir,
que sepa bordar,
que sepa abrir la puerta
para ir a jugar.
Con ésta sí,
con ésta no,
con ésta señorita
me caso yo.

Rice with milk,
I want to marry,
with a woman
from this place.
Who knows how to write,
who knows how to embroider,
who knows how to open the door
to go out to play.
To this one yes,
to this one no,
To this woman
I will get married.

Don Melitón

Don Melitón

Don Melitón era muy chato.
Le llamaban narices de gato.
Pero los gatos se le han
   escapado

Don Melitón was very snub-nosed
They called him cat nose.
But the cats have escaped,

comiendo ratones a medio
  bocado.

and are eating rats, their mouths
  half full.

Luna

Luna, luna, dame una tuna

la que me diste
se cayó a la laguna.

Moon

Moon, moon, give me
  a tuna.
The one you gave me
fell in the lagoon.

La Luna

Mira la luna
comiendo su tuna,
echando las cáscaras
en esta laguna.

The Moon

Look at the moon,
eating his tuna,
throwing the scales
into this lagoon.

Los Dias De La Semana

Lunes, martes, miércoles,
  tres.
Jueves, viernes, sábado, seis.
Y domingo siete.

Days of the Week

Monday, Tuesday, Wednesday,
  three.
Thursday, Friday, Saturday, six.
And Sunday, seven.

A-b-c-d

A-B-C-D
la burra se me fué por la calle
  de mi Tía Merced.

A-b-c-d

A-B-C-D
The burro left me in my Aunt
  Merced's street.

A-e-i-o-u

A-E-I-O-U
El burro sabe mas que tú.

A-e-i-o-u

A-E-I-O-U
The donkey knows more than
  you.

Simon Bribon

Simon bribón,
comió mi melón
y luego me dijo
¡Que calveron!

Lazy Simon

Lazy Simon
ate my melon
and later said to me
How greedy I was!

Goodnight Rhymes

Sueño

Éste niño tiene sueño
y no se puede dormir
tiene un ojo cerrado
y el otro no puede abrir.

Sleepy

This child is sleepy
But he can't go to sleep
He has one eye closed
And he can't open the other.

El Dia Que Tu Naciste

El día que tú naciste
nacieron las cosas bellas
nació el sol, nació la luna

y nacieron las estrellas.

The Day You Were Born

The day you were born
All the beautiful things were born
The sun was born, the moon was
    born
And the stars were born.

Arrorro Me Nene

Arrorró, mi nene,
arrorró, mi sol,
duérmete pedazo de mi
    corazón.
Éste niño lindo no quiere
    dormir
porque no le traen
la flor del jardín.

Lullaby

Go to sleep my child,
go to sleep my sun,
sleep little piece of my heart.

This beautiful child doesn't want
    to sleep
because no one is bringing him
a flower from the garden.

Nanita

Nanita, nana,
duérmete lucerito
de la mañana.

Lullaby

Lullaby, and goodnight
Sleep little light
of the morning.

Tongue Twisters

These tongue twisters are fun to say, but virtually untranslatable!

El Arzobispo (The Archbishop)

El arzobispo de Constantiopla
que quiere desarzobisconstantinopolitanizar;
el desarzobisconstantinopolitanizador

que lo desarzobisconstantinopolitanizare
buen desarzobisconstantinopolitanizador será.

Tengo Una Guitarilla (I have a guitar)

Tengo una guitarilla mal enguitarillada.
El que la enguitarillo no la supo enguitarillar.
Voy a buscar un enguitarillador que la enguitarille mejor.

Tengo Un Guacalito (I have a crate)

Tengo un guacalito mal enguacalitado.
El que lo enguacalito no lo supo enguacalitar.
Voy a buscar un enguacalitador que lo enguacalite mejor.

Fui Al Perejil (I went to the parsley)

Fuí al perejil
y me emperejilé
para desemperejilarme
cómo me desemperejilaré.

En Un Jucal De Junquier (In the rushes of Junquier)

En un jucal de Junquier
juncos juntaba Julián
Juntóse Juan a juntarlos
y juntos juncos juntaron.

Si Cien Sierras Asseran Cien (If ten saws saw ten)

Si cien sierras asserán cien
siprese, sescientas sierras
asserán seisceintos cipreses.

Un Dicho (A saying)

Me han dicho que has dicho un dicho
que han dicho que he dicho yo,
el que lo ha dicho mintió
y en caso que hubiese dicho
ese dicho que tu has dicho
que han dicho que he dicho yo
dicho y redicho quedo

y estaría muy bien dicho,
siempre que yo hubiera dicho
que se dicho que tu has dicho
que han dicho que he dicho yo.

Piñata Rhymes

Dale, Dale, Dale

Dale, dale, dale, no pierdas el tino.

Mide la distancia que hay en el camino.

Hit It, Hit It, Hit It

Hit it, hit it, hit it, don't loose your skill.

Measure the distance there is in the path.

Bolita

Bolita, bolita
te llaman piñatita
eres muy redondita,
y yo con esta varita
te destrozaré ahorita.

Little Ball

Little, ball, little ball
they call you piñata
you are very round,
and with this stick
I will break you right now.

ADIVINANZAS (RIDDLES)

This book would not be complete without mentioning an extremely popular form of Latino folklore: the riddle. Almost every book that has collected Latino folklore includes some adivinanzas. Here are some examples:

Blanca Por Dentro

Blanca por dentro,
verde por fuera;
si quieres saber mi nombre,
espera.

White Inside

White inside
Green on the outside.
If you want to know my name,
wait.

Solution: Pera (pear) This riddle is a play on words, since the letters that make the word "espera" (wait), form the phrase "es pera" or "it's a pear."

Oro Parece

Oro parece,
plata no es,

It Looks Like Gold

It looks like gold,
Silver it's not,

el que no lo acierte	He that doesn't know this
bien bobo es.	is a dolt.

Solution: Plátano (Banana) Again, a play on words. "plata no es" means, "silver it is not," but if you combine "plata" and "no," you get "plátano" or banana! Some adivinanzas are more poetic.

Un Pajarito Voló, Voló	*A Bird Flew, Flew*
Un pajarito voló, voló,	A bird flew, flew,
pasó por los ojos	Past in front of our eyes
y nadie lo vio.	And no one saw it.

Solution: El sueño (A dream)

Que Cosa Es	*What Is It*
¿Que cosa es?	What is it?
Una cosa muy bonita	A very beautiful thing
que tiene alas	it has wings
y se pone en la cabeza.	and you put it on your head.

Solution: El sombrero (a hat).

Tito, Tito	*Tito, Tito*
Tito, tito, capodito	Tito, tito, with a little cap
sube al cielo y pega un grito.	rises to the sky and shouts.

Solution: Triquictraque (Firecrackers).

SOURCES FOR FINGERPLAYS

Many of the above fingerplays at the beginning of chapter 7 were gathered from colleagues, miscellaneous handouts, and copies which have come into my possession over the years. The following are some of the published sources for fingerplays which I have found most useful. In the bibliography, I have noted where books have included any of the fingerplays and rhymes mentioned here.

Bernier-Grand, Carmen T. **Shake It, Morena!: And Other Folklore from Puerto Rico**. Illustrated by Lulu Delacre. Brookfield, CT: Millbrook Press, 2002. ISBN: 0761319107.
    A brightly illustrated collection of games, songs, tales and other folklore from Puerto Rico.

Bravo-Villasante, Carmen. **Colorín colorete**. Madrid: Ediciones Didascolia, 1983.
A book of riddles, rhymes, tongue twisters, lullabies, carols and prayers.

Ebinger, Virginia Nylander. **Spanish Songs, Games and Stories of Childhood**. Santa Fe, NM: Sunstone, 1993.
Particularly notable for its explanations of how to play the various games. Includes the music for all the songs.

Fernández, Laura. **De tin marín: cantos y rondas infantiles** (Children's Songs and Rhymes, picture book). Mexico: Editorial Trillas, 1983.
Nursery rhymes and songs enhanced by Fernández's delicate illustrations.

Flint Public Library. **Ring a Ring O'Roses: Fingerplays for Preschool Children**. Edited by Cynthia Stilley and Charles Hansen.
This book includes 25 Spanish-language fingerplays. The cost is approximately $7.00 and the book can be ordered from: Flint Public Library Business Office, 1026 East Kearsley, Flint, Michigan 48502-1994, 810-232-7111.

Griego, Margot C., Besty L. Bucks, Sharon S. Gilbert, and Laurel H. Kimball, translators. **Tortillitas Para Mama and Other Nursery Rhymes/ Spanish and English** (picture book). Illustrated by Barbara Cooney. New York: Holt, 1981.
This classic should be in the collection of any librarian or teacher working with Latino children. Includes some of the most common rhymes.

Jiménez, Emma Holgun, and Chonchita Morales Puncel. **Para chiquitines: cancioncitas, versitos y juegos meñiques** (For Little Ones: Songs, Verses and Fingerplays). Illustrated by Gilbert T. Martinez. Glendale, California: Bowmar, 1969.
A book of songs, poems and fingerplays with colorful illustrations. Includes music and guitar chords for the songs. Some are traditional, others are new creations of the authors.

Llimona, Mercedes. **Juegos y canciones para los niños**. (Games and Songs for Children). Barcelona: Ediciones Hymnsa, 1984.
A selection of fingerplays with illustrations that suggest how to act them out. Includes "Este niño tiene sueño," "Cinco lobitos," "Éste compró un huevito," "Que llueva," "La gallina ponicana," "Arroz con leche," and many others.

Lubbock Public Schools. **Kindergarten Bilingual Resource Handbook**. Austin, TX: Dissemination and Assessment Center for Bilingual Education, 1973.
Includes a fairly large selection of nursery rhymes and fingerplays.

Medina, Arturo. **Pinto maraña: juegos populares infantiles** (Popular Children's Games). Illustrated by Carmen Andrada. Spain: Editorial Miñón, 1987.

Children's games, such as hopscotch, some with accompanying rhymes. Also some song lyrics at the end.

Moguel, Margarita Robleda. **Trabalenguas, colmos, tantanes, refranes, y un pilón de Margarita Robleda Moguel** (Tongue Twisters, Wordplays, Nursery Rhymes, Verses, and Something Extra from Margarita Robleda Moguel). Illustrated by Laura Fernández. Mexico, D.F.: Sitesa, 1989. ISBN: 9686048103.

Cartoon-like drawings illustrate word games, tongue twisters, questions and answers, all calculated to make children laugh.

————. **Y va de nuez (adivinanzas, colmos, juegos y pilónes de Margarita Robleda Moguel)** (And It Goes Nuts: Riddles, Wordplays, Games and Something More from Margarita Robleda Moguel). Illustrated by Laura Fernández. Mexico, D.F.: Sitesa, 1989. ISBN: 9686048545.

A book full of jokes, riddles and wordplay that has immense kid appeal. Includes simple line drawings.

Orozco, José-Luis. **De Colores and Other Latin-American Folk Songs for Children** (music). Illustrated by Elisa Kleven. New York: Dutton, 1994.

Selected, arranged and translated by José-Luis Orozco. Orozco includes background on the origins of the songs as well as some related games.

Includes "El chocolate," "La araña pequeñita"/The Eensy, Weensy Spider, and "Los Pollitos."

————. **Diez Deditos and Other Play Rhymes and Action Songs from Latin America** (picture book). Illustrated by Elisa Kleven. New York: Dutton, 1997.

The book that teachers and librarians have been waiting for forever. Rhymes in Spanish and English, with line drawings which show how to do the actions. Includes "Este compró un huevito," and many others.

Sandoval, Ruben. **Games, Games, Games/Juegos, Juegos, Juegos: Chicano Children at Play—Games and Rhymes**. Illustrated by David Strick. New York: Doubleday, 1977.

Black and white photos of children illustrate this collection of traditional rhymes used in children's games such as jump rope.

Schon, Isabel. **Tito, Tito: Rimas, Adivinanzas y Juegos Infantiles** (Tito, Tito: Rhymes, Riddles and Children's Games). Illustrated by Victoria Monreal. Mexico: Editorial Everest, 1995. Poetry for ages 7–11.

Isabel Schon collects the rhymes games she loved the best as a child. The book is complemented by beautiful watercolor illustrations.

El silbo del aire: Antología lírica infantil—1 (A Breath of Air: Anthology of Children's Songs). Barcelona: Editorica Vicens-Vivas, 1985.

A collection of songs in Spanish that caregivers, teachers, and librarians can use with children. Includes music.

Zwick, Louise Yarian, and Oralia Garza de Cortés. **Rimas y cancioncitas para niños** (Rhymes and Songs for Children). Houston Public Library, 1984.

A small pamphlet with rhymes and songs gathered by these librarians.

Part III.   Resources for Evaluating and Locating Books and Materials for Bilingual and Spanish-Speaking Children

Chapter 8

Other Notable Selections
of Books and Materials

The following additional selections are designed to help you move beyond the basic core collection and expand your collection with a wide range of materials. They are arranged by type, just like the core list. I've included one extra list, a sampling of "Latino Classics." These are books which have shaped Latino children's literature. I have also included a warning list of books that should be omitted because of inferior translations or other issues. The definitions of the categories for these selections are the same as those for the Core Collection.

BOARD BOOK

Alcántara, Ricardo. **El pirata valiente** (The Brave Pirate). Illustrated by Gusti. Madrid: Ediciones SM, 1989. ISBN: 0843482809X.
A board book in which a little boy plays at being a pirate until his mother calls him to diner.

PICTURE BOOKS

Ada, Alma Flor. **The Lizard and the Sun/La lagartija y el sol**. Illustrated by Felipe Dávalos. New York: Doubleday, 1997. ISBN: 0440415314.
When the sun disappears from the sky, all the animals try to find it to wake it up. The lizard is the one who finds it after all the other animals have given up.

Anaya, Rudolfo. **The Santero's Miracle: A Bilingual Story**. Illustrated by Amy Córdova. Albuquerque: University of New Mexico Press, 2004. ISBN: 0826328474.

Andrés's grandfather, Don Jacobo, carves wooden saints. Don Jacobo helps his grandson carve his own saint, which is then the catalyst for a miracle in the snow.

Argueta, Manlio. **Magic Dogs of the Volcanoes/Los perros mágicos de los volcanes**. Illustrated by Elly Simmons. San Francisco, CA: Children's Book Press, 1990. ISBN: 0892390646.

Set in El Salvador, this is an original story about the mythic characters, the cadejos, or magic volcano dogs. The cadejos function like guardian angels, except for Don Tonio and his thirteen brothers who do not like them. They send their lead soldiers to get the dogs, but the soldiers begin to melt when they get too near the volcanoes.

Balzoa, Asun. **Guillermo, un ratón de biblioteca** (Guillermo, A Library Rat). Spain: Anaya, 2001. ISBN: 0846670292X.

A rat named Shakespeare tries to escape from his library. A cat threatens the rat.

Balzoa, Asun. **Los zapatos de Munia** (Munia's Shoes). Barcelona: Ediciones Destino, 1988. ISBN: 08423312437.

Munia worries because her shoes are too tight. She is concerned that they might have shrunk. When she gets the chance to go into town, she asks the shoemaker, and learns that her feet are growing bigger, along with the rest of her body.

Berenguer, Carmen. **El rey mocho** (The King Without an Ear). Illustrated by Carmen Salvador. Adapted by Verónica Uribe. Caracas, Venezuela: Ediciones Ekaré/Banco Del Libro, 1981. ISBN: 9802570680.

Once there was a king who lacked an ear, but this fact was covered up by his long curly black wig. The only person who knew the secret is his barber. When his barber got sick and died, the king searched for a new barber. The new barber could not keep the secret and told it to a hole. Later a shepherd boy made a flute from cane that grew there, and it began to sing, "El rey es mocho." Now the whole country knew, and the king decided that wigs were too hot.

Note: Includes the music for a brief song.

Bertrand, Diane Gonzales. **Family, Familia**. Illustrated by Pauline Rodriguez Howard. Houston: Piñata (Arte Público), 1999. ISBN: 1558852697.

Daniel is dragged reluctantly to a family reunion. He gains a greater appreciation for his family connections, however, when he is given a picture of his great-great-grandparents.

————. **Sip, Slurp, Soup, Soup/Caldo, caldo, caldo**. Illustrated by Alex Pardo DeLange. Houston: Piñata (Arte Público), 1997. ISBN: 1558851836.

This book captures a warm family ritual. Mama pulls out the large soup pot, and the children know it is caldo day. Everyone helps Mama make the soup; then they go to buy tortillas to make the soup complete. Includes a recipe.

Calders, Pere. **Cepillo**. Illustrated by Carme Solé Vendrell. Barcelona: Ediciones Hymsa, 1981. ISBN: 8471831813.

English edition: **Brush**. Translated by Marguerite Feitlowitz. Brooklyn, NY: Kane Miller, 1986. ISBN: 0916291057.

When Little Sala's dog Turco is banished for bad behavior, he searches for a new companion. He tries a bird, ". . . but the number of really fun things he could do with a bird were so few, he immediately knew they could never be close friends." He tries to create lasting friendships with a ball of string, and an American-made top, without success. He finally finds a brush in the attic. It becomes his companion and begins acting like a dog.

Casteneda, Omar S. **Abuela's Weave**. Illustrated by Enrique O. Sanchez. New York: Lee & Low, 1993. ISBN: 1880000008.

Spanish edition: **El tapiz de abuela**. Translated by Aida E. Marcuse. ISBN: 1880000083.

Esperanza and her grandmother sell traditional woven items. Because grandmother's birthmark discourages people from buying, they pretend not to know each other. Esperanza finds buyers while grandmother stays in the background.

Colón-Villa, Lillian. **Salsa**. Illustrated by Roberta Collier-Morales. Houston: Arte Públic Press, 1998. ISBN: 1558852204.

Rita loves salsa music. Her family teaches her all they know, and she dreams of becoming a band director.

Fernández, Laura. **De tin marín: cantos y rondas infantiles** (Children's Songs and Rhymes). Mexico: Editorial Trillas, 1983. ISBN: 9682414695.

Nursery rhymes and songs enhanced by Fernández's delicate illustrations.

————. **Luis y su genio** (Luis and His Genie). Mexico: Editorial Trillas, nd. ISBN: 9682419166.

Luis's genie magically appears in his room. He is a bread genie. Instead of granting you wishes, bread genies ask you to grant their wishes. Luis genie wants to play ball and then go to school as Luis. All the kids love him when he makes three goals in the soccer game. The genie's final wish is to go to a bakery where he disappears.

Garcia, María. **The Adventures of Connie and Diego/Las aventuras del Connie y Diego**. Illustrated by Malaquias Montoya. San Francisco: Children's Book Press, 1987. ISBN: 089239028X.

The twins Connie and Diego run away because everyone makes fun of them. They meet various animals try to live with them. Eventually they discover they are humans, and it is with people that they belong.

García, Richard. **My Aunt Otilia's Spirits/Los espiritus de me Tía Otilia**. San Francisco: Children's Book Press, 1987. ISBN: 0892390298.

Aunt Otilia is the quintessential weird aunt who comes from Puerto Rico to visit her family in San Francisco each year. When Aunt Otilia tries to contact the spirit world one evening, she precipitates a funny series of events, which end up with her going away, never to return.

Hayes, Joe. **La llorona/The Weeping Woman**. El Paso, TX: Cinco Puntos Press, 1997. ISBN: 0938317024.

The fact that it is a written rendition of the version Joy Hayes tells makes this the best choice for a version of this classic tale to be told or read aloud.

———. **Mariposa, mariposa** (Butterfly, Butterfly). Illustrated by Lucy Jelinek. Santa Fe, NM: Trails West, 1988. ISBN: 0939729083.

This book is bilingual—the title is just not translated. A variation on "Perez and Martina." Mariposa finds some money and gets a beautiful dress (her wings). She asks various animals who want to marry her how they will talk when they are married. She likes the mouse. Mouse gets eaten by cat. Friends bring flowers and she likes them so much that she flies from flower to flower to this day.

———. **Monday, Tuesday, Wednesday, Oh!/Lunes, Martes, Miercoles, ¡Oh!** Illustrated by Lucy Jelinek. Santa Fe, NM: Trails West, 1987. ISBN: 0939729040.

A poor woman is forced to work for a rich, snobby woman for pay that consists of stale tortillas. The poor woman finds some little men whom she hears singing. She inadvertently adds to their day-of-the-week song. They only knew the first three verses for Monday, Tuesday, and Wednesday. They give her gold in thanks.

———. **No Way, José! ¡De ninguna manera, José!** Illustrated by Lucy Jelinek. Santa Fe, NM: Trails West, 1986. ISBN: 0939729008.

A rooster named José goes to the wedding of his Uncle Perico. Jose gets his beak dirty through eating, but no one will help him clean it so he can be presentable.

Herrera, Juan Felipe. **The Upside Down Boy/El niño de cabeza**. San Francisco: Children's Book Press, 2000. ISBN: 0892391626.

An autobiographical story about Herrera's experiences going to school for the first time. He has difficulty with English, but encounters a sensitive teacher.

Jaffe, Nina. **The Golden Flower: A Taino Myth from Puerto Rico**. Illustrated by Enrique O. Sánchez. New York: Simon and Schuster, 1996.

Pura Belpré Illustrator Award, 1998. A Puerto Rican creation myth that describes how water came to the world.

Johnston, Tony. **My Mexico/México mío**. Illustrated by F. John Sierra. New York: Putnam, 1996. ISBN: 0399222758.

Poems about Mexico that are filled with a love of the country, which developed over the fifteen years the author lived there.

Kiefer, Eduardo Gudiro. **Giraluna**. Illustrated by Maia Miller. New York: Lectorum (Emece), 2005. ISBN: 9500426684.

A moonflower lives in a field of sunflowers.

Krahn, Fernando. **Bernardo y Canelo**. Caracas, Venezuela: Ediciones Ekaré, 1998. ISBN: 9802572071.

Bernardo wants to perform in the circus, but his dog beats him to the punch.

Kurusa. **El cocuyo y la mora** (The Firebug and the Berry Bush). Illustrated by Veronica Uribe. Caracas, Venezuela: Ediciones Ekaré/Banco del Libro, 1983. ISBN: 9802570427.

Lachtman, Ofelia Dumas. **Big Enough/Bastante grande**. Illustrated by Enrique O. Sánchez. Houston: Piñata (Arte Publico), 1998. ISBN: 1558852212.

Lupita's mother tells her that she is too little to help out in the restaurant that her mother owns. She is able to show that she is big enough to be able to do some things when she apprehends a thief.

————. **Pepita Talks Twice/Pepita habla does veces**. Illustrated by Alex Pardo DeLange. Houston: Piñata (Arte Público), 1995. ISBN: 1558850775.

Pepita is frustrated that she is bilingual and has to translate for everyone. She decides to stop speaking Spanish, but the problems she then encounters lead her to realize the value of both languages.

————. **Pepita Thinks Pink/Pepita y el color rosado**. Illustrated by Alex Pardo DeLange. Houston: Piñata (Arte Público), 1998. ISBN: 1558852220.

In this sequel to *Pepita Talks Twice*, Pepita cannot stand the new neighborhood girl, Sonya, who dresses entirely in pink, even though her family and her friend Mr. Hobbs urge her to make friends.

————. **Pepita Takes Time/Pepita, siempre tarde**. Illustrated by Alex Pardo DeLange. Houston: Piñata (Arte Público), 2001. ISBN: 1558853049.

Pepita always takes her time, and is late for everything. She realizes that this habit impacts others, when she misses a school field trip to the zoo, and disappoints a friend.

————. **Tina and the Scarecrow Skins/Tina y las pieles de espantapajaros**. Houston, TX: Arte Publico Press, 2002. ISBN: 1558853731.

Tina's new friend, Campanita or "Little Bell," is very unusual. She speaks in her own invented language and puts flowers in her hair. Tina's mother is not necessarily approving of Campanita. When a sack of corn husks to be used to make tamales goes missing, Campanita tries to help by bringing in some "scarecrow skins," which turn out to be corn husks as well.

Leclercq, Jean Paul, and Carme Solé Vendrell. **Peluso y la cometa** (Peluso and the Kite). Valladolid: Editorial Miñón, 1979. ISBN: unavailable.

Peluso is a small, gray bird, not very exciting. When he sees a colorful kite, he wants to be like it. He meets a little boy who tries to help him. A Venezuelan legend about how the firebug got the light on its tail.

Levert, Claude, and Carme Solé Vendrell. **Pedro y su roble** (Pedro and His Tree). Valladolid: Editorial Miñón, 1979. ISBN: 8430571981.

A boy cares for his tree through the four seasons. In autumn, he mistakenly thinks that it is dying. He wraps a blanket around it during winter, and in spring experiences the miracle of new life.

Martínez, Alejandro Cruz. **The Woman Who Outshone the Sun/La mujer que brillaba aún mas que el sol**. Illustrated by Fernando Olivera. San Francisco, CA: Children's Book Press, 1991. ISBN: 0892391014.

Story by Rosalma Zubizaretta, Harriet Rohmer, and David Schecter. When Lucia Zenteno arrives in a small village, the villagers are awed but jealous of her dazzling beauty. The river that flows through the village falls in love with Lucia, and runs through her black hair. When the villagers treat her cruelly, Lucia leaves, taking the river with her. Only then do the villagers see their folly.

Menéndez, Margarita. **Un abrigo crecedero** (The Overcoat that Got Bigger). Madrid: Ediciones SM, 1989. ISBN: unavailable.

Rita has a slightly-too-big-for-her overcoat which grows. She uses it to create shadows that make her look like an elephant or a ghost. She can hide all her toys in it. When it rains, she does not need an umbrella. She can hide in it when she does not want to see anybody. And she can jump without a parachute. This board book is told in rhyme.

Mora, Pat. **A Birthday Basket for Tía**. Illustrated by Cecily Lang. New York: Macmillan, 1992. ISBN: 0027674002.

Spanish edition: **Una canasta de cumpleaños para Tía**. ISBN: 06142 90821.

Cecelia searches for the perfect present for her great aunt's ninetieth birthday, and ends up putting together a memory book representing their favorite activities together.

————. **Confetti**. Illustrated by Enrique O. Sanchez. New York: Lee & Low, 1996. ISBN: 1880000253.

Poems that mix English and Spanish, and touch on familiar things in Latino life. Told from the perspective of a Mexican American girl, they celebrate the landscape of the American southwest. Mora's best book to date.

————. **Delicious Hullabaloo/Pachanga deliciosa**. Illustrated by Francisco X. Mora. Translated by Alba Nora Martínez and Pat Mora. Houston: Piñata (Arte Público), 1998. ISBN: 1558852468.

Birds, armadillos, and an assortment of other creatures cavort at night in a kitchen to the music of a lizard mariachi band. They are all very hungry and will eat anything.

————. **The Desert Is My Mother/El desierto es mi madre**. Illustrated by Daniel Lechon. Houston: Piñata (Arte Público), 1994. ISBN: 1558851216.

A simple text narrated by a girl with long, dark hair evokes the power of the desert.

————. **Uno, dos, tres: One, Two, Three**. Illustrated by Barbara Lavalee. New York: Clarion, 1996. ISBN: 0395672945.

A bilingual rhyme with girls going to the market to buy birthday presents for their mother.

————, and Charles Ramírez Berg. **The Gift of the Poinsettia/El regalo de la flor de nochebuena**. Illustrated by Daniel Lechón. Houston: Piñata (Arte Público), 1995. ISBN: 1558851372.

Takes place in the Mexican town of San Bernando. Carlos worries about what gifts he will have for las posadas. He has songs. He gives a plant by a favorite rock—it turns into a poinsettia. Use with Tomie DePaola's *The Legend of the Poinsettia*.

Nazoa, Aquiles. **El libro de los cochinitos** (The Pig Book). Venezuela: Playco Editores, 1999. ISBN: 980074247.

A tongue-in-cheek book in rhyming verse that explains different types of pigs. Fun for reading aloud.

Orozco, José-Luis. **Rin, Rin, Rin/Do, Re, Mi**. Illustrated by David Diaz. New York: Orchard (Scholastic), 2005. ISBN: 0439649412.

A simple rhyme presented bilingually with bold illustrations by Caldecott medal-winner David Diaz. Includes the music.

Pérez, Amada Irma. **My Very Own Room/Mi propio cuartito**. Illustrated by Maya Christina Gonzalez. San Francisco: Children's Book Press, 2000. ISBN: 0892391642.

A little girl's wish for her very own room comes true.

Posadas Mañé, Carmen De. **Señor Viento Norte** (Mr. North Wind). Illustrated by Alfonso Ruano. Madrid: Ediciones SM, 1984. ISBN: 8434812258.

The animals tell Arthur that they are suffering because Mr. North Wind is not letting spring come. He sets out for the North Wind's house, but finds that his friend, María, went before him so he would not have to go. Together they convince Mr. North Wind to blow south so that spring can come.

Rodríguez, Luis J. **No tiene que ser así, una historia del barrio** (It Doesn't Have to Be Like This: A Barrio Story). Illustrated by Daniel Galvez. San Francisco: Children's Book Press, 1999. ISBN: 0892391618.

An authority on gangs tells the story of Mochi, who gets drawn in to the gang lifestyle. It take a tragic event for Mochi to see the truth of what it means to be involved in gangs.

Rohmer, Harriet. **The Legend of Food Mountain/La leyenda de la montaña de alimento**. Illustrated by Graciela Carrillo. Translated by Alma Flor Ada and Rosalma Zubizaretta. San Francisco, CA: Children's Book Press, 1982. ISBN: 0892390220.

This Aztec legend explains why the people pray to the rain god for food.

———. **Uncle Nacho's Hat/El sombrero del tío Nacho**. Illustrated by Veg Reisberg. San Francisco: Children's Book Press, 1989. ISBN: 0892390433.

A Nicaraguan folktale about a little girl who teaches her uncle to overcome an old habit.

Ruano, Moises. **El caballo fantastico** (The Fantastic Horse). Illustrated by Alfonso Ruano. Madrid: Ediciones SM, 1985. ISBN: 8434816814.
Juan believes that he has seen a unicorn, driven by a man with a beard and a turban, as he goes to school. No one believes him until the next morning.

Saenz, Benjamin Alire. **A Gift from Papá Diego/Un regalo de Papá Diego**. Illustrated by Geronimo Garcia. San Antonio: Cinco Puntos Press, 1998. ISBN: 0938317334.
Diego receives a surprise visit from his Grandfather for his birthday. A predictable, repetitive text makes this a good choice for storytimes.

Sanromán, Susana. **Señora Regañona: A Mexican Bedtime Story** (Old Grouch). Illustrated by Domi. Toronto: Groundwood Books/Douglas & McIntyre, 1997. ISBN: 088899320X.
A frightened child keeps a light under the covers to scare away the night. In a dream she becomes a friendly playmate.

Sarda, Rosa. **I Like Acting Grown Up/Me gusta hacer como los mayors**. New York: Lectorum Publications Inc., 2002. ISBN: 1930332335.
———. **I Like Getting Dirty/Me gusta ensuciarme**. New York: Lectorum Publications Inc., 2002. ISBN: 1930332327.
———. **I Like Growing Up/Me gusta ser mayor**. Lectorum Publications Inc., 2002. ISBN: 1930332319.
———. **I Like Hiding/Me gusta esconderme**. New York: Lectorum Publications Inc., 2002. ISBN: 1930332300.

Sastrías, Marta. **Queta la vaca coqueta**. Illustrated by Enrique Martínez. México, DF.: Fondo de Cultura Económica, 1999. ISBN: 9681657578.
Queta is a very vain cow who learns a lesson the day she loses her tail and a tooth.

Slate, Joseph. **The Secret Stars**. Illustrated by Felipe Dávalos. New York: Marshall Cavendish, 1998. ISBN: 0761450270.
Pura Belpré Illustrator Honor Book, 2000. In a story set in New Mexico capturing the anticipation of a visit from the Three Kings, *The Secret Stars* tells the story of two children who worry that the Kings will not find them. Through the skillful use of acrylics, Dávalos has created an exquisite work of art.

Soto, Gary. **Snapshots from the Wedding**. Illustrated by Stephanie Garcia. New York: Putnam, 1997. ISBN: 0698117522.
Pura Belpré Illustrator Award, 1998. Unique three-dimensional illustrations tell the story of a typical Latino wedding.

————. **Too Many Tamales**. Illustrated by Ed Martinez. New York: Putnam, 1993. ISBN: 0399221468.

Spanish edition: **¡Qué montón de tamales!** Illustrated by Ed Martinez. Translated by Alma Flor Ada and F. Isabel Campos. ISBN: 0698114132.

This delightful story centers around an important cultural tradition—making tamales on Christmas Eve. Since tamales take so much effort to make, homemade tamales are a special event. Maria tries on mother's ring, which she is taken off while making the tamales. It slips off her finger and into the masa (dough). Horrified when she makes the discovery, Maria and her cousins secretly eat all the tamales trying to find the missing ring. This is Soto's first picture book, and one of the first picture books to provide an authentic cultural experience.

Torres, Leyla. **Saturday Sancocho**. New York: Farrar, Straus and Giroux, 1995. ISBN: 0374364184.

Spanish edition: **El sancocho del sábado**. (Mirasol). ISBN: 0374420858.

On a day when there are only eggs in the house, María Lilí and her mother barter in the market for the ingredients to make a delicious chicken dish.

Vallejo-Nájera, Alejandra. **¡No tengo sueño!** (I'm Not Sleepy). Miami, FL: Alfaguara Infantil, 2002. ISBN: 1589865464.

Series: "Las aventuras de Ricardete y Lola."

Lola finds every excuse she possibly can to get out of going to sleep. She has to go to the bathroom, she has to feed her turtle, and she has a spider in her bed. Her father tries to read her a long story that puts *him* and not Lola to sleep. Her cousin Ricardete even makes an appearance to stage a sleep-delaying pillow fight. The payoff comes the next morning when Lola's parents try to wake her, and *now* she is sleepy. This book has a spark that makes it ideal for reading aloud to children in storytimes and will be a favorite with parents—especially ones with children who share Lola's dislike for bedtime. Another title in this series is: *¡Cuanto me quieren!* (How Much They Love Me!).

Wolf, Ema. **Hay que enseñarle a tejer el gato** (You Have to Teach a Cat to Knit). Buenos Aires: Editorial Sudamericana S. A., 1991, 1997. ISBN: 950071261X.

A genuinely funny book about teaching your pet cat how to knit.

Picture Book Anthology

An anthology including different types of literature such as poetry and folk tales. Appropriate for ages 18 months through 7 years, preschool through 2nd grade.

Ada, Alma Flor, and F. Isabel Campoy. **¡Pío Peep!: Traditional Spanish Nursery Rhymes**. English adaptation by Alice Schertle. Illustrated by Viví Escrivá. New York: HarperCollins, 2003. ISBN: 068816019.

An excellent resource for rhymes from the Latino oral tradition that will provide material for storytimes and other early childhood programs. One caveat is that the English translations are not literal. Use those just to understand more or less what the Spanish is saying, and stick to sharing the Spanish versions.

Chapter Fiction, ages 7–11

Shorter novels with content appropriate for ages 7–11 (grades 3–5).

Anza, Ana Luisa. **El misterio de la casa chueca (y el bulto color mugre)** (The Mystery of the Crooked House and the Dirt-colored Lump). Illustrated by Antonio Rocha Escobar. Monterrey, México: Ediciones Castillo, 2004. ISBN: 9702002001.

Pedro and his family have recently moved into a new neighborhood full of odd characters whom Pedro gives nicknames such as "The Witch" and "The Extraterrestrial." With his Chinese immigrant friend, Chi-son, Pedro navigates a neighborhood full of odd characters, and the mystery of a dirt-colored lump that he sees in the strange crooked house. At the end of the book, Chi-son and Pedro discover the "lump" is actually the bed-ridden wife of one of the persons in the house, and that these mysterious folks are all real people, with actual names, and with a fascinating story that brought them all together.

Cameron, Ann. **Colibrí**. New York: Farrar, Straus and Giroux/Frances Foster, 2003. ISBN: 0374315191.

Kidnapped by an abusive man, Colibrí must endure life as a beggar as she tries to find out who she really is.

————. **The Most Beautiful Place in the World**. Illustrated by Thomas B. Allen. New York: Knopf, 1988. ISBN: 0394804244.

Seven-year-old Juan grows up with his grandmother in a small Guatemalan village. He enjoys the beauty of his surroundings, but is afraid to communicate to her his desire to go to school.

Malpica, Toño. **Las mejores alas** (The Best Wings). México, D.F.: Ediciones Castillo, 2004. ISBN: 970200179X.

Gus is a street kid. He is also an angel, not meaning that he is a sweet thoughtful kid, but that he is actually an angel, of the sort that has wings. Only Gus does not know it. This story is narrated by Dunedinn, who is also an angel. Dunedinn was a police officer on earth, and has been permitted to continue to wear his uniform in eternity. The story begins as Dunedinn fails in his mission to take Gus to heaven. Gus has decided that the sky is not as far away as people think, and begins to wonder about ways to get there. His first thought is to purchase an airplane. Everyone thinks Gus is crazy, but he perseveres despite all the obstacles to find his own way of reaching the sky.

Martínez, Floyd. **Spirits of the High Mesa**. Houston: Piñata Books (Arte Público Press), 1997. ISBN: 1558851984.

Pura Belpré Author Honor Book, 1998. A historical novel about life in a village in New Mexico, that intertwines the story of the boy Flavio coming of age, with the end of an era marked by the coming of technology.

Mohr, Nicolasa. **The Magic Shell**. Illustrated by Rudy Gutierrez. Scholastic, 1995. ISBN: 0590471104.

Spanish edition: **El regalo mágico**. ISBN: 0590502107.

Jamie Ramos has to leave the Dominican Republic when his dad gets a good job in New York City. He does not like the cold, and he cannot speak English. He has a shell, which takes him back to his island in his imagination.

Montes, Graciela. **La venganza en el mercado** (Vengeance in the Market). Illustrated by Claudia Legnazzi. Mexico, D.F.: Fondo de cultura económica, 1998. ISBN: 968-16-5800-0.

When Ema goes to market, she finds a unique way of making sure she gets waited on before anybody else.

Puelles, Vicente Muñoz. **Óscar y el león de correos** (Oscar and the Mail Lion). Illustrated by Noemí Villamuza. Madrid: Anaya, 1998. ISBN: 8420789860.

Óscar learns to deal with the fears engendered by a mailbox in the shape of a lion's head. You deposit your letters in the lion's mouth.

FICTION ANTHOLOGY

Ada, Alma Flor. Series: **Puertas al sol** (Gateways to the Sun) (picture books). Miami, Santillana USA, 1999.

This new series is designed for classroom use but also should be in public libraries. These books anthologize literature and art from Latin American authors and illustrators. The titles are in three categories: Poetry, Art, and Biography.

Poetry:
Pimpón. ISBN: 1581054017.
Antón Pirulero. ISBN: 1581054033.
Mambrú. ISBN: 158105405X.
Chuchurumbé. ISBN: 1581054076.

Art:
Azul y verde (Blue and Green). ISBN: 1581054173.
Brocha and Pincel (Paintbrush). ISBN: 158105419X.
Caballete (Easel). ISBN: 1581054211.
Lienzo y papel (Canvas and Paper). ISBN: 1581054238.

Biography:
Sonrisas (Smiles). ISBN: 1581054092.
Pasos (Footsteps). ISBN: 1581054114.
Voces (Voices). ISBN: 1581054130.
Caminos (Paths). ISBN: 1581054157.

POETRY (AGES 7–11)

Alarcón, Francisco X. **Poems to Dream Together/Poemas para sonar juntos**. Illustrated by Paula Barragán. New York: Lee & Low, 2005. ISBN: 158430233X.
Bilingual poems that all address the themes of dreams that can make the world better.

Medina, Jane. **My Name Is Jorge: On Both Sides of the River**. Illustrated by Fabricio Vanden Broeck. New York: Boyds Mills Press, 2000.
A series of bilingual poems that explore the life of a border child.

Stavans, Ilan, ed. **Wáchale: Poetry and Prose About Growing Up Latino in America**. Chicago: Cricket Books, 2001. ISBN: 0812647505.
While uneven, this new anthology includes works by Latinos representing many different countries and backgrounds.

Sullivan, Charles, ed. **Here Is My Kingdom: Hispanic-American Literature and Art for Young People**. New York: H. N. Abrams, 1993. ISBN: 0810934221.
An anthology primarily of children's poetry.

SHORT STORY COLLECTIONS (AGES 7–11)

Como surgieron los seres y las cosas (How People and Things Came to Be). Lima, Peru: PIESA Coedicíon Latinoamericana, 1986. ISBN: 9507011633.
A collection of Latin "porquei" tales. A Puerto Rican tale describes the origin of the island itself. A Nicaraguan tale tells how mosquitoes came to a great river.

Cuentos de animales fantasticos para niños (Stories of Fantasic Animals for Children). Sao Paulo, Brazil: Editorial Atica, Coedición Latinoamericana, 1984. ISBN: 09684940149.

Includes the stories: "El caballito de siete colores" (The Seven-Colored Horse), from Guatemala, and "El murciélago" (The Bat), from Mexico.

Cuentos de enredos y travesuras (Stories of Tangled-up Mischief). Stories of Bolivia: Centro Pedagogico y Cultural de Portales, Coedición Latinoamericana, 1986. ISBN: 0950701165X.

Stories about playing tricks from many Latin American countries. Brief notes regarding cultural background preface each story. Glossaries also explain the meaning of any unusual words.

Cuentos de espantos y aparecidos (Stories of Ghosts and Apparitions). Edited by Veronica Uribe. Sao Paulo, Brazil: Editorial Atica, Coedición Latinoamericana, 1984. ISBN: 09507011617.

A great place to find scary stories for Halloween like "El barco negro" (The Black Boat), from Nicaragua, "María Angula," from Ecuador, and "Abad Alfau y la calavera" (Abad Alfau and the Skeleton), from the Dominican Republic.

Cuentos, mitos y leyendas para niños de américa latina (Stories, Myths and Legends for Latin American Children). Buenos Aires, Argentina: Editorial Plus Ultra, Coedición Latinoamericana, 1981. ISBN: 09507011609.

Includes a version of "La Leyenda del Dorado" (The Legend of El Dorado or the Golden One), from Colombia.

Cuentos picarescos para niños de america latina (Adventure Stories for Latin American Children). Coedición Latinoamericana, 1983. ISBN: 09802571377.

Includes the stories: "Domingo siete" (. . . And Sunday Makes Seven), from Colombia; "Tío Conejo y Tío Lobo" (Uncle Rabbit and Uncle Wolf), from Ecuador; "Pedro Urdemalas," from Guatemala; "Juan Bobo y el secreto de la Princesa" (Juan Bobo and the Princesses Secret), from Dominican Republic; and "Pedro Rimales, Curandero" (Pedro Rimales, Healer), from Venezuela.

Cuentos y leyendas de amor para niños (Stories and Legends of Love for Children). Buenos Aires, Argentina: Editorial Plus Ultra, Coedición Latinoamericana, 1984. ISBN: 09507011595.

Love stories from all over Latin America.

Delacre, Lulu. **Salsa Stories**. New York: Scholastic, 2000. ISBN: 0590631187.

Spanish edition: **Cuentos con sazón**. ISBN: 043922649X.
As they come together for the holidays, each member of Carmen Teresa's extended family tells a story about their childhoods. The book is rounded out with family recipes.

> Roldan, Gustavo. **Cuentos de Pedro Urdemales** (Stories of Pedro Urdemales). Argentina: Sudamericana, 2000. ISBN: 9500717603.

Stories of the quintessential trickster with a distinctly Argentine ambiance.

DRAMA (AGES 7–11)

> Armijo, Consuelo. **Bam, bim, bom, arriba el telon** (Up Goes the Curtain). Valladolid: Editorial Miñón, 1984. ISBN: 08435505618.

Plays for kids to put on:
"Gorros y Botas" (Caps and Boots); "Cumpleaños de Verano" (A Summer Birthday); "Una Historia de Sacos" (A History of Sacks); "Pájaros de Invierno" (Birds in Winter); "Un Duende en Palacio" (A Goblin in the Palace); and "Disimulando" (Hiding).

> Torices, José González. **Cuatro estaciones: teatro para niños** (Four Seasons: Theater for Children). Illustrated by Carmen Lucini. Madrid: Ediciones SM, 1998. ISBN: 8434862948.

An anthology of plays and poems that kids can perform.

NONFICTION (AGES 7–11)

Many of these books are heavily illustrated photo essays, with plenty of color pictures.

> Ancona, George. **Charro: The Mexican Cowboy**. New York: Harcourt, 1999. ISBN: 0152010475.

Spanish edition: **Charro**. ISBN: 0152020268.
Ancona describes all the traditions that surround the celebration of the Mexican cowboys and cowgirls.

> ———. **Pablo Remembers: The Fiesta of the Day of the Dead**. New York: HarperCollins, 1993. ISBN: 0688112498.

Spanish edition: **Pablo recuerda: La fiesta de el día de los muertos**. ISBN: 0688128947.
Pura Belpré Illustrator Honor Book 1996. Pablo and his family participate in Day of the Dead celebrations in Mexico.

Horenstein, Henry. **Baseball in the Barrios**. San Diego, CA: Harcourt, 1997. ISBN: 015201263X.
Spanish edition: **Béisbol en los barrios**. Translated by Alma Flor Ada and F. Isabel Campoy.
Young boys playing baseball in Venezuela hope to break into the big leagues.

King, Elizabeth. **Quinceañera: Celebrating Fifteen**. New York: Dutton, 1998. ISBN: 0525456384.
Spanish edition: **Quinceañera: celebrando los quince**. ISBN: 0525458441.
King traces the history of this tradition, and recounts the real-life quiceañera of Cindy Chávez.

Vara, Ana Serna. **Juegos para viajes y días de lluvia** (Games for Travel and Rainy Days). Madrid: Ediciones SM, 1997. ISBN: 8434856654.
A compilation of children's games, arranged alphabetically.

NOVELS (AGES 8–12)

Charles, Francois, Julia Mercedes Castilla, and Daniel Garcia. **Aventuras de un niño de la calle (Adventures of a Child on the Street)**. Colombia: Grupo Editorial Norma, 1997. ISBN: 9580409455.
This book recounts the daily struggle of a child abandoned in the streets and forced to make it on his own. A very popular book in Latin America that discusses a reality that is all too common.

Danticat, Edwidge. **Tras las montañas** (Behind the Mountains). Translated by Mercedes Guhl. Bogota, Colombia: Grupo Editorial Norma, 2003. ISBN: 9580474818 pap.
Danticat has created a poetic, first person narrative in the form of a journal. Danticat weaves some of her personal experience into this tale of Celiane Espérance, a Haitian girl who moves to Brooklyn to be with her father after realizing the danger she faces from the political upheaval in Haiti.

Ortiz Cofer, Judith. **Call Me María: A Novel in Letters, Poems and Prose**. New York: Orchard, 2004. ISBN: 043938577.
María lives with her apartment superintendent father in New York and struggles to express herself in writing as she misses her home in Puerto Rico and her mother who remained there.

DRAMA (AGES 8–12)

Soto, Gary. **Novio Boy: A Play**. San Diego, CA: Harcourt, 1997. ISBN: 0152015310.

Rudy does not believe it when an older woman (in 11th grade) accepts a date with him. Now he needs to know what to say, how to behave, and money. And then, everyone shows up at the restaurant during the date itself. Could be presented fully staged, or as a reading.

POETRY (AGES 8–12)

Nye, Naomi Shihab. **The Tree Is Older Than You Are: A Bilingual Gathering of Poems and Stories From Mexico With Paintings by Mexican Artists**. New York: Simon and Schuster, 1995. ISBN: 0689802978.

A bilingual collection which includes works of varying lengths and difficulty, making it possible to find something appropriate for all ages.

YOUNG ADULT FICTION (AGES 12 AND UP)

Sometimes mature content is included.

Alvarez, Julia. **Before We Were Free**. New York: Knopf, 2002. ISBN: 0375915443.
Spanish translation: **Antes de ser libres**. ISBN: 0375915451.
Pura Belpré Author Award 2004.

Anita de la Torre witnesses firsthand the atrocities committed during the 1961 Dominican Revolution. She has to endure her father and uncle being imprisoned; and she has to go into hiding herself along with her mother Anita. They live in fear because of the political situation in her beloved Dominican Republic.

————. **Finding Miracles**. New York: Knopf, 2004. ISBN: 0375827609.

Milly Kaufman, from an unnamed Central American country, comes to terms with her adoption by an Anglo family in Vermont. She loves them, but wants to uncover the mystery of her past. When Pablo, who happens to be from Milly's native country, arrives at her school, an opportunity opens up for Milly to travel home and find out about herself.

Anaya, Rudolfo. **Serafina's Stories**. Alburquerque: University of New Mexico Press, 2004. ISBN: 0826335691.

Taken prisoner by the Governor of New Mexico, Serafina tells him stories, and he promises to release a prisoner for each story.

Herrera, Juan Felipe. **Cinnamon Girl: Letters Found Inside a Cereal Box**.
    New York: Joanna Cotler (HarperCollins), 2005. ISBN: 0060276045.
In this free verse novel, Yolanda tries to find hope in the dust left behind
by the fall of the World Trade Center towers on September 11, 2001.

Núñez, Luchy. **Esa extraña vergüenza** (This Strange Feeling of Shame).
    Leon, Spain: Editorial Everest, 2004. ISBN: 8424183835.
Premio "Leer es Vivir" (To Read Is to Live)
The title *Esa extraña vergüenza*, or "This Strange Feeling of Shame" refers
to the shame felt by victims of abuse. This powerful novel by Luchy Núñez
tells the story of one such victim, and according to the publisher, this story
was inspired by a real event. Marina is a typical twenty-first century teen,
who likes to watch Brad Pitt movies and play video games. Marian is sexu-
ally abused by a man in the elevator of her apartment, and the novel explores the impact this act has on various members of the family.

Santiago, Danny. **Famous All Over Town**. New York: Simon and Schus-
    ter, 1983. ISBN: 0606034242.
Tells the story of Rudy Medina, better known as Chato, who lives on
Shamrock Street in East L. A. The story begins on Rudy's 14th birthday. To
prove his manhood, his father asks him to kill a chicken. Rudy can not man-
age to slit its throat, so he gets a gun and shoots it instead. Of course, Rudy's
father is furious. The neighborhood is abuzz. When asked what all the con-
fusion is about, people reply: "Medina's kid just shot a chicken."

Villaseñor, Victor. **Walking Stars: Stories of Magic and Power**. Hous-
    ton: Piñata (Arte Público), 1994. ISBN: 1558851186.
Stories of triumph over difficulty about the author's parents. "Bullfighting
the Train" tells how his father Juan catches up with a train taking his family
away by running 100 miles in one day. "Woman's Greatest Power" is the
story of Villaseñor's mother and how she helps deliver twins in primitive settlements.

YOUNG ADULT POETRY (AGES 12 AND UP)

Carlson, Lori M., ed. **Cool Salsa: Bilingual Poems on Growing Up
    Latino in the United States**. New York: Holt, 1994. Introduced by
    Oscar Hijuelos. ISBN: 0805031359.
A book that celebrates challenges of growing up Latino in the United
States with two languages and two cultures. "Speaking more than one lan-
guage, I have found, enriches life, broadens perspective, extends horizons of

opportunity, and makes us more sensitive to nuance, difference, contrast," from the Introduction (p. xiv).

————. **Red Hot Salsa: Bilingual Poems on Being Young and Latino in the United States**. New York: Holt, 2005. Introduced by Oscar Hijuelos. ISBN: 0805076166.

A follow up to Carlson's previous anthology, *Cool Salsa*. The poems are presented in both Spanish and English with a notation of which version is the translation.

YOUNG ADULT ANTHOLOGY

Carlson, Lori M., ed. **Barrio Streets, Carnival Dreams: Three Generations of Latino Artistry**. New York: Holt, 1996. ISBN: 0805041206.

A collection of poetry, literature, artwork, and essays that celebrate Latino contributions.

YOUNG ADULT SHORT STORY COLLECTION

Griego y Maestas, José, and Rudolfo A. Anaya. **Cuentos: Tales from the Hispanic Southwest**. Bilingual Stories in Spanish and English. Illustrated by Jaime Valdez. Santa Fe: The Museum of New Mexico Press, 1980. ISBN: 0890131112.

Based on stories originally collected by Juan B. Rael.

BOOKS NOT RECOMMENDED

The following Spanish-language books should be avoided. The English version may be really good, but the Spanish translation may be inferior. They may, as in the case with the Robles Boza books, be overly didactic. They may have incorrect or insensitive approaches to cultural issues, or simply not have any reader appeal.

Ada, Alma Flor. **Under the Royal Palms: A Childhood in Cuba**. New York: Atheneum, 1998. ISBN: 0689806310 (nonfiction, for ages 7–11). Spanish edition. **Bajo las palmas reales**. Miami: Santillana USA, 2001. ISBN: 1581056567.

Pura Belpré Author Award, 2000. In a heartwarming and loving portrayal of her childhood days in Cuba, Ada describes her deep friendship with a

(continued on page 204)

Recommended Latino Classics

Araujo, Orlando. **Miguel Vicente, pata caliente** (Miguel Vicente, Hot-foot). Illustrated by Morelle Fuenmayor. Caracas, Venezuela: Ediciones Ekaré/Banco del Libro, 1992. ISBN: 9802571024 (picture book).

Miguel Vincente, the shoe-shine boy, dreams of being able to travel places and see things. He knows that he will probably never able to make his dreams a reality. It especially bothers him at Christmastime that his family is so poor that all he receives is a used shoe-shine brush and cream. At the end of the story his mother becomes ill, and his older brother picks him up and he begins a new adventure.

Dario, Ruben. **Margarita**. Illustrated by Monkia Doppert. Caracas, Venezuela: Ediciones Ekaré/Banco del Libro, 1979. ISBN: 09802570532 (picture book).

An illustrated version of Dario's classic mystical poem about a princess.

del Amo, Montserrat. **Rastro de Dios y otros cuentos** (The Face of God and Other Stories). Madrid: Ediciones SM, 1981. ISBN: 08434809060 (short story collection, for ages 7–11).

Three stories about angels. The title story won several prizes.

Farias, Juan. **Los caminos de la luna** (The Paths of the Moon). Illustrated by Alicia Cañas Cortázar. ISBN: 8420782939 (chapter fiction, for ages 7–11).

Juan, the "old one," shares stories and wisdom with his niece Maroliña, to prepare her for the time when he will no longer be with her.

Fernández, Laura. **Pajaros en la cabeza** (Birds in Your Head). Mexico: Trillas, 1983. ISBN: unavailable (picture book).

Premio Antoniorobles. Based on a popular folk expression usually referring to big hair, this is the story of a girl who wakes up with real bluebirds dancing in her head. They stay with her during the day, but at night they go to their tree house to sleep. The girl is consoled by the knowledge that they are just outside her window.

García Lorca, Federico. **Canciones y poemas para niños** (Songs and Poems for Children). Illustrated by Daniel Zarza. Barcelona: Editorial Labor, 1990. ISBN: 1887578595 (poetry, for ages 7–11).

A volume that collects all of García Lorca's children's poetry, some humorous, others lyrical.

Hinojosa, Francisco. **A golpe de calcetin** (By Means of a Sock). Illustrated by Carmen Parra. Mexico: Editorial Novaro, 1982 (chapter fiction, for ages 7–11).

Manuel has to take care of his family in Mexico City during the 1930s, while his father is on strike. Then a strange man buys all his papers and asks him to deliver a letter to a man in the hospital. Manuel finds himself in the middle of a bank heist, and becomes a hero.

>Jiménez, Juan Ramón. **Platero y yo/Platero and I**. Translated by Myra Cohn Livingston. Illustrated by Antonio Frasconi. New York: Clarion, 1957, 1994. ISBN: 068571523X (novel, for ages 8–12).

Bilingual selections from the children's classic from Spain about a boy and his beloved donkey who wander through the landscape of southern Spain.

>Machado, Ana Maria. **El perro del cerro y la rana de la sabana** (The Dog from the Hill and the Frog from the Plains). Caracas, Venezuela: Ediciones Ekaré/Banco del Libro, 1981, 1986. ISBN: 9802570214 (picture book).

Frog and Dog argue that each is braver than the other. A Lion scares them both.

>———. **Historia medio al réves** (Reversed Story). Translated by Mónica Mansour. Illustrated by Rafael Barajas. Mexico, D.F.: Fondo de cultura económica, 1998. ISBN: 9681645456 (chapter fiction, for ages 7–11).

A story of a misguided king that begins with the "happily ever after."

>Martí, José. **La edad de oro** (The Age of Gold). Río Piedras, Puerto Rico: Editorial San Juan, 1976. ISBN: 0897299477 (short story collection, for ages 8–12).

A collection of all the articles which appeared in the 4 issues of the magazine, *The Age of Gold*, where José Martí published in New York between July and October 1889.

>Mateos, Pilar. **Historias de ninguno** (Stories of Nobody). Madrid: Ediciones SM, 1981. ISBN: 8434809079 (novel, for ages 8–12).

Stories about a child named "Nobody." He is very small and refuses to grow. He has to put stones in his pocket so he won't blow away on a windy day. His classmates do not give him much attention.

>———. **Jeruso quiere ser gente** (Jeruso Wants to Be a Person). Madrid: Ediciones SM, 1998. ISBN: 8434810026 (novel, for ages 8–12).

Jeruso delivers for the shopkeeper, Julian, but one day his box of items for the Señora de Rodríguez is stolen. He has to solve the mystery before he gets into trouble.

>———. **La bruja Mon** (Mon, the Witch). Illustrated by Viví Escrivá. Madrid: Ediciones SM, 2000. ISBN: 8434814617 (chapter fiction, for ages 7–11).

La Bruja Mon no longer changes children into frogs, after she finds she can not travel anywhere with a frog. In the final story she gets angry at an echo and turns herself into a fish.

>Mistral, Gabriela. **Ronda de astros**. Madrid: Editorial Espasa, 1992. ISBN: 8423990192 (poetry, for ages 7–11).

Lyrical poems for children by the Nobel Prize-winner for Literature.

Muria, Anna. **El maravilloso viaje de Nico Huehuetil a través de México** (The Marvelous Voyage of Nico Huehuetl Across Mexico). Illustrated by Felipe Dávalos. Amecameca, Mexico: Editorial Amaquemecan, 1986. ISBN: 9687205199 (novel, for ages 8–12).

Nico wants to discover the marvels of his country, like the Scandinavian children's book hero, Nils Holgerson. He gets his wish, and is able to take a magical journey through Mexico's past.

Osorio, Marta. **La mariposa dorada** (The Golden Butterfly). Spain: Editorial Miñón, 1978. ISBN: unavailable (picture book).

Literatura Infantil. 2nd Premio a la Mejor Labor de Creación 1978.

A caterpillar turns into a butterfly. A particularly well-written book:

¿Qué habrá más allá de las hojas? . . . —seguía pensando–. El mundo no puede ser sólo esto . . . tiene que haber muchas cosas mas, aunque yo no alcanzo a verlas . . . tengo que llegar a discubrirlo . . . Pero el camino era trabajoso y difícil. (" 'What is out there beyond the leaves?' he continued thinking. 'The world cannot be just this . . . there have to be many more things, even though I have not seen them . . . I have to discover it' . . . But the path was tiring and difficult.")

Paz, Marcela. **Papelucho**. Santiago, Chile: Universitaria, 1983. ISBN: 956110850X (novel, for ages 8–12).

This is one of the most beloved classics of Chilean children's literature. Papelucho's diaries give insight into the world and mind of a school-age child. The other "Papelucho" books are: *Papelucho casi húerfano* (Papelucho Almost An Orphan), *Papelucho en la clínica* (Papelucho in the Clinic), *Papelucho, misionero* (Papelucho, Missionary), and *Papelucho y el marciano* (Papelucho and the Martian).

Perera, Hilda. **El automóvil de mi abuelo** (My Grandfather's Car). Illustrated by Carlos Rodrmguez Rosillo. Leon, Spain: Editorial Everest (picture book).

As they build a car together, a little boy helps his uncle discover that he needs glasses to help him read.

———. **La pata Pita: libro primero de lectura** (The Duck Pita: My First Reader). Mana F. Fraga; Illustrated by Olivia Robain. New York: Minerva Books, 2001. ISBN: 0805601376 (picture book).

The landmark Spanish reader, the "Dick and Jane" of Latino children. Sequel *La pata Pita vuelve : libro segundo de lectura*, 1984. ISBN: 0805601414.

Pierini, Fabio. **El niño que queria volar** (The Boy Who Wanted to Fly). Illustrated by Carme Solé Vendrell. Valladolid: Editorial Miñón, 1979. ISBN: 84-355-0504-9 (picture book).

A little boy wants to fly, and looks for someone to teach him how. He looks in important books, he looks everywhere. He asks animals, and finally realizes that he was not made to fly.

Roldan, Gustavo. **Cuentos de Pedro Urdemales** (Stories of Pedro Urdemales). Argentina: Sudamericana, 2000. ISBN: 9500717603 (short stories, ages 7–11).

Stories of the quintessential trickster with a distinctly Argentine ambiance.

Uribe, Maria de la Luz. **El primer pájaro de piko-niko** (The First Piko-Niko Bird). Illustrated by Fernando Krahn. Barcelona: Editorial Juventud, 1987. ISBN: 8426123074 (picture book).

The piko-niko bird is born, but does not know his name, or what he is for. He asks a monster in a cave: "Who are you and what am I?" The monster answers: "I am the one who pushes you, and you are the one who falls!" There is a delightful illustration of the piko-niko bird plummeting through space upside-down. He says to himself, "Now I'm going to die, and that's all I know."

Vázquez-Vigo, Carmen. **Caramelos de menta** (Mint Candies). Madrid: Ediciones SM, 1981. ISBN: 8434808986 (chapter fiction, for ages 7–11).

Pepito and his friends have to raise money to repair the hole they have created in the awning of Don Joaquin's store.

Walsh, Maria Elena. **El reino del reves** (The Backwards Kingdom). Illustrated by Vilar. Buenos Aires, Argentina: Editorial Sudamericana, 1986 (poetry, for ages 7–11).

Delightful poems with illustrations reminiscent of Ellen Raskin.

———. **Zoo Loco** (Crazy Zoo). Illustrated by Eduardo and Ricardo Fuhrman. Buenos Aires, Argentina: Espasa Calpe, 1965, 1996. ISBN: 950852085X.

A series of limericks about zoo animals.

Perera, Hilda. **Cuentos para chicos y grandes** (Stories for Young and Old). Illustrated by Ana Bermejo. Valladolid: Editorial Miñón, 1985. ISBN: 8430561277 (short story collection, for ages 8–12).

Premio Lazarillo. Stories include the following:

"Los burritos" (The Burros). Burros wreck havoc in a small village. Bumbling politicians say that they will do something about it. Children save the burros from death by sending them away, then everybody misses them. An amusing read-aloud.

"Chichi la osita panda" (Chichi the Panda Bear). Chichi is a small panda bear. None of the animals will play with Chichi. They all marry. When An An is brought from China to be Chichis's mate, at first he will have nothing to do with her because he thinks he is the only one of his kind.

"Pedrin y la garza" (Pedrin and the Crane). This story is about a poor boy who finds a crane and tries to keep it like a toy. The crane discovers that it is a bird, and needs to fly free. The boy follows it to the sea, and goes into the ocean as the crane flies out. The boy nearly drowns. The crane sees this and gives up its freedom to rescue the boy.

Other stories are "Tatica," about a dog, and "Quintin," about a gnome who invents sleep.

———. **Podría ser que una vez** (It Could Be That Once). Madrid: Everest, 2000. ISBN: 8424132742 (short story collection, for ages 8–12).

Six contemporary stories. A particularly notable one is "Kilo," which concerns a young boy who desires a pet.

Quiroga, Horacio. **Cuentos de la selva** (Tales of the Jungle). Mexico: Anaya, 2001. ISBN: 8466700919 (short story collection, for ages 8–12).

Short stories about jungle animals.

Sanchez Silva, José María. **Marcelino, pan y vino** (Marcelino, Bread and Wine). Editorial Miñón, 1982. ISBN: 8420793280 (chapter fiction, for ages 7–11).

An orphan appears at the door of a monastery. Named Marcelino, he is raised and cared for by the friars. A beloved story known throughout the Spanish-speaking world.

Sierra i Fabra, Jordi. **Los mayores están locos, locos, locos** (The Adults are Crazy, Crazy, Crazy). Illustrated by Federico Delicado. Madrid: Ediciones SM, 1994. ISBN: 8434842645 (young adult).

Series: Los libros de Víctor y Cía.

Victor does not understand. His father is shouting, his mother is preoccupied and is considering giving him socks, underpants, and undershirts for his birthday when what he really wants is a John Lennon T-shirt, a chemistry set, and skates. His sister will not speak and his brother will not stop complaining. They all blame him for what happened, but he is convinced they are all crazgy.

beloved dance teacher. Readers meet relatives and share the tragedy of the loss of Ada's beloved uncle. Photographs enhance the diary-like portrayal of Ada's early years. The concern here is that, while it is about a child, feels more like a memoir directed at adults.

Cisneros, Sandra. **Hairs/Pelitos**. Illustrated by Terry Ybáñez. Translated by Liliana Valenzuela. New York: Apple Soup (Alfred A. Knopf), 1984, 1994. ISBN: 0679890076 (picture book).

Adapted from the book *The House on Mango Street*. Cisneros describes the hair of each person in her family.

Hayes, Joe. **Watch Out for Clever Women!/¡Cuidado con las mujeres astutas!** Illustrated by Vicky Trego Hill. El Paso, TX: Cinco Puntos Press, 1994. ISBN: 0938317210 (short story collection, for ages 7–11).

Texas Bluebonnet Award Nominee. Stories that celebrate the strength of Latina women. Includes "The Day it Snowed Tortillas."

The following Eduardo Robles Boza books tend to be very much on the didactic side, though he still holds a place in my heart for providing the first really useful book I found, *Cuatro letras que escaparon.*

Robles Boza, Eduardo. **Barranco el rebelde** (Barranco the Rebel). León, Spain: Editorial Everest, 1985. ISBN: 8424158156 (picture book).

Una escoba es una escoba y se pone a barrer, pero hay escobas differentes . . . ¡No me van a creer! (A broom is a broom and they are used for sweeping. But there are different sorts of brooms . . . You won't believe me!)

A story about an unusual broom the moves on its own, and causes complications until it is discovered that it is actually a horse. A broom can also be a horse in the imagination of a child.

————. **Cajon de los tiliches** (The Box of Junk). León, Spain: Editorial Everest, 1985. ISBN: 8424158148 (picture book).

Lo que no sirve o estroba lo metemos a un cajón. A eso le llaman tiliches y viven en un rincón. (Whatever is of no use any more, we put in a box. We call them, and they live in a corner.)

A story about a special box, like all houses have. One day a boy opened it and marbles, a string, and an electric plug came out among other miscellaneous objects. These objects talk to the boy, and one of them, a top, helps him when they stop talking.

————. **Carlota es una pelota** (Carlota is a Ball). León, Spain: Editorial Everest, 1985. ISBN: 8424158113 (picture book).

Carlota es una pelota de teni de campeonato y desertó, ¡vaya broma! a causa de un raquetazo. (Carlota is a championship tennis ball, who left, what a joke, all because of a racquet).

A story about a super ball that broke things and caused problems. It follows the storyteller, and gets caught up in a game of tennis, which it does not like. It spends the rest of its days on the storyteller's shelf with his books.

————. **Chispa de luz** (A Spark of Light). Illustrated by Gloria Calderas Lim. Trillas, 1984. ISBN: 9682416345 (picture book).

A spark of light leaves its light bulb in its desire to be free. It finds its place sparkling in a child's eyes.

Stevens, Jan Romero. **Carlos and the Cornfield/Carlos y la milpa de maiz**. Illustrated by Jeanne Arnold. Translated by Patricia Hinton Davison. Flagstaff, AZ: Northland Publishing, 1995. ISBN: 0873585968 (picture book).

Carlos gets in too much of a hurry to finish planting the cornfield. Trying to fix his mistake when the corn sprouts, he pawns his knife but accidentally buys blue corn. You reap what you sow.

―――. **Carlos and the Skunk/Carlos y el zorillo**. Illustrated by Jeanne Arnold. Translated by Patricia Hinton Davison. Flagstaff, AZ: Rising Moon (Northland), 1997. ISBN: 0873585917 (picture book).

The success of the first book led to this sequel in which Carlos gets sprayed by a skunk. He clears out the church when he forgets to remove the smell from his shoes.

Chapter 9

Sources for Latino Children's Theatre, Music, and Magazines

LATINO CHILDREN'S THEATRE

Theater has always been an especially popular Latino art form, especially suited to the culture. Throughout Latin America you will find many examples of religious folk theater. These plays depicting religious stories hinge on interaction between the audience and the actors and are acted out in spaces other than the traditional proscenium. This type of theater, which is really almost a pageant, brings a community together and forms an important part of Latino culture.

In Latin America, theater has also provided a voice for disenfranchised. This is especially apparent in the *Teatro Campesino*, or farmworkers theater, which was born out of the Chicano movement and farmworkers strike led by César Chávez in the 60s. Teatro Campesino was founded by Luis Valdez, who also became its principal playwright. Their initial efforts were known as *Actos*, or acts. These short plays were often very political in nature and meant to motivate the audience to social action. Valdez later gained fame as the author of *Zoot Suit*, a full scale musical that was produced to great acclaim.

The following are sources of plays that might be presented in school and library settings. When performing these plays, please pay close attention to copyright notices. Even if you are presenting a reading or staging for which no admission is charged, most playrights will still require written permission. Addresses of agents or other parties from whom this permission may be obtained is usually found on the copyright page for each play.

Armijo, Consuelo. **Bam, bim, bom, arriba el telon** (Up Goes the Curtain). Valladolid, Spain: Editorial Miñón, 1984.

Plays for kids to present:

"Gorros y Botas" (Caps and Boots).
"Cumpleaños de Verano" (A Summer Birthday).
"Una Historia de Sacos" (A History of Sacks).
"Pájaros de Invierno" (Birds in Winter).
"Un Duende en Palacio" (A Goblin in the Palace).
"Disimulando" (Hiding).

Otero, Clara Rose. **La cena de tío tigre y otras obras de teatro para niños** (Uncle Tiger's Dinner and Other Theater Pieces for Children). Caracas, Venezuela: Ediciones Ekaré, 1993.

Rosenberg, Joe, ed. **¡Aplauso!** (Applause!) Houston: Piñata (Arte Público), 1995.
An anthology of plays by Latino authors. Includes three plays in separate English and Spanish versions, one in Spanish, one in English, and three bilingual plays:
"Fred Menchaca and Filemón/Fred Menchaca y Filemón" by José G. Gaytán.
"The Caravan/La caravana" by Alvan Colón.
"¡Bocón!" by Lisa Loomer.
"The Day They Stole All the Colors/El día que robaron todos los colores" by Héctor Santiago.
"The Legend of the Gold Coffee Bean" by Manuel Martín Jr.
"El gato sin amigos / The Cat Who Had No Friends" by Joe Rosenberg.
"Song of the Oak / El canto del roble" by Roy Conboy.
"La lente maravillos / The Marveous Lens" by Emilio Carbadillo.
This play teaches the principal of personal hygiene in an amusing way. It makes the teaching of science concepts fun.

Rivera, José. Maricela de la Luz Lights the World. *American Theater*, December 1996: 25–38.
Based on bedtime stories this well-known Puerto Rican playwright told his daughter, this play tells the story of Maricela and her brother Riccardo who become involved in an apocalyptic conflict involving figures from many of the world's mythologies. Set in present day Los Angeles, this play presents a typical blend of magic realism. These recognizable contemporary Latino young people become heroes and save the world from the cold grip of snow creatures.

Valdez, Luis. "Los Vendidos." In **Luis Valdez—Early Works: Actos, Bernabe and Pensamiento serpentino**. Houston: Arte Público, 1990, 1971.
This would be an excellent play for young teens to present, although since it was written in 1967 and refers to Governor Reagan, you might desire to

update it or make some mention of the historical context. It satirizes various Mexican stereotypes such as the migrant farmworker, the Zoot-Suited Pachuco, the sombrero-clad revolucionario Pancho Villa clone, and the business-suited Mexican-American. The setting is Honest Sancho's Used Mexican Lot and Mexican Curio Shop. A secretary from Governor Reagan's office enters and is seeking a "Mexican type" for the administration. Sancho shows off his models. The humor hits home, as when Sancho describes the farmworker model to the secretary: "Economical? Señorita, you are looking at the Volkswagon of Mexicans. Pennies a day is all it takes. One plate of beans and tortillas will keep him going all day. That, and chile. Plenty of chile. Chile jalapeños, chile verde, chile colorado. But of course, if you do give him chile, then you have to change his oil filter once a week" (42, 43). The twist ending is that it is Honest Sancho who is really a robot; the others are fully alive and simply pulling a scam.

Vigil, Angel. **¡Teatro! Hispanic Plays for Young People**. Englewood, CO: Teacher Ideas Press (Libraries Unlimited), 1996.

This book provides scripts for plays that are easy to produce. Especially nice are the scripts provided for holidays and Cinco de Mayo.

The following is an original play by Latino playwright José Cruz González. I became acquainted with Jose as I worked with him on his stage adaptation of Pat Mora's book, Tomas and the Library Lady which was presented by Childsplay, a children's theater company based in Tempe, Arizona in schools and libraries throughout Maricopa County during the spring of 2006. This play, "A Lincoln Heights Tale (La Casa De Las Luzes)" ("The House of Lights") is one of the three one-act plays that Jose wrote to be performed by children in an elementary school setting. He gave permission for it to be reprinted here with the thought that it could be presented in library settings as well. It can be presented staged with costumes and sets, or as a readers theater. It is simple enough for children to learn and perform. I am very grateful to Jose for providing this script for library programs.

(La Casa De Las Luzes) (The House of Lights: A Lincoln Heights Tale)
By   **José Cruz González**   *Characters*   STORYTELLER   MARCOS

MANDI
PATTI
YOUNG SHADOW PEOPLE
SMALLEST SHADOW PERSON
EL BIG MAL OJO HELICOPTER
LITTLE SCARY WOLVES
NIGHTHAWK
LA RED
CHICKENS, PIGS and COWS
OLD WOMAN
COMADRES

(A hip-hop beat is heard. Our STORYTELLER appears.)

STORYTELLER
Our tale shifts gears when a Chevy lowrider appears driving through the 'hood. An evil troll if you recall brought the neighborhood to a downfall. His wicked mirror shattered across the 'hood and now everything's misunderstood. Myths have turned real, reality has become myth. Kids aren't supposed to be out at night and the 'hood is locked up tight. This tale is called La Casa de las Luzes, The House of Lights. And it is going to take place near a park where a teenage brother named—

(MARCOS, MANDI and PATTI sit on tires. MARCOS is driving.)

MARCOS: ¡Marcos!
STORYTELLER: His little sister—
PATTI: ¡Patti!
STORYTELLER: And their little brother—
MANDI: ¡Mandi!
STORYTELLER: Fight!

(Storyteller snaps her fingers.)

MANDI: Give me my toy, ¡Patti!
PATTI: No, you can't play with jugetes, ¡Mandi!
MANDI: But it's mine!
MARCOS: Hey!
PATTI: It's against the law to play!
MARCOS: Cut it out!
MANDI: I don't care!
PATTI: El Big Mal Ojo might be watching!
MARCOS & MANDI: ¿El BIG MAL OJO?
MANDI: WHERE?

MARCOS: IS IT FOLLOWING US?!
MANDI: ¡MAMÍ!
PATTI: I said it might be watching us!
MARCOS: Stop freaking us out, ¡Patti!
PATTI: There's a curfew tonight.
MANDI: We're going to be in big trouble.

(STORYTELLER holds up a broken piece of mirror.)

STORYTELLER: Oh, no, a broken piece of mirror!
MARCOS: We wouldn't be in this mess but I had to take my sick carnal Miguel to L.A. County. A friend is a friend. Por vida. Now, keep your eyes peeled!
STORYTELLER: Oh-oh!

(She tosses the broken mirror in front of them. A car tire is heard exploding.)

MARCOS: WATCH OUT!
PATTI: HOLD ON!
MANDI: ¡MAMÍ!

(The car screeches to a stop.)

PATTI: What happened?
MARCOS: We got a flat tire.
MANDI: Where did the glass come from?
PATTI: We got no spare.
MARCOS: There's has to be auto repair shops around here somewhere it's Lincoln Heights. Hey, where are you two going?
PATTI & MANDI: With you.
MARCOS: No way! You have to stay with the car. I don't want it jacked. I can pass like a grown up out because I'm taller than you.
MANDI: Hey, I'm going to be tall!
MARCOS: Well, not today little brother. Look, I don't want the chotas getting suspicious. Remember, we're kids and we aren't trusted.
PATTI: Marcos, what do we do?
MARCOS: Pretend you're grown ups hanging out in a dark parked car en el parque. Nobody is going to get suspicious 'cause nobody cares what grown ups do. I'll be back as soon as I get la llanta fixed.

(MARCOS exits with the tire. MANDI and PATTI quickly huddle together. Eerie music. YOUNG SHADOW PEOPLE appear. They wear grey sweatshirts with hoods. They stand watching PATTI and MANDI.)

PATTI: (Scared) Did you hear that?
MANDI: (Scared) Hear what?

PATTI: It's probably nothing.
MANDI: Yeah, probably nothing.

(Beat)

PATTI: There it is again!
MANDI: My stomach's growling. Tengo hambre.
PATTI: Me too. (Dreamingly) Oh, French fries!
MANDI: Hot dog and a soda!
PATTI: Pepperoni pizza!
MANDI: Nachos!
PATTI: ¡Churros!
ALL YOUNG SHADOW PEOPLE: ¡Churros!
PATTI: Who said that?
MANDI: No me!
YOUNG SHADOW PERSON #1: Gummy worms!
YOUNG SHADOW PERSON #2: Chili cheese dog!
YOUNG SHADOW PEOPLE: ¡Tamales!

    (MANDI and PATTI see the YOUNG SHADOW PEOPLE.)

PATTI & MANDI: AAGGHHH!

    (YOUNG SHADOW PEOPLE see MANDI and PATTI.)

ALL YOUNG SHADOW PEOPLE: AAGGHHH! AAGGHHH!

    (PATTI and MANDI hide while YOUNG SHADOW PEOPLE run off except for the SMALLEST SHADOW PERSON.)

SMALLEST SHADOW PERSON: ¡Me gusta Skiddles!
PATTI: Hey, get out of here!
SMALLEST SHADOW PERSON: ¡Tengo miedo! (I'm scared!)
PATTI: ¡Vayase! (Go!)
MANDI: Stop it, ¡Patti! You're scaring her!
PATTI: ¡Vayase! (Go!)

    (SMALLEST SHADOW PERSON cries.)

MANDI: You made her cry.
SMALLEST SHADOW PERSON: Quiero mi mami y papi.
PATTI: I'm sorry. Lo siento.

    (YOUNG SHADOWS PEOPLE begin to emerge.)

PATTI: Son sombras. You're shadows.
YOUNG SHADOW PERSON #3: An evil spell was put on us.

YOUNG SHADOW PERSON #4: An ice cream truck drove down our street.

YOUNG SHADOW PERSON #5: We ran out to buy an ice cream—

ALL YOUNG SHADOW PEOPLE: And we looked into ¡el espejo grande!

YOUNG SHADOW PERSON #6: Now we hide in the shadows.

PATTI: Everything's loco.

MANDI: No one can laugh and play no more.

SMALLEST SHADOW PERSON: Ayudanos. (Help us.)

PATTI: We don't know how to help.

YOUNG SHADOW PERSON #1: If only the spell can be broken—

YOUNG SHADOW PERSON #2: —then we can be ourselves again!

YOUNG SHADOW PERSON #3: And everything can be like it was!

PATTI: Okay, we'll help!

MANDI: We promise!

ALL YOUNG SHADOW PEOPLE: Hurray!

   (A puppet EL BIG MAL OJO HELICOPTER enters.)

MANDI: Oh, no, ¡El Big Maj Ojo!

PATTI: ¡CORRELE! (RUN!)

   (EL BIG MAL OJO HELICOPTER chases after YOUNG SHADOW PEO-
PLE while PATTI and MANDI hide onstage.)

MANDI: Where are we now?

PATTI: We're lost.

MANDI: ¡MAMÍ!

PATTI: BE QUIET!

   (A wolf howl is heard offstage.)

PATTI: What was that?

MANDI: It wasn't my stomach growling!

   (LITTLE SCARY WOLVES rush in.)

LITTLE SCARY WOLVES: Awoo!

PATTI: ¡Son lobos!

MANDI: ¡Correle!

PATTI: No! It's too late! Freeze!

MANDI: What?

PATTI: Don't move! Just do it!

   (They freeze in place. LITTLE SCARY WOLVES come up to them. They
sniff.)

LITTLE SCARY WOLVES: Awoo!

(They exit. PATTI and MANDI unfreeze.)

MANDI: Why didn't they eat us?
PATTI: Maybe they thought we were statues!

(A piercing cry of a bird is heard.)

PATTI: What now?

(NIGHTHAWK flies in circling PATTI and MANDI. Cool music is heard as LA RED enters riding a tricycle. She wears a red hooded sweatshirt. On her bike is a small colorful Mexican shopping bag. NIGHTHAWK lands on LA RED's shoulder.)

LA RED: (Loudly) Hey, what are you chamacos doing out here?
MANDI: Is that your ¿pájaro? (Bird?)
LA RED: This is Nighthawk. I raised him myself. Nighthawk is my eye in the sky.
PATTI: Do you own any pet wolves?
LA RED: No. Why?
MANDI: Never mind.
LA RED: Hey, can't you read the placas on the walls? This is a no man's land of
    gangsters, strangers, and winos. Bad company for little people like you.
PATTI: We just want to go home.
MANDI: Do I smell ¿tacos?
LA RED: Yeah, so?
MANDI: Tengo hambre.
PATTI: He's always hungry.
LA RED: I'll give you some. My nana don't eat much.
MANDI: Your nana?
LA RED: Yeah, she's sick in bed, and I'm taking her some tacos, Vicks, hot canela,
    and big bag of my favorite M&M's. Here.
    (LA RED hands them each a taco.)
PATTI & MANDI: Thank you.
LA RED: Look, you chamacos gotta be careful tonight. Something's up. I don't
    know what but watch your back.

(A helicopter sound is heard. EL BIG MAL OJO HELICOPTER enters.)

LA RED: ¡El BIG MAL OJO! Run for it!
PATTI & MANDI: Duck and cover!

(NIGHTHAWK flies off as LA RED exits on her bike. EL BIG MAL OJO HELICOPTER chases her while PATTI and MANDI hide. They see a house lit up with lights.)

MANDI: Look at that beautiful casa on the hill!

PATTI: Maybe some one there can help us!

(CHICKENS, PIGS and COWS appear. They make sounds and gestures trying to warn them.)

MANDI: Where did they come from?

PATTI: What are they saying? Shoo!

MANDI: Look, it's a little pan dulce house cooling on the window!

(CHICKENS, PIGS and COWS try to warn them again.)

MANDI: Come on let's eat it!

PATTI: No, we can't. It don't belong to us!

MANDI: But I'm hungry!

(An OLD WOMAN appears. She is played by our STORYTELLER.)

OLD WOMAN: ¡AY, MIS HIJOS!

PATTI & MANDI: ¡LA LLORONA!

OLD WOMAN: No, no, little ones! I'm not La Llorona but a little old sweet viejita who lives solita at the end of this dark and lonely street. I see you are very hungry and cold. Don't your parents know where you are?

MANDI: No.

PATTI: We're lost.

OLD WOMAN: ¡AY, MIS HIJOS!

MANDI: ¡MAMÍ!

PATTI: YOU'RE SCARING US!

OLD WOMAN: ¡Ay, lo siento! Forgive me old habits never die. I use to have many children but . . . they . . . they went away! Yes, that's right, they went away and left me solita at the end of this dark and lonely street.

PATTI: Did they become shadows?

OLD WOMAN: Shadows?

MANDI: Are they in hiding too?

OLD WOMAN: My children are not lawbreakers! Children today have no respect for their elders. My sweet angels are resting peacefully—

PATTI: Huh?

OLD WOMAN: I mean they're sleeping. After all, it's late, you know? Why don't you come inside my casita and I'll make you some hot chocolate to drink with pan dulce.

MANDI: Okay!

(CHICKENS, PIGS and COWS make noises trying to warn them.)

PATTI: Mandi don't go!

MANDI: It's okay, Patti, she's a little old sweet viejita who lives solita at the end of this dark and lonely street. Come on! What's the worse that can happen?

(MANDI goes behind the house.)

PATTI: No!

(OLD WOMAN returns with MANDI now turned into a cow.)

MANDI: Moo!

PATTI: ¡Mandi!

OLD WOMAN: (to Patti) Yes, that's right I've turned you're brother into a cow, and if you don't pipe down I'll turn you into a pig and make chicharrones out of you just like all the others I'm going to eat!

(The CHICKENS, PIGS and COWS faint.)

PATTI: You're a witch!

OLD WOMAN: Duh!

PATTI: I knew it!

OLD WOMAN: You can call me Llorona or 'Rona.

PATTI: You tricked us!

OLD WOMAN: Don't you children know that your worst nightmares are free roaming the world like on T.V., and that you're the stars on this reality show?

PATTI: What are you going to do to my ¿hermano?

OLD WOMAN: Well, we'll just have to see what our judges say!

(COMADRES enter. They are a chorus of old women.)

OLD WOMAN: These are my comadres ¡La Nina, La Pinta, y la Santa Maria!

OLD WOMAN & COMADRES: ¡AY, MIS HIJOS!

PATTI: ¡MAMÍ!

MANDI: MOO!

(OLD WOMAN and COMADRES burst out in wicked laughter.)

OLD WOMAN: We just love scaring kids to death! Well, what do you say, ¿Comadres?

(Brief music while they think. The COMADRES turn their thumbs upside down.)

OLD WOMAN: Oh, my, your brother has been voted off the farm!

OLD WOMAN & COMADRES: Goodbye and ¡Adios!

(The COMADRES exit as YOUNG SHADOW PEOPLE appear. The OLD WOMAN doesn't notice them.)

PATTI: What does that mean?

OLD WOMAN: I'm going to fatten up your hermano because I'm in the mood for some menudo tonight!

MANDI: MOO!

OLD WOMAN: Be quiet you dumb cow!

PATTI: No, you can't eat him!

OLD WOMAN: Watch me!

MANDI: MOO!

(An oven appears. MANDI faints. OLD WOMAN holds up a large match.)

OLD WOMAN: Now go turn on the oven with this mecha or I'll turn you into my next meal, kung pao chicken!

PATTI: I'm not supposed to play with matches.

OLD WOMAN: Oh, you dumb girl! Just crawl in, light it, and—

YOUNG SHADOW PERSON #1: (Whispering) Pretend you don't know how!

PATTI: But I don't know how!

YOUNG SHADOW PERSON #2: (Whispering) If you show me I'll do it!

PATTI: If you show me I'll do it!

OLD WOMAN: Oh, very well!

(OLD WOMAN crawls into the oven. She lights the match.)

OLD WOMAN: See? What's so hard about that?

YOUNG SHADOW PERSON #3: Then what do I do?

PATTI: Then what do I do?

OLD WOMAN: You turn the gas to full, ¡Tonta!

PATTI: Like this?

OLD WOMAN: That's right!

YOUNG SHADOW PERSON #4: And then?

OLD WOMAN: You shut the door!

PATTI: Shut the door?

OLD WOMAN: You're as thick as a two by four!

PATTI: Okay, I'm shutting the door! Goodbye and ¡Adios!

OLD WOMAN: Goodbye and ¡Adios?

(PATTI slams the oven door closed.)

OLD WOMAN: ¡AY, MIS HIJOS!

(MANDI, the CHICKENS, PIGS, COWS and YOUNG SHADOW PEOPLE are magically transformed back into humans.)

YOUNG SHADOW PERSON #5: You freed us!

YOUNG SHADOW PERSON #6: You broke the witch's spell!

(MARCOS enters rolling a tire.)

PATTI: ¡Marcos!

MARCOS: Hey!

PATTI: What are you doing here?

MARCOS: I got lost!

MANDI: And we found you big brother!

MARCOS: I guess you did.

ALL YOUNG PEOPLE: Hi.

MARCOS: Who are they?

PATTI: Our friends.

MANDI: Look, there's our old school Loreto Elementary!

PATTI: Then I know where we are! We got to tell the other kids what we know!

YOUNG PERSON #1: The kids were no longer afraid.

ALL: And they spoke out loud!

YOUNG PERSON #2: I'm a super granddaughter!

YOUNG PERSON #3: I'm a best friend!

YOUNG PERSON #4: I'm a good drawer!

MARCOS: I'm a big brother!

YOUNG PERSON #5: I wish the universe were water 'cause I could swim everywhere!

SMALLEST SHADOW PERSON: ¡Me gusta Skiddles!

MARCOS: And so ends our 3/7/11: A Lincoln Heights Tale (La Casa de las Luzes)!

3/7/11: A Lincoln Heights Tale was commissioned by Cornerstone Theater Company. © José Cruz González 2005. Partial Draft (5/29/2006).

LATINO CHILDREN'S MUSIC

Happily there are numerous recordings available featuring Latino artists which can be utilized on their own, or as part of other programming. These recordings help reinforce and celebrate Latino cultural heritage. On a more practical level they can be used to teach children how a particular rhyme or song should be sung, or as a resource for the librarian or teacher who wishes to perform some of these traditional songs themselves. Many of the traditional songs provide a tune for folk rhymes, as is the case with Mother Goose rhymes as well. They are a wonderful vehicle through which Latino children and families can celebrate their cultural heritage and traditions. I have found that many adults may say that they do not remember any rhymes, but when they hear them, they smile and remember, all of a sudden, something nearly forgotten from their childhood. The recordings mentioned should surely strike a chord in children, especially those who are new immigrants.

Fiesta Musical

Fiesta Musical: A Musical Adventure Through Latin America for Children (Music for Little People 42525D), http://www.musicforlittlepeople.com/ is a good way to begin a journey through the different musical styles of Latin America. The album is narrated by Emilio Delgado who plays "Luis" on Sesame Street. A number of different Latin artists appear on the record and the songs are delightful, representing numerous countries and styles of Latin music. There is an excellent booklet that goes along with this album that gives the lyrics and describes the types of instruments played and even some ideas for activities such as making your own instruments and dances. It includes the following:

"Fiesta Musical" (Musical Party)—María Medina Serafín (Puerto Rico—Bilingual Rap)
"A La Escuela" (To School)—Bobí Céspedes (Cuba—Rumba)
"La Acamaya" (The Crawdad)—Eugene Rodriguez and Artemio Posadas Jimenez (Mexico-Huapango)
"Tonadas de Quitiplas" (Sounds of Quitiplas Drums)—Jackeline Rago (Venezuela)
"Salaque"—Sukay (Bolivia)
"Happy Bomba"—Carolyn Brandy (Puerto Rico—Bomba)
"Los Pollitos" (The Little Chicks)—María Márquez (Venezuela)
"De La Puna"—Sukay (Peru)
"Los Enanos" (Little People)—Eugene Rodriguez and Artemio Posadas Jimenez (Jarojcho region of Mexico)
"El Gallo Pinto" (The Painted Rooster)—Claudia Gomez (Argentina)
"Una Melodía" (A Melody)—Bobí Céspedes (Cuba)
"No Llora Má" (Don't Cry Anymore)—María Márquez (Carribean)

Available from Music For Little People P.O. Box 1460 Redway, CA 95560.

Tish Hinojosa

Tish Hinojosa is an artist based in Austin, Texas. http://www.mundotish.com/ Her parents came to this country from Mexico. Her work, primarily for adults, reflects her bicultural heritage. Her one children's album is a gem.

CADA NIÑO/EVERY CHILD

This CD contains eleven bilingual songs for young children. There are play-ful songs, story songs, and lullabies. They are all about "the rich mixture of Latino and American culture and traditions." Lyrics in both languages are available. It includes the following:

Cada Niño/Every Child
Escala Musical/Music Scale
Siempre Abuelita/Always Grandma
Baile Vegetal/Barnard Dance
Nina Violina/Magnolia
Simplemente por amor/Simply for Love
Hasta Los Muertos Salen a Bailer/Even the Dead Are Rising Up to Dance
Quien/Who
Las Fronterizas/The Frontier Woman
Señora Santa Ana

Cada Niño is put out by Rounder Records, One Camp Street, Cambridge, MA 02140.

José-Luis Orozco

José-Luis Orozo is a native of Mexico City. http://www.joseluisorozco.com/. He perhaps has made the single greatest contribution to Latino children's music through his continuing series of CDs and cassettes of children's songs, rhymes, and singing games. They include some of the classic rhymes men-tioned in chapter 2. If you are not bilingual, you could perhaps play Orozco's renditions for your children. I have noted where an album includes songs or poems or fingerplays that are mentioned elsewhere in this manual.

LATIN AMERICAN CHILDREN'S SONGS, GAMES AND RHYMES BY JOSÉ-LUIS OROZCO.

Vol. 1. Lírica Infantil (Children's Lyrics)
Includes Chocolate, Pin Una . . . , Sana, Sana, Aserrin, Los Pollitos.
Vol. 2. Lírica Infantil (Children's Lyrics)
Includes Nanita nana, and La Vibora de la Mar.
Vol. 3. Latin American Children's Songs, Games and Rhymes
Vol. 4. Animales y Bailes (Animals and Dances)
Vol. 5. Letras, Numeros y Colores (Letters, Numbers and Colors)
Includes Chocolate, and Diez Perritos.
Vol. 6. Fiestas/Holidays

Vol. 7. Navidad y Pancho Claus (Christmas)
Vol. 8. Arrullos/Lullabies
Vol. 9. De Colores (accompanies the book the book *De Colores*)
Includes El chocolate, La vibora de la mar, and Los pollitos.
Vol. 10. Corridos Mexicanos y Chicanos (Mexican and Chicano Ballads)
Vol. 11. Esta es mi tierra (This Land Is My Land)
Vol. 12. Diez Deditos
Includes Tortillitas, Esté compró un huevo, Asserín, Asserán.

Orozco's recordings are available through Arcoiris Records, P.O. Box 7428, Berkeley, CA 94707, 510-527-5539.

José-Luis Orozco also now has a Web site which lists all the tracks for each of his albums. They can be ordered over the web as well. The address is http://www.joseluisorozco.com

Suni Paz

Suni Paz is an Argentine singer, composer, and guitarist. Her Web site address is http://www.sunipaz.com/. She has worked extensively with Alma Flor Ada, creating the accompaniment for a series of books and tapes, which were especially designed as readers for schools. She has also produced other book and cassette pairs in conjunction with the Santillana publishing company. These contain many songs and rhymes taken from Latino sources.

Canciones para el recreo (Children's Songs for the Playground), FC7850, 1977.
Alerta Sings: Children's Songs in Spanish and English from Latin America, the Carribean and the United States, FC7714, 1980.

These recordings are available from Folkways Records, Distributed by Birch Tree Group, 180 Alexander Street, Princeton, NJ 08540.

Maria Elena Walsh

Maria Elena Walsh has delighted generations of Argentine children with her music, which sadly has been difficult to obtain in the United States. It is now possible to purchase a number of her CDs on the Internet at the "Music and More" site: http://www.w3ar.com.ar/mmore/dbmore/Mus0063.htm. This is a good site to find Latino children's music other than Walsh's, as well. It is available in English.

Notable Recording

Here is another notable recording for children in Spanish:

Arroz con leche (Rice With Milk): Popular Songs and Rhymes from Latin America. Selected by Lulu Delacre. Performed and Produced by Carl and Jennifer Shaylen. New York: Scholastic, 1992. ISBN: 0590600354.

This is a recording which accompanies Delacre's outstanding book.

LATINO CHILDREN'S MAGAZINES

The following is a representative list of Latino-oriented children's magazines. These are an essential part of a balanced collection and provide popular reading for Latino children. For some, they may help them keep in touch with what is popular in their home countries. Many of these magazines can be obtained through a subscription service such as EBSCO. I have provided the ISSN where available and the addresses of the publishers for these titles. However, it is generally easier to obtain them through a jobber, than direct from the publisher. A good reference source for magazines in Spanish, including children's, is the reference work *Magazines for Libraries* by Bill Katz. Note that the international phone numbers are in the following format: (Country Code) City Code followed by the 7 digit phone number.

Billiken. Editorial Atlántida, S. A., Azopardo 579, 1307 Buenos Aires, Argentina. Editor: Carlos Silveyra. (54)1-130-7040. ISSN: 0006-2553. Internet http://www.billiken.com.ar/.

Eres (For young adults. Similar to Tiger Beat or Teen People). Bi weekly, Editorial Eres, S. A., Andres Bello, 45, piso 14, Polanco, 11560 México, D.F., (52)5-709-7302, (52)5-281-3200 fax. No ISSN. Internet http://www.esmas.com/eres/.

Iguana (a new educational magazine for children ages 7–12 written in Spanish). P.O. Box 26432, Scottsdale, AZ 85255, 541-342-4956. ISSN: 1554-916X. E-mail info@NicaGal.com, http://www.iguanarevista.com/.

Skipping Stones (a multicultural children's magazine with articles often written in Spanish). P.O. Box 3939, Eugene, Oregon 97403, 541-342-4956. ISSN: 0899-529X. E-mail info@skippingstones.org, http://www.skippingstones.org/

Tu Internacional (Similar to *Seventeen*. Covers health, beauty fashion, relationships, entertainment and psychology). Editorial America, S. A. 6355 N.W. 36th Street, Virginia Gardens, Florida 33166. Subscription address, Box 10950, Des Moines, IA 50347-0950, 305-871-6400. ISSN: 0746-9691. Internet http://www.esmas.com/revistatu/.

Zoo Books (Spanish-language edition of this familiar kids' magazine). Wildlife Education, Ltd., 12233 Thatcher Court, Poway, CA 92064-6880, 858-513-7600, 858-513-7660 fax. Internet http://www.zoobooks.com/.

Louis Yarian Zwick. "Recordings in Spanish for Children." *School Library Journal*, February 1989: 23–26.

Chapter 10

Major Book Awards

PURA BELPRÉ AWARD

"Honors Hispanic writers and illustrators whose work best portrays, affirms and celebrates the Hispanic cultural experience in a work of literature for children and youth. The award is named in honor of Pura Belpré, the first Latina librarian from the New York Public Library, who as a children's librarian, puppeteer, author and storyteller, enriched the lives of Puerto Rican children through her pioneer work in preserving and disseminating Puerto Rican folklore."

The first Pura Belpré awards were given at the first annual REFORMA National Conference held in Austin, Texas, in 1996. This biennial award has now taken its place alongside all the other awards given by the Association for Library Service to Children, and is announced together with the Newbery, Caldecott and other awards at the American Library Association Midwinter Meeting. The first award jury considered approximately eighty books written or illustrated by Latino authors who were residents of the United States in the period 1990–1995. The 1998 and all future awards were and will be given to books published only within a two-year time frame. It is important to note the stipulation that besides being written or illustrated by a Latino, the books must also exhibit cultural content. In other words, they must be relevant to Latino culture.

The Web site for the Pura Belpré award can be found at http://www.ala.org/ala/alsc/awardsscholarships/literaryawds/belpremedal/belprmedal.htm.

Pura Belpré Medal Winners 2006–1996

2006

For Narrative

Viola Canales for **The Tequila Worm**. Wendy Lamb Books (Random House), 2005.

For Narrative Honor Books

Carmen T. Bernier-Grand for **César: ¡Sí, Se Puede! Yes, We Can!** Illustrated by David Diaz. Tarrytown, NY: Marshall Cavendish, 2005.

Pat Mora for **Doña Flor: A Tall Tale About a Giant Woman with a Great Big Heart**. Illustrated by Raul Colón. Alfred A. Knopf (Random House), 2005.

Pam Muñoz Ryan for **Becoming Naomi León**. Scholastic Press, 2004.

For Illustration

Raul Colón for **Doña Flor: A Tall Tale About a Giant Woman with a Great Big Heart**. Written by Pat Mora. Alfred A. Knopf (Random House), 2005.

For Illustration Honor Books

Lulu Delacre for **Arrorró, Mi Niño: Latino Lullabies and Gentle Games**. Lee & Low Books, Inc., 2004.

David Diaz for **César: ¡Sí, Se Puede! Yes, We Can!** Written by Carmen T. Bernier-Grand. Tarrytown, NY: Marshall Cavendish, 2005.

Rafael López for **My Name is Celia: The Life of Celia Cruz/Me llamo Celia: La vida de Celia Cruz**. Written by Monica Brown. Luna Rising (Rising Moon), 2004.

2004

For Narrative

Julia Alvarez for **Before We Were Free**. Alfred A. Knopf, 2002.

For Narrative Honor Books

Nancy Osa for **Cuba 15**. Delacorte Press, 2003.

Amada Irma Pérez for **My Diary from Here to There/Mi Diario de Aquí Hasta Allá**. Children's Book Press, 2002.

For Illustration

Yuyi Morales for **Just a Minute: A Trickster Tale and Counting Book**. Chronicle Books, 2003.

For Illustration Honor Books

Robert Casilla for **First Day in Grapes**. Written by L. King Pérez. Lee & Low Books, Inc., 2002.

David Diaz for **The Pot That Juan Built**. Written by Nancy Andrews-Goebel. Lee & Low Books, Inc., 2002.

Yuyi Morales for **Harvesting Hope: The Story of César Chávez**. Written by Kathleen Krull. Harcourt, Inc., 2003.

2002

For Narrative

Pam Muñoz Ryan for **Esperanza Rising**. Scholastic Press, 2000.

For Narrative Honor Books

Francisco Jiménez for **Breaking Through**. Houghton Mifflin Company, 2001.

Francisco X. Alarcón for **Iguanas in the Snow**. Illustrated by Maya Christina González. Children's Book Press, 2001.

For Illustration

Susan Guevara for **Chato and the Party Animals**. Written by Gary Soto. G.P. Putnam's Sons, 2000.

For Illustration Honor Book

Joe Cepeda for **Juan Bobo Goes to Work: A Puerto Rican Folk Tale**. Retold by Marisa Montes. HarperCollins, 2000.

2000

For Narrative

Alma Flor Ada for **Under the Royal Palms: A Childhood in Cuba**. Atheneum Books, 1998.

For Narrative Honor Books

Francisco X. Alarcón for **From the Bellybutton of the Moon and Other Summer Poems/Del ombligo de la luna y otros poemas de verano**. Illustrated by Maya Christina González. San Francisco: Children's Book Press, 1998.

Juan Felipe Herrera for **Laughing out Loud, I Fly: Poems in English and Spanish**. Illustrated by Karen Barbour. HarperCollins, 1998.

For Illustration

Carmen Lomas Garza for **Magic Windows/Ventanas mágicas**. Children's Book Press, 1999.

For Illustration Honor Books

George Ancona for **Barrio: José's Neighborhood**. Harcourt Brace, 1998.
Amelia Lau Carling for **Mama & Papa Have a Store**. Dial Books, 1998.
Felipe Dávalos for **The Secret Stars**. Written by Joseph Slate. Tarrytown, NY: Marshall Cavendish, 1998.

1998

For Narrative

Victor Martinez for **Parrot in the Oven: Mi Vida**. Joanna Cotler Books (HarperCollins), 1996.

For Narrative Honor Books

Francisco X. Alarcón for **Laughing Tomatoes and Other Spring Poems/Jitomates risueños y otros poemas de primavera**. Illustrated by Maya Christina González. San Francisco: Children's Book Press, 1997.
Floyd Martinez for **Spirits of the High Mesa**. Houston: Arte Público Press, 1997.

For Illustration

Stephanie Garcia for **Snapshots from the Wedding** by Gary Soto. Putnam, 1997.

For Illustration Honor Books

Carmen Lomas Garza for **My Family/Mi Familia**. Children's Book Press, 1996.
Enrique O. Sanchez for **The Golden Flower** by Nina Jaffe. Simon and Schuster, 1996.
Simon Silva for **Gathering the Sun: An Alphabet in Spanish and English** by Alma Flor Ada. Lothrop, 1997.

1996

For Narrative

Judith Ortiz Cofer for **An Island Like You: Stories of the Barrio**. Orchard Books, 1995.

For Narrative Honor Books

Lucía Gonzales for **The Bossy Gallito/El gallo de bodas: A Traditional Cuban Folktale**. Scholastic, Inc., 1994.

Gary Soto for **Baseball in April and Other Stories**. Harcourt Brace, 1994.

For Illustration

Susan Guevara for **Chato's Kitchen** by Gary Soto. G. P. Putnam's Sons, 1995.

For Illustration Honor Books

George Ancona for **Pablo Remembers: The Fiesta of the Day of the Dead/Pablo Recuerda: La Fiesta de el Día de los Muertos**. Lothrop, Lee & Shepard Books, 1993.

Lulu Delacre for **The Bossy Gallito/El Gallo de Bodas: A Traditional Cuban Folktale** by Lucía Gonzales. Scholastic, Inc., 1994.

Carmen Lomas Garza for **Family Pictures/Cuadros de familia**. Children's Book Press, 1990.

AMÉRICAS AWARD

"The Américas Award is given in recognition of U.S. works of fiction, poetry, folklore, or selected non-fiction (from picture books to works for young adults) published in the previous year in English or Spanish that authentically and engagingly portray Latin America, the Caribbean, or Latinos in the United States. By combining both and linking the Americas, the award reaches beyond geographic borders, as well as multicultural-international boundaries, focusing instead upon cultural heritages within the hemisphere. The award is sponsored by the national Consortium of Latin American Studies Programs (CLASP).

"The award winners and commended titles are selected for their 1) distinctive literary quality; 2) cultural contextualization; 3) exceptional integration of text, illustration and design; and 4) potential for classroom use. The winning books are honored at a ceremony held each summer at the Library of Congress, Washington, D.C."

The coordinator for the Américas Award is Julie Kline of the University of Wisconsin-Milwaukee. She can be reached at the CLASP Committee on Teaching and Outreach, c/o The Center for Latin America, University of Wisconsin-Milwaukee, P.O. Box 413, Milwaukee, Wisconsin 53201, (414) 229-5986, fax (414) 229-2879, and E-mail cla@csd.uwm.edu

The Center for Latin America's Web site has a complete annotated list of the awards, and can be consulted annually as the award is presented, http://www.uwm.edu/Dept/CLACS/outreach/americas.html.

Annotated references to the Américas award-winning books can be found in the bibliography. Please note that this list includes books, which are set in non-Spanish-speaking Caribbean countries. While they fall outside the scope of this manual, I included them so that you had a complete list of winners. They may also be useful for other collection development.

Américas Award Winners 2004–1993

2004

Winners

Alire Sáenz, Benjamin. **Sammy & Juliana in Hollywood**. El Paso: Cinco Puntos, 2004.

Brown, Monica. **My Name Is Celia/Me llamo Celia**. Illustrated by Rafael López. Flagstaff: Rising Moon (Northland), 2004.

Honorable Mention

Cofer, Judith Ortiz. **Call Me María**. New York: Orchard, 2004.

Commended List

Anaya, Rudolfo. **The Santero's Miracle**. Illustrated by Amy Córdova. Spanish translated by Enrique Lamadrid. Albuquerque: University of New Mexico Press, 2004.

Geeslin, Campbell. **Elena's Serenade**. Illustrated by Ana Juan. New York: Atheneum, 2004.

Medina, Jane. **The Dream on Blanca's Wall/El sueño pegado en la pared de Blanca**. Illustrated by Robert Casilla. Honesdale, PA: Boyds Mill, 2004.

Russell, Barbara Timberlake. **The Remembering Stone**. Illustrated by Claire B. Cotts. New York: Farrar, Straus and Giroux, 2004.

Ryan, Pam Muñoz. **Becoming Naomi León**. New York: Scholastic, 2004.

Youme. Sélavi, **That Is Life: A Haitian Story of Hope**. El Paso: Cinco Puntos, 2004.

2003

Winners

Cofer, Judith Ortiz. **The Meaning of Consuelo**. New York: Farrar, Straus and Giroux, 2003.

Morales, Yuyi. **Just a Minute: A Trickster Tale and Counting Book**. San Francisco: Chronicle Books, 2003.

Honorable Mention

Krull, Kathleen. **Harvesting Hope: The Story of César Chávez**. Illustrated by Yuyi Morales. San Diego: Harcourt, 2003.
Osa, Nancy. **Cuba 15**. New York: Delacorte, 2003.

Commended List

Ancona, George. **Murals: Walls That Sing**. Tarrytown, NY: Marshall Cavendish, 2003.
Argueta, Jorge. **Xochitl and the Flowers**. Illustrated by Carl Angel. San Francisco: Children's Book Press, 2003.
Comino, Sandra. **Little Blue House**. Toronto: Groundwood, 2003.
Endredy, James. **The Journey of Tunuri and the Blue Deer**. Illustrated by María Hernández de la Cruz and Casimiro de la Cruz López. Rochester: Bear Cub Books, 2003.
Soto, Gary. **The Afterlife**. San Diego: Harcourt, 2003.

2002

Winner

Alvarez, Julia. **Before We Were Free**. New York: Knopf, 2002.

Honorable Mention

Danticat, Edwidge. **Behind the Mountains**. New York: Orchard, 2002.
Winter, Jonah. **Frida**. Illustrated by Ana Juan. New York: Scholastic, 2002.

Commended List

Ada, Alma Flor. **I Love Saturdays y Domingos**. Illustrated by Elivia Savadier. New York: Atheneum, 2002.
Andrews-Goebel, Nancy. **The Pot that Juan Built**. Illustrated by David Diaz. New York: Lee and Low, 2002.
Herrera, Juan Felipe. **Grandma and Me at the Flea/Los meros meros remateros**. Illustrated by Anita DeLucio-Brock. San Francisco: Children's Book Press, 2002.
Lee, Claudia M., comp. **Messengers of Rain and other Poems from Latin America/Mandaderos de la lluvia y otros poemas de América Latina** (dual edition). Illustrated by Rafael Yockteng. Toronto: Groundwood, 2002.

Machado, Ana Maria. **Me in the Middle**. Illustrated by Caroline Merola. Translated by David Unger. Toronto: Groundwood, 2002. (Originally published as **Bisa Bia Bisa Bel**. Rio de Janeiro: Salamandra, 1982.)

Mora, Pat. **A Library for Juana**. Illustrated by Beatriz Vidal. New York: Knopf, 2002.

Pérez, Amada Irma. **My Diary from Here to There/Mi diario de aquí hasta allá**. Illustrated by Maya Christina González. San Francisco: Children's Book Press, 2002.

Veciana-Suarez, Ana. **Flight to Freedom**. New York: Orchard, 2002.

2001

Winners

Argueta, Jorge. **A Movie in My Pillow/Una película en mi almohada**. Illustrated by Elizabeth Gómez. San Francisco: Children's Book Press, 2001.

Jiménez, Francisco. **Breaking Through**. Boston: Houghton Mifflin Company, 2001.

Honorable Mention

Freedman, Russell. **In the Days of the Vaqueros: America's First True Cowboys**. New York: Clarion Books, 2001.

Commended List

Alarcón, Francisco X. **Iguanas in the Snow and Other Winter Poems/Iguanas en la nieve y otros poemas de invierno**. Illustrated by Maya Christina González. San Francisco: Children's Book Press, 2001.

Ancona, George. **Harvest**. Tarrytown, NY: Marshall Cavendish, 2001.

Johnston, Tony. **Uncle Rain Cloud**. Illustrated by Fabricio Vanden Broeck. Watertown, MA: Charlesbridge, 2001.

Leiner, Katherine. **Mama Does the Mambo**. Illustrated by Edel Rodríguez. New York: Hyperion, 2001.

Saldaña, René, Jr. **The Jumping Tree**. New York: Delacorte Press, 2001.

2000

Winners

Joseph, Lynn. **The Color of My Words**. New York: Joanna Cotler (HarperCollins), 2000.

Skármeta, Antonio. **The Composition**. Illustrated by Alfonso Ruano. English Trans. Elisa Amado. Toronto: Groundwood, 2000.

Honorable Mention

Pérez, Amada Irma. **My Very Own Room/Mi propio cuartito**. Illustrated by Maya Christina González. San Francisco: Children's Book Press, 2000.
Ryan, Pam Muñoz. **Esperanza Rising**. New York: Scholastic Press, 2000.

Commended List

Anaya, Rudolfo. **Roadrunner's Dance**. Illustrated by David Diaz. New York: Hyperion, 2000.
Ancona, George. **Cuban Kids**. Tarrytown, NY: Marshall Cavendish, 2000.
Castillo, Ana. **My Daughter, My Son, The Eagle, The Dove: An Aztec Chant/Mi hija, mi hijo, el aguila, la paloma: un canto Azteca** (dual edition). Illustrated by S. Guevara. New York: Dutton, 2000.
Delacre, Lulu. **Salsa Stories**. New York: Scholastic, 2000.
Galindo, Mary Sue. **Icy Watermelon/Sandía fria**. Illustrated by Pauline Rodriguez Howard. Piñata Books (Arte Público), 2000.
Jiménez, Francisco. **The Christmas Gift/El regalo de Navidad**. Illustrated by Claire B. Cotts. Boston: Houghton Mifflin, 2000.
Winick, Judd. **Pedro and Me: Friendship, Loss, and What I Learned**. New York: Henry Holt, 2000.

1999

Winners

Herrera, Juan Felipe. **Crashboomlove: A Novel in Verse**. Albuquerque: University of New Mexico Press, 1999.

Honorable Mention

Garza, Carmen Lomas. **Magic Windows/Ventanas mágicas**. Spanish translated by Francisco X. Alarcón. San Francisco: Children's Book Press, 1999.
Wolf, Bernard. **Cuba: After the Revolution**. New York: Dutton, 1999.

Commended List

Alarcón, Francisco X. **Angels Ride Bikes and Other Fall Poems/Los angeles andan en bicicleta y otros poemas de otoño**. Illustrated by Maya Christina González. San Francisco: Children's Book Press, 1999.
Ancona, George. **Carnaval**. San Diego: Harcourt Brace, 1999.

Belafonte, Harry, and Lord Burgess. **Island in the Sun**. Illustrated by Alex Ayliffe. New York: Dial, 1999.

Chin-Lee, Cynthia, and Terri de la Peña. **A Is for Americas/A es para decir Américas** (dual edition). Illustrated by Enrique O. Sanchez. New York: Orchard, 1999.

Holtwijk, Ineke. **Asphalt Angels**. English translated from Dutch by Wanda Boeke. Asheville, NC: Front Street Press, 1999.

Holzwarth, Werner, and Yatiyawi Studios. **I'm José and I'm Okay: Three Stories from Bolivia**. English translated from German by Laura McKenna. La Jolla, CA: Kane/Miller, 1999.

Madrigal, Antonio Hernández. **Erandi's Braids**. Illustrated by Tomie dePaola. New York: G.P. Putnam's Sons, 1999.

Rodríguez, Luis J. **It Doesn't have to Be This Way: A Barrio Story/No tiene que ser así: Una historia del barrio**. Illustrated by Daniel Galvez. San Francisco: Children's Book Press, 1999.

Taylor, Harriet Peck. **Two Days in May**. Illustrated by Leyla Torres. New York: Farrar, Straus and Giroux, 1999.

1998

Winners

Ancona, George. **Barrio: José's Neighborhood/Barrio: El barrio de José** (dual edition). San Diego: Harcourt Brace, 1998.

Carling, Amelia Lau. **Mama and Papa Have a Store**. New York: Dial, 1998.

Honorable Mention

San Souci, Robert D. **Cendrillon: A Caribbean Cinderella**. Illustrated by Brian Pinkney. New York: Simon and Schuster, 1998.

Commended List

Ada, Alma Flor. **Under the Royal Palms: A Childhood in Cuba**. New York: Atheneum, 1998.

Alarcón, Francisco X. **From the Bellybutton of the Moon and Other Summer Poems/Del ombligo de la luna y otros poemas de verano**. Illustrated by Maya Christina González. San Francisco: Children's Book Press, 1998.

Ancona, George. **Fiesta Fireworks**. New York: Lothrop, Lee and Shepard, 1998.

Chambers, Veronica. **Marisol and Magdalena: The Sound of Our Sisterhood**. New York: Hyperion, 1998.

Cowley, Joy. **Big Moon Tortilla**. Illustrated by Dyanne Strongbow. Honesdale, PA: Boyds Mill, 1998.

Gershator, Phillis, and David Gershator. **Greetings, Sun**. Illustrated by Synthia Saint James. New York: DK Ink, 1998.

Hausman, Gerald. **Doctor Bird: Three Lookin' Up Tales from Jamaica**. Illustrated by Ashley Wolff. New York: Philomel, 1998.

Heide, Florence Parry, and Roxanne Heide Pierce. **Tío Armando**. Illustrated by Ann Grifalconi. New York: Lothrop, Lee and Shepard, 1998.

Isadora, Rachel. **Caribbean Dream**. New York: Putnam, 1998.

Jiménez, Francisco. **La mariposa**. Illustrated by Simón Silva. Boston: Houghton Mifflin, 1998.

Loya, Olga. **Momentos Mágicos/Magic Moments: Tales from Latin America Told in English and Spanish**. Little Rock: August House, 1998.

Luenn, Nancy. **A Gift for Abuelita: Celebrating the Day of the Dead/Un regalo para Abuelita: En celebración del Día de los Muertos**. Illustrated by Robert Chapman. Flagstaff: Rising Moon, 1998.

Reeve, Kirk. **Lolo and Red-Legs**. Flagstaff: Rising Moon, 1998.

Slate, Joseph. **The Secret Stars**. Illustrated by Felipe Dávalos. Tarrytown, NY: Marshall Cavendish, 1998.

Soto, Gary. **Big Bushy Mustache**. Illustrated by Joe Cepeda. New York: Knopf, 1998.

————. **Petty Crimes**. San Diego: Harcourt Brace, 1998.

Torres, Leyla. **Liliana's Grandmothers**. New York: Farrar Straus Giroux, 1998.

Van Laan, Nancy. **The Magic Bean Tree: A Legend From Argentina**. Illustrated by Beatriz Vidal. Boston: Houghton Mifflin, 1998.

Van West, Patricia E. **The Crab Man/El hombre de los cangrejos** (dual edition). Illustrated by Cedric Lucas. New York: Turtle Books, 1998.

1997

Winners

Hanson, Regina. **The Face at the Window**. Illustrated by Linda Saport. New York: Clarion, 1997. (Picture Book Category.)

Jiménez, Francisco. **The Circuit: Stories from the Life of a Migrant Child**. Albuquerque: University of New Mexico Press, 1997. (Fiction Category.)

Honorable Mention

Ancona, George. **Mayeros: A Yucatec Maya Family**. New York: William Morrow, 1997.

Bloom, Valerie. **Fruits: A Caribbean Counting Poem**. Illustrated by David Axtell. New York: Henry Holt, 1997.

Commended List

Ada, Alma Flor. **Gathering the Sun: An Alphabet in Spanish and English**. Illustrated by Simón Silva. New York: Lothrop, 1997.

———. **The Lizard and the Sun/La largartija y el sol**. Illustrated by Felipe Dávalos. New York: Doubleday Dell, 1997.

Alarcón, Francisco X. **Laughing Tomatoes and Other Spring Poems/Jitomates risueños y otros poemas de primavera**. Illustrated by Maya Christina González. San Francisco: Children's Book Press, 1997.

Almada, Patricia. **From Father to Son**. Illustrated by Marianno de López. Crystal Lake, IL: Rigby, 1997.

Cappellini, Mary. **The Story of Doña Chila/El cuento de Doña Chila** (dual edition). Illustrated by Gershom Griffith. Crystal Lake, IL: Rigby, 1997.

Carden, Mary, and Mary Cappellini, eds. **I Am of Two Places/Soy de dos lugares** (dual edition). Illustrated by Christina González. Crystal Lake, IL: Rigby, 1997.

Corpi, Lucha. **Where Fireflies Dance/Ahi, donde bailan las luciernagas**. Illustrated by Mira Reisberg. San Francisco: Children's Book Press, 1997.

Ehlert, Lois. **Cuckoo/Cucu**. Translated by Gloria de Aragón Andújar. New York: Harcourt Brace, 1997.

Garay, Luis. **Pedrito's Day**. New York: Orchard, 1997.

González, Lucía M. **Señor Cat's Romance and Other Favorite Stories from Latin America**. Illustrated by Lulu Delacre. New York: Scholastic, 1997.

González-Jensen, Margarita. **Mexico's Marvelous Corn/El maravilloso maíz de México** (dual edition). Crystal Lake, IL: Rigby, 1997.

Hernández, Jo Ann Yolanda. **White Bread Competition**. Houston: Piñata Books (Arte Público), 1997.

Hornstein, Henry. **Baseball in the Barrios**. New York: Gulliver (Harcourt Brace), 1997.

Johnston, Tony, and Jeanette Winter. **Day of the Dead**. New York: Harcourt Brace, 1997.

Keane, Sofía Meza. **Dear Abuelita**. Illustrated by Enrique O. Sanchez. Crystal Lake, IL: Rigby, 1997.

Kroll, Virginia. **Butterfly Boy**. Illustrated by Gerado Suzán. Honesdale, PA: Boyds Mills, 1997.

Lopez, Loretta. **Birthday Swap/¡Que sorpresa de cumpleaños!** (dual edition). New York: Lee and Low, 1997.

Martinez, Floyd. **Spirits of the High Mesa**. Houston: Arte Público, 1997.

Mora, Pat. **Tomás and the Library Lady/Tomás y la Señora de la biblioteca** (dual edition). Illustrated by Raul Colón. New York: Knopf, 1997.

Moreton, Daniel. **La Cucaracha Martina: A Caribbean Folktale/La cucaracha Martina: un cuento folklórico del Caribe**. New York: Turtle, 1997.

Orozco, José-Luis. **Diez deditos/Ten Little Fingers and Other Play Rhymes and Action Songs from Latin America**. Illustrated by Elisa Kleven. New York: Dutton, 1997.

Rahaman, Vashanti. **A Little Salmon for Witness: A Story from Trinidad**. Illustrated by Sandra Speidel. New York: Lodestar, 1997.

Sisnett, Ana. **Grannie Jus' Come**. Illustrated by Karen Lusebrink. San Francisco: Children's Book Press, 1997.

Solá, Michèle. **Angela Weaves a Dream: The Story of a Young Maya Artist**. Illustrated by Jeffrey Jay Foxx. New York: Hyperion, 1997.

Soto, Gary. **Buried Onions**. New York: Harcourt Brace, 1997.

Stevens, Jan Romero. **Carlos and the Skunk/Carlos y el Zorillo**. Illustrated by Jeanne Arnold. Flagstaff: Rising Moon, 1997.

Viesti, Joe, and Diane Hall. **Celebrate in Central America**. Illustrated by Joe Viesti. New York: Lothrop, Lee & Shepard, 1997.

1996

Winners

Garza, Carmen Lomas. **In My Family/En Mi Familia**. San Francisco: Children's Book Press, 1996.

Martinez, Victor. **Parrot in the Oven: Mi vida**. New York: HarperCollins, 1996.

Honorable Mention

Becerra de Jenkins, Lyll. **So Loud a Silence**. New York: Lodestar, 1996.

Hallworth, Grace, comp. **Down by the River: Afro-Caribbean Rhymes, Games and Songs for Children**. Illustrated by Caroline Binch. New York: Scholastic, 1996.

Commended List

Albert, Burton. **Journey of the Nightly Jaguar**. Illustrated by Robert Roth. New York: Atheneum, 1996.

Aldana, Patricia, ed. **Jade and Iron: Latin American Tales From Two Cultures**. Translated by Hugh Hazelton. Illustrated by Luis Garay. Toronto: Groundwood/Douglas & McIntyre, Ltd., 1996.

Alphin, Elaine Marie. **A Bear for Miguel**. Illustrated by Joan Sandin. New York: HarperCollins, 1996.

Anzaldúa, Gloria. **Prietita and the Ghost Woman/Prietita y la llorona**. Illustrated by Christina González. San Francisco: Children's Book Press, 1996.

Belpré, Pura. **Firefly Summer**. Houston: Arte Público, 1996.

Bunting, Eve. **Going Home**. Illustrated by David Diaz. New York: HarperCollins, 1996.

Calhoun, Mary. **Tonito's Cat**. Illustrated by Edward Martínez. New York: Morrow, 1996.

Carlson, Lori Marie, ed. **Barrio Streets, Carnival Dreams: Three Generations of Latino Artistry**. New York: Henry Holt, 1996.

Charles, Faustin, comp. **A Caribbean Counting Book**. Illustrated by Roberta Arenson. Boston: Houghton Mifflin, 1996.

Cooper, Martha, and Ginger Gordon. **Anthony Reynoso: Born to Rope**. New York: Clarion, 1996.

Delacre, Lulu. **Golden Tales: Myths, Legends, and Folktales from Latin America/De oro y esmeraldas: mitos, leyendas y cuentos populares de Latino América** (dual edition). New York: Scholastic, 1996.

Delgado, María Isabel. **Chave's Memories/Los recuerdos de Chave**. Illustrated by Yvonne Symank. Houston: Arte Público, 1996.

Gage, Amy Glaser. **Pascual's Magic Pictures**. Illustrated by Karen Dugan. Minneapolis: Carolrhoda, 1996.

Geeslin, Campbell. **In Rosa's Mexico**. Illustrated by Andrea Arroyo. New York: Knopf, 1996.

Gershator, Phillis. **Sweet, Sweet Fig Banana**. Illustrated by Fritz Millevoix. Morton Grove, Illinois: Albert Whitman, 1996.

Gollub, Matthew. **Uncle Snake**. Illustrated by Leovigildo Martínez. New York: Tambourine, 1996.

Huth, Holly Young. **Darkfright**. Illustrated by Jenny Stow. New York: Atheneum, 1996.

Jaffe, Nina. **The Golden Flower: A Taino Myth from Puerto Rico**. Illustrated by Enrique O. Sanchez. New York: Simon & Schuster, 1996.

Johnston, Tony. **The Magic Maguey**. Illustrated by Elisa Kleven. San Diego: Harcourt Brace, 1996.

———. **My Mexico/México mío**. Illustrated by F. John Sierra. New York: G.P. Putnam's Sons, 1996.

Kleven, Elisa. **Hooray, a Pinata!** New York: Dutton, 1996.

Kurtz, Jane. **Miro in the Kingdom of the Sun**. Illustrated by David Frampton. Boston: Houghton Mifflin, 1996.

Lauture, Denizé. **Running the Road to ABC**. Illustrated by Reynold Ruffins. New York: Simon and Schuster, 1996.

Machado, Ana Maria. **Nina Bonita: A Story**. Illustrated by Rosana Faría. Translated by Elena Iribarren. Brooklyn, NY: Kane/Miller, 1996.

Mohr, Nicholasa. **Old Letivia and the Mountain of Sorrows**. Illustrated by Rudy Gutiérrez. New York: Viking, 1996.

Mora, Pat. **Confetti**. Illustrated by Enrique O. Sanchez. New York: Lee & Low, 1996.

Myers, Walter Dean. **Toussaint L'ouverture: The Fight for Haiti's Freedom**. Illustrated by Jacob Lawrence. New York: Simon and Schuster, 1996.

Schecter, Ellen. **The Big Idea**. Illustrated by Bob Dorsey. New York: Hyperion, 1996.

Silverman, Sarita Chavez. **Good News!** Illustrated by Melinda Levine. Carmel, CA: Hampton-Brown, 1996.

Soto, Gary. **The Old Man and His Door**. Illustrated by Joe Cepeda. New York: G.P. Putnam's Sons, 1996.

Stanley, Diane. **Elena**. New York: Hyperion, 1996.

Tamar, Erika. **Alphabet City Ballet**. New York: HarperCollins, 1996.

————. **The Garden of Happiness**. Illustrated by Barbara Lambase. San Diego: Harcourt Brace, 1996.

Van Laan, Nancy. **La boda: A Mexican Wedding Celebration**. Illustrated by Andrea Arroyo. Boston: Little, Brown, 1996.

Wing, Natasha. **Jalapeno Bagels**. Illustrated by Robert Casilla. New York: Atheneum, 1996.

Winter, Jeanette. **Josefina**. San Diego: Harcourt Brace, 1996.

OTHER NOTABLE 1996 PUBLICATIONS INCLUDE THE FOLLOWING:

Presilla, Maricel E., and Gloria Soto. **Life Around the Lake: Embroideries by the Women of Lake Patzcuaro**. New York: Henry Holt, 1996.

Presilla, Maricel E. **Mola: Cuna Life Stories and Art**. New York: Henry Holt, 1996.

1995

Winner

Temple, Frances. **Tonight By Sea**. New York: Orchard Books, 1995.

Honorable Mention

Cofer, Judith Ortiz. **An Island Like You: Stories of the Barrio**. New York: Orchard Books, 1995.

Soto, Gary. **Chato's Kitchen**. Illustrated by Susan Guevara. New York: G. P. Putnam's Sons, 1995.

Talbert, Marc. **Heart of a Jaguar**. New York: Simon and Schuster, 1995.

Commended List

Ada, Alma Flor. **Mediopollito/Half-Chicken**. Illustrated by Kim Howard. New York: Doubleday, 1995.

Agard, John, and Grace Nichols. **A Caribbean Dozen: Poems From Caribbean Poets**. Illustrated by Cathie Felstead. Cambridge, MA: Candlewick Press, 1994.

Anaya, Rudolfo. **The Farolitos of Christmas**. Illustrated by Edward Gonzales. New York: Hyperion, 1995.

Ancona, George. **Fiesta U.S.A.** New York: Lodestar, 1995.

Bertrand, Diane Gonzales. **Sweet Fifteen**. Houston: Arte Público Press, 1995.

Brusca, Maria Cristina, and Tona Wilson. **Pedro Fools the Gringo, and Other Tales of a Latin American Trickster**. Illustrated by Maria Cristina Brusca. New York: Henry Holt, 1995.

————. **When Jaguars Ate the Moon and Other Stories about Animals and Plants of the Americas**. Illustrated by Maria Cristina Brusca. New York: Holt, 1995.

Ciavonne, Jean. **Carlos, Light the Farolito**. Illustrated by Donna Clair. New York: Clarion, 1995.

Crespo, George. **How Iwariwa the Cayman Learned to Share: A Yanomami Myth**. New York: Clarion, 1995.

Dorros, Arthur. **Isla/La isla** (dual edition). Illustrated by Elisa Kleven. New York: Dutton, 1995.

Garland, Sherry. **Indio**. San Diego: Harcourt Brace, 1995.

Gerson, Mary-Joan. **People of Corn: A Mayan Story**. Illustrated by Carla Golembe. Boston: Little, Brown and Company, 1995.

Gonzalez, Ralfka, and Ana Ruiz. **My First Book of Proverbs/Mi primer libro de dichos**. Emeryville, CA: Children's Book Press, 1995.

Gregory, Kristiana. **The Stowaway: A Tale of California Pirates**. New York: Scholastic, 1995.

Hanson, Regina. **The Tangerine Tree**. Illustrated by Harvey Stevenson. New York: Clarion, 1995.

Hernandez, Irene Beltran. **The Secret of Two Brothers**. Houston: Pinata Books (Arte Público Press), 1995.

Herrera, Juan Felipe. **Calling the Doves/El canto de las palomas**. Illustrated by Elly Simmons. Emeryville, CA: Children's Book Press, 1995.

Keister, Douglas. **Fernando's Gift/El regalo de Fernando**. Illustrated by Douglas Keister. San Francisco: Sierra Club Books for Children, 1995.

Levy, Janice. **The Spirit of Tío Fernando: A Day of the Dead Story/El espíritu de tío Fernando: Una historia del Día de los Muertos**. Illustrated by Morella Fuenmayor. Morton Grove, IL: Albert Whitman & Company, 1995.

Mike, Jan. **Juan Bobo and the Horse of Seven Colors: A Puerto Rican Legend**. Illustrated by Charles Reasoner. Mahwah, NJ: Troll Associates, 1995.

Mohr, Nicholasa, and Antonio Martorell. **The Song of El Coqui and Other Tales of Puerto Rico**. New York: Viking, 1995.

Nye, Naomi Shihab, ed. **The Tree Is Older Than You Are: A Bilingual Gathering of Poems and Stories From Mexico With Paintings By Mexican Artists**. New York: Simon and Schuster, 1995.

Paulsen, Gary. **The Tortilla Factory/La tortilleria** (dual edition). Illustrated by Ruth Wright Paulsen. San Diego: Harcourt Brace, 1995.

Rojany, Lisa. **The Magic Feather: A Jamaican Legend**. Illustrated by Philip Kuznicki. Mahwah, NJ: Troll Associates, 1995.

Rossi, Joyce. **The Gullywasher**. Flagstaff: Northland Publishing, 1995.

San Souci, Robert D. **The Faithful Friend**. Illustrated by Brian Pinkney. New York: Simon and Schuster, 1995.

Scott, Ann Herbert. **Hi**. Illustrated by Glo Coalson. New York: Philomel, 1994.

Shute, Linda. **Rabbit Wishes**. New York: Lothrop, Lee & Shepard, 1995.

Soto, Gary. **Canto Familiar**. Illustrated by Annika Nelson. San Diego: Harcourt Brace, 1995.

———. **Summer On Wheels**. New York: Scholastic, 1995.

Talbert, Marc. **A Sunburned Prayer**. New York: Simon and Schuster, 1995.

Torres, Leyla. **Saturday Sancocho**. New York, Farrar, Straus and Giroux, 1995.

1994

Winners

Joseph, Lynn. **The Mermaid's Twin Sister: More Stories From Trinidad**. Illustrated by Donna Perrone. New York: Clarion, 1994.

Commended List

Ada, Alma Flor. **Where the Flame Trees Bloom**. Illustrated by Antonio Martorell. New York: Atheneum, 1994.

Albert, Richard E. **Alejandro's Gift**. Illustrated by Sylvia Long. San Francisco: Chronicle Books, 1994.

Atkin, S. Beth. **Voices From the Fields: Children of Migrant Farmworkers Tell Their Stories**. Boston: Little, Brown, 1993.

Bernhard, Emery, and Durga Bernhard. **The Tree That Rains: The Flood Myth of the Huichol Indians of Mexico**. New York: Holiday House, 1994.

Bernier-Grand, Carmen T. **Juan Bobo: Four Folktales from Puerto Rico**. Illustrated by Ernesto Ramos Nieves. New York: HarperCollins, 1994.

Blanco, Alberto. **Angel's Kite/La estrella de Angel**. Illustrated by Rodolfo Morales. Emeryville, CA: Children's Book Press, 1994.

Bunting, Eve. **A Day's Work**. Illustrated by Ronald Himler. New York: Clarion, 1994.

Carlson, Lori, ed. **Cool Salsa: Bilingual Poems On Growing Up Latino in the United States**. New York: Holt, 1994.

Castaneda, Omar S. **Imagining Isabel**. New York: Lodestar, 1994.

Czernecki, Stefan, and Timothy Rhodes. **The Hummingbirds' Gift**. Illustrated by Juliana Reyes de Silva and Juan Hilario Silva. New York: Hyperion, 1994.

Dawson, Mildred Leinweber. **Over Here It's Different: Carolina's Story**. Illustrated by Geroge Ancona. New York: Macmillan, 1993.

DePaola, Tomie. **The Legend of the Poinsettia**. New York: Putnam, 1994.

Franklin, Kristine L. **When the Monkeys Came Back**. Illustrated by Robert Roth. New York: Atheneum, 1994.

Gershator, Phillis. **Rata, Pata, Scata, Fata: A Caribbean Story**. Illustrated by Holly Meade. Boston: Little, Brown and Company, 1994.

———. **Tukama Tootles the Flute: A Tale from the Antilles**. Illustrated by Synthia Saint James. New York: Orchard Books, 1994.

González, Lucía M. **The Bossy Gallito: A Traditional Cuban Folktale**. Illustrated by Lulu Delacre. New York: Scholastic, 1994.

Gordon, Ginger. **My Two Worlds**. Illustrated by Martha Cooper. New York: Clarion, 1993.

Grossman, Patricia. **Saturday Market**. Illustrated by Enrique O. Sanchez. New York: Lothrop, Lee & Shepard, 1994.

Gunning, Monica. **Not a Copper Penny in Me House: Poems from the Caribbean**. Illustrated by Frane Lessac. Honesdale, PA: Boyds Mill Press, 1993.

Jaramillo, Nelly Palacio. **Grandmother's Nursery Rhymes: Lullabies, Tounge Twisters, and Riddles from South America/Las nanas de abuelita: Canciones de cuna, trabalenguas y adivinanzas de Surámerica**. Illustrated by Elivia Savadier. New York: Holt, 1994.

Jekyll, Walter. **I Have a News: Rhymes from the Caribbean**. Compiled by Neil Philip. Illustrated by Jacqueline Mair. New York: William Morrow and Company, 1994.

Jiménez, Juan Ramón. **Platero y yo/Platero and I**. English translated by Myra Cohn Livingston and Joseph F. Dominguez. Illustrated by Antonio Frasconi. New York: Clarion, 1994.

Johnston, Tony. **The Tale of Rabbit and Coyote**. Illustrated by Tomie de Paola. New York: Putnam, 1994.

Kendall, Sarita. **Ransom for a River Dolphin**. Minneapolis: Lerner Publications Company, 1993.

Lessac, Frane. **Caribbean Alphabet**. New York: William Morrow and Company, 1994.

Mathews, Sally Schofer. **The Sad Night: The Story of an Aztec Victory and a Spanish Loss**. New York: Clarion Books, 1994.

Merino, Jose Maria. **Beyond the Ancient Cities**. English translated by Helen Lane. New York: Farrar, Straus and Giroux, 1994. (Originally published in Spain in 1987.)

Meyer, Carolyn. **Rio Grande Stories**. San Diego: Harcourt Brace, 1994.

Mora, Pat. **Pablo's Tree**. Illustrated by Cecily Lang. New York: Macmillan, 1994.

Ober, Hal. **How Music Came to the World: An Ancient Mexican Myth**. Illustrated by Carol Ober. Boston: Houghton Mifflin, 1994.

Orozco, José-Luis. **De Colores and Other Latin-American Folk Songs for Children**. Illustrated by Elisa Kleven. New York: Dutton, 1994.

Pico, Fernando. **The Red Comb**. Illustrated by Maria Antonia Ordonez. Mahwah, NJ: BridgeWater Books, 1994. (Originally published in Puerto Rico and Venezuela in 1991.)

Presilla, Maricel E. **Feliz Nochebuena, Feliz Navidad**. Illustrated by Ismael Espinosa Ferrer. New York: Holt, 1994.

Roybal, Laura. **Billy**. Boston: Houghton Mifflin, 1994.

Thomas, Jane Resh. **Lights on the River**. Illustrated by Michael Dooling. New York: Hyperion, 1994.

Villasenor, Victor. **Walking Stars: Stories of Magic and Power**. Houston: Arte Público Press, 1994.

Williams, Karen Lynn. **Tap-Tap**. Illustrated by Catherine Stock. New York: Clarion Books, 1994.

1993

Winners

Delacre, Lulu. **Vejigante Masquerader**. New York: Scholastic, 1993.

Commended List

Becerra de Jenkins, Lyll. **Celebrating the Hero**. New York: Lodestar Books, 1993.

Castaneda, Omar. **Abuela's Weave**. Illustrated by Enrique O. Sanchez. New York: Lee & Low, 1993.

Dorros, Arthur. **Radio Man: A Story in English and Spanish**. Translated by Sandra Marulanda Dorros. New York: HarperCollins, 1993.

Hodge, Merle. **For the Life of Laetitia**. New York: Farrar, Straus and Giroux, 1993.

Markun, Patricia Maloney. **The Little Painter of Sabana Grande**. Illustrated by Robert Casilla. New York: Bradbury, 1993.

Mitchell, Rita Phillips. **Hue Boy**. Illustrated by Caroline Binch. New York: Dial Books for Young Readers, 1993.

PREMIO LAZARILLO

With the object of stimulating the production of good books, especially destined for children and young people, the Organización para el Libro Infantil y Juvenl (OEPLI) (Organization for Children's and Young Adult Books), with the patronage of the Spanish Ministry of Culture, gives the "Lazarillo" prize annualy to the best children's and young adult works written in any of the Spanish tongues and published especially for readers under 15 years of age.

Since 1986 OEPLI has been charged with giving this prize annualy, with the patronage of the Ministry of Education and Culture. This prize, the oldest and one of the most prestigious in children's literature, was given for the first time by INLE (Instituto Nacional del Libro Español National Institute of the Spanish Book) in 1958, with the goal of stimulating the creation and production of good books for children and young people. Prizes are given to authors, illustrators and publishing houses. You should note that in Spain there is publishing not only in Spanish, but also in the Catalán language. Some of the winners were written originally in Catalán, and the titles here are given in that language. However, many of these Catalán titles have been translated into Spanish. A list of winners and honor books can now be found at this Web site: http://www.oepli.org/esp/actividades/laz_premios.htm. The main page for the governing body, OEPLI, is at http://www.oepli.org.

Many of these Lazarillo award-winners are out of print, and many others are in Catalán. While I wanted to include this list for reference and historical purposes, it is probably not as useful for collection development. For this reason, citations for these titles have not been included as is the case with the other award titles.

Lazarillo Prize Winners 2005–1958

2005

Author

Angeles Alfaya for **A ollada de Elsa**.

Illustrator

Manuel Hidalgo for **La casita de chocolate**.

2004

Author

Xosé Antonio Niera Cruz for **A noite da raíña Berenguela**.

Illustrator

Adrià Gòdia for **El último día de otoño**.

2003

Author

Juan Carlos Mártin Ramos for **Poemamundi**.

Honorable Mention

Consuelo Morales Fernandez for **Barasingha**.

Illustrator

Tae Mori Rivas for **Los alimentos**.

2002

Author

Laida Martínez Navarro for **Max**.

Honorable Mention

Daniel Nesquens for **Días de clase**.
José Ramírez Lozano for **El tren de los aburridos**.

Illustrator

Carles Arbat for **La Ciutat dels Ignorants**.

Honorable Mention

Luis Castro Enjamio for **Ocho hermosos cuentos de los hermanos Grimm**.
Mercé Sendino for **Sueños de lana**.

2001

Author

Ana María Fernández Martínez for **Amar e outros verbos**.

Honorable Mention

Luchy Núñez for **Corriendo niño, llegando hombre**.
Luchy Núñez for **Llenaría tu cara tenure**.

Illustrator

Saúl Oscar Rojas for **Los siete domingos**.

Honorable Mention

José Antonio Tàssies for **El secreto**.
Rocío Martinez for **La gallina Catalina**.

2000

Author

Gloria Sánchez for **Chinto e Tom**.

Honorable Mention

Gloria Sánchez Cándida for **Viladecruces**.
Miguel Ángel Mendo for **Mi abuela la bruja**.

Illustrator

Fernando Gómez Díaz for **El acertijo de Pópol**.

Honorable Mention

Anna Clariana for **Somriures**.
Federico Delgado for **La espera**.

1999

Author

Marilar Alexandre for **A banda sin futuro**.

Honorable Mention

Carmen Gómez Ojea for **Hija de muerta**.
Jordi Sierra ì Fabra for **Los hombres de la silla**.

Illustrator

Pablo Amargo for **No todas las vacas son iguales**.

Honorable Mention

Rocío Martínez for **Ratoncito Miguel arregla palampalatas**.
José Antonio Tássies for **Volando al revés**.

1998

Author

Emilio Pascual for **Día de Reyes Magos**.

Honorable Mention

Carles Cano for **La mar de elefantes**.
Alicia Borrás Sanjurjo **Versos graciosos, sabrosos y jugosos**.

Illustrator

Judit Morales Villanueva for **No eres más que una pequeña hormiguita**.

Honorable Mention

Accésit Carles Arbat for **El traspás de l'Isidre**.
Angels Ruiz for **Com gat i gos**.

1997

Author

Elacier Cansino for **El misterio Velázquez**.

Honorable Mention

Concha Blanco for **A mi que me importa**.
Empar de Lanuza for **Versos per a ossets**.

Illustrator

Manuel Barbero Richard for **El niño que dejó de ser pez**.

Honorable Mention

Angels Ruíz for **La pequeña costrurera**.
Montse Tobella for **El mond Rar de L'Estrafo**.

1996

Author

Miguel Fernández Pacheco for **Los zapatos de Murano**.

Honorable Mention

Francisco Alonso Villaverde for **Cidades**.
Teresa Aretzaga for **Las montañas del cielo**.

Illustrator

Isidro Ferrer for **El verano y sus amigos**.

Honorable Mention

Garbriela Rubio for **La bruja Tiburcia**
Manuel Hidalgo for **El terrible tragafuegos**.

1995

Author

José Zafra Castro for **Tres historias de Sergio**.

Honorable Mention

Santiago García-Clariac for **El señor que quería ser Tintín**.
Isabel Molina for **El señor del cero**.

Illustrator

Luis Farré Estrada for **Una casa com un cabás**.

Honorable Mention

Sofía Balzola for **La mariposa azul**.
Angels Ruiz for **Un domingo de perros**.

1994

Author

José Zafra Castro for **The agafat caputxeta**.

Honorable Mention

Paloma Bardons for **Hojas de líneas rojas**.
Rafael Estrada Delgado for **El extraño caso de Comisario Olegario**.

Illustrator

Samuel Velasco for **Chumplufated** . . . .

Honorable Mention

Josep Montserrat for **El viento del mar**.
J. A. Tàssies for **Hora carabola**.

1993

Author

Prize not given.

Honorable Mention

Ana Guillemi for **En la cola del aire**.
José M. Plaza for **Que alguien me quiera cinco minutos**.

Illustrator

Gabriela Rubio for **Bzzz . . . Grijalbo**.

Honorable Mention

Monica Verena Kesuch for **Un curioso ratoncito**.

1992

Author

Francisco A. Díaz Guerra for **Nacido del verbo oscuro**.

Honorable Mention (Poetry)

Eduardo Galán Font for **La silla voladora**.

Honorable Mention (Theater)

Anton Cortizas for **Historias a algún percance, todas ditas en romance**.

Illustrator

José M. Carmona for **Entre el juego y el frugo**.

1991

Author

Enrique Páez for **Devuelve el anillo, pelo cepillo**.

Illustrator

Gusti for **La pequeña Wu-lli**.

1990

Author

Agustín Fernández Paz for **Contos por palabras**.

Illustrator

Marta Balaguer for **¡Qina nit de Reis!**.

1989

Author

Miguel Angel Mendo for **Por un maldito anuncio**.

Illustrator

Pablo Echevarría for **Camilón, comilón**.

1988

Author

Manuel Alfonseca Moreno for **El rubí del Ganges**.

Illustrator

Francisco Giménez for **Historia de una receta**.

1987

Author

Beatriz Doumercy for **Un cuento grande como una casa**.

Illustrator

Montse Ginesta for **Gargantua**.

1986

Author

Fernando Martínez Gil for **El juego del pirata**.

Honorable Mention

Manuel Alonso Erausquin for **Encuentro con los contrarios**.

Illustrator

Angel Esteban for **Los norks**.

Honorable Mention

Paula Reznickova for **El conqur i la nena**.

1985

Author

Francisco Climent Carrau for **El tesoro del Capitán Nemo**.

Honorable Mention

Alfredo Gómez Cerdá for **El bloc de Timo**.

Illustrator

Constantino Gatagán for **La reina de las nieves**.

Honorable Mention

Irene Bordoy for **El comillo**.

1984

Author

Concha Lópe Narvaez for **El amigo oculto y los espíritus de la tarde**.

Honorable Mention

Juan Antonio de Laiglesia for **¡Chuic!.**

Illustrator

Alfonso Ruano Martín for **El camino de Juan**.

Honorable Mention

Josep Montserrat for **El caballo fantástico**.
Montse Ginesta Clavell for **El mag dels estels**.

1983

Author

Miguel M. Fdez. de Velasco for **Las tribulaciones de Pabluras**.

Honorable Mention

Rodolfo Guillermo Otero for **La travesía**.

Illustrator

Juan Carlos Eguillor for **El saco de leña**.

Honorable Mention

Jesús Gabán Bravo for **El ciervo que fué a buscar la primavera**.

1982

Author

Pilar Mateos for **Capitanes de plástico**.

Honorable Mention

Enrique Gainza for **Wela y otros cuentos**.

Illustrator

Clara Pérez Escrivá for **La hija del sol**.

Honorable Mention

Constantino Gatagán for **Ping y pong y los animales** and **Ping y Pong navegantes**.

1981

Author

José A. del Cañizo for **Las cosas del abuelo**.

Honorable Mention

Juan Gómez Saavedra for **Ristra de cuentos**.

Illustrator

Carme Solé Vendrell for **Cepillo**.

1980

Author

Joan Manuel Gisbert for **El misterio de la isla de Tokland**.

Honorable Mention

María Puncel for **Abuelita Opalina**.

Illustrator

Viví Escrivá for **Dos cuentos de princesas**.

1979

Author

No prize given.

Honorable Mention

Graciela Montes for **Amadeo y otros cuentos**.

Illustrator

Ulises Wensell for **Cuando sea mayor seré marino** and **Cuando sea mayor seré enfermera**.

1978

Author

Hilda Perera for **Podría ser que una vez . . . .**

Illustrator

José Ramón Sánchez for **Los libros del aprendiz de brujo**.

1977

Author

Fernando Alonso for **El hombrecito vestido de gris y otros cuentos**.

Illustrator

No prize given.

1976

No awards given.

1975

Author

Hilda Perera for **Cuentos para chicos y grandes**.

Illustrator

Margarita Vazquez de Praga for **La ventana de María**.

Publisher

Beginning in 1975, the publisher's prize was discontinued.

1974

Author

Consuelo Armijo for **Los Bautautos**.

Illustrator

Miguel Calatayud for **Cuentos del año 2100**.

Publisher

No prize given.

1973

Author

Carmen Vázquez Vigo for **Caramelos de menta**.

Illustrator

Miguel Angel Pacheco for **Maestro de la fantasía**.

Publisher

No prize given.

1972

Author

Aaron Cupit for **Cuentos del año 2100**.

Illustrator

Manuel Boix for **El país de las cosas perdidas**.

Publisher

No prize given.

1971

Author

María Puncel for **Operación pata de oso**.

Illustrator

Fernando Sáez for **Goya**.

Publisher

No prize given.

1970

Author

Fernando Sadot Pérez for **Cuentos del Zodíaco**.

Illustrator

Felicidad Montero for **Los músicos de Bremen**.

Publisher

Editorial Teide.

1969

Author

José Javier Aleixandre for **Froilán, el maigo de los pájaros**.

Illustrator

Fernando Sáez for **El Lazarillo de Tormes**.

Publisher

Editorial Verón.

1968

Author

Jaime Ferrán for **Angel en Colombia**.

Illustrator

María Rius for **¿Por qué cantan los pájaros?**.

Publisher

Editorial Cantábrica.

1967

Author

Lita Tiraboschi for **Historia del gato que vino con Solís**.

Illustrator

Roque Riera Rojas for **El Ingenioso Hidalgo Don Quixote de la Mancha**.

Publisher

No prize given.

1966

Author

Marta Osorio for **El caballito que quería volar**.

Illustrator

Luis de Horna for **Gino, comino y el camello Moja-Jamón**.

Publisher

No prize given.

1965

Author

Ana María Matute for **El polizónde Ulises**.

Illustrator

Asunción Balzola Elorza for **Cancionero infantil universal**.

Publisher

Santillana S. A.

1964

Author

Carmen Kurtz for **Color de fuego**.

Illustrator

Daniel Zarza Ballugera for **Fiesta en Marilandia**.

Publisher

Ediciones Anaya.

1963

Author

Angela C. Ionescu for **De un país lejano**.

Illustrator

Celedonio Perellón for **Cuentos del ángel custodio**.

Publisher

No prize given.

1962

Author

Concha Fernández-Luna for **Fiesta en Marilandia**.

Illustrator

José Picó for **Fantasía**.

Publisher

Ediciones Gaisa.

1961

Author

Joaquín Aguirre Bellver for **El juglar del Cid**.

Illustrator

José Narro Celorio for **Robinson Crusoe**.

Publisher

Editorial Doncel.

1960

Author

Montserrat del Amo for **Rastro de Dios**.

Illustrator

M. Jiménez Arnalot for **Yo soy el gato**.

Publisher

Ediciones Gamma.

1959

Author

Miguel Buñuel for **El niño, la golondrina y el gato**.

Illustrator

Rafael Munoa for **Exploradores en Africa**.

Publisher

Dalmau y Jover.

1958

Author

Alfonso Iniesta for **Dicen de las florecillas**.

Illustrator

José F. Aguirre for **El libro del desierto**.

Publisher

Editorial Mateu.

Chapter 11

Review Sources, Publishers, and Vendors

The task of identifying and then aquiring Spanish-language and bilingual materials has always been challenging, but it is certainly becoming less so. The major trend that I have seen most recently is a consolidation among distributors of Spanish-language materials. This is both good and bad news. Scholastic acquired Lectorum Publications, which is both a publisher and distributor, in order to position itself as a major source of Spanish-language books for children through all their distribution channels, including book fairs. The major book distributors, Baker and Taylor, Ingram, Brodart, BWI and others have also seen that there is a substantial market and therefore money to be made in carrying Spanish-langauge books. They are also responding to the many requests from their library customers with whom they have accounts. This has been a learning process, but to their credit, these distributors have been listening. What this has meant is that to meet the demand, the distributors have looked for people who have experience in acquiring Spanish-language titles. An example of how this has worked can be found in the recent acquisition of distributor *Libros Sin Fronteras* by Baker and Taylor. They have employed *Libros Sin Fronteras*'s founder, Michael Shapiro, to head up their Spanish-language department. With a knowledgable expert such as Shapiro, this is probably a good bet. Brodart now sends selectors to the International Book Fair in Guadalajara and publishes "Best of Guadalajara" lists.

The downside is that through this culture of merger and consolidation, many of the mom and pop distributors are fading away, and with that the personal touch you could get from a small company. I recently had a conversation with the founder of Nana's Book Warehouse, who was getting ready to go out of business. He was holding what basically amounted to a fire sale to liquidate his remaining inventory. He said that he had made no money for a while, and that he and his wife had continued only out of love for the books. The bottom line is, for better or worse, acquiring Spanish-language and bilingual titles has probably never been easier because of the involvement of the major distributors. In fact, many of these distributors offer to do much of the selection for you.

PRINT REVIEW SOURCES

School Library Journal, *Booklist* and *The Horn Book* all publish semi-regular lists of Spanish-language books for children. I've made a habit of keeping these on file. Isabel Schon's periodic pieces for *Booklist* are especially helpful, because she includes books that are not recommended because of poor, inaccurate translations or for other reasons. This is extremely useful for the librarian who is not familiar with Spanish. Isabel Schon is the director for the Barahona Center for the Study of Books in Spanish for Children and Adolescents based out of California State University, San Marcos, which maintains a Web site with an extensive list of recommended titles and includes complete bibliographic information as well as grade levels and subject headings. It updates titles monthly. Schon also publishes books that compile the reviews the Center has done in print form. Her most recent book, which is highly recommended as a source for up-to-date titles: Isabel Schon. *Recommended Books in Spanish for Children and Young Adults: 2000–2004*. Lanham, Maryland: Scarecrow Press, 2004.

Another excellent source for recommended books is the Consortium of Latin American Studies Programs (CLASP) annual "Americas" award for children's and young adult literature. These can be books in English or Spanish, but must be works published in the United States. Available on its Web site are lists of each year's awards with brief reviews. Do not forget to peruse the catalogs of the mainstream New York publishers for their Spanish-language titles, as well as titles in English that relate to Hispanic culture. Following is an annotated list of review sources. Note that international telephone numbers are in the following format: (Country Code) City Code-7 digit number.

Américas Award List,
http://www.uwm.edu/Dept/CLA/.
The list is prepared annually by the national Consortium for Latin American Studies Programs.

Banco del Libro,
Avenida Luis Roche, Edificio Banco del Libro, Altamira Sur, Caracas

1062, Venezuela. (58)2-266-1566/266-5077/265-3136, (58)2-266-3621/264-1391 fax, http://www.bancodellibro.org.ve/, e-mail info@bancodellibro.org.ve.

Banco del Libro, or "Bank of the Book," is a Venezuelan institution which is a model for Latin America in terms of conceiving, implementing, and diffusing programs and services related to the promotion of children's literature. Banco de Libro sponsors a publication, *Tres estrellas y más* (Three Stars and More), which is a bulletin published twice a year (in September and March) with reviews of recommended Spanish-language books. This includes critical reviews which rank books with from three to five stars. An annual subscription can be obtained for $5.

Barahona Center of the Study of Books in Spanish for Children and Adolescents,
California State University San Marcos, Kellogg Library, 5th Floor, 333 S. Twin Oaks Valley Road, San Marcos, CA 92096-0001, Isabel Schon, Director, 760-750-4070, 760-750-4073 fax, e-mail ischon@csusm.edu, http://www.csusm.edu/csb/.

This center is a major clearinghouse for information related to children's books in Spanish.

Bilingual Review, ISSN: 0094-5366,
Hispanic Research Center, Arizona State University, P.O. Box 872702, Tempe, AZ 85287-2702, 480-965-3867, 480-965-8309 fax, e-mail brp@asu.edu
Includes book reviews and creative writing by Latino writers.

Booklinks: Connecting Books, Libraries and Classrooms,
P.O. Box 607 (subscription address), Mt. Morris, IL 61054-7564, 888-350-0949, http://www.ala.org/ala/productsandpublications/periodicals/booklinks/booklinks.htm.
Booklinks occasionally includes bibliographies that relate to Latino interests.

Booklist, P.O. Box 607 (subscription address), Mt. Morris, IL 61054-7564, 888-350-0949, http://www.ala.org/ala/booklist/booklist.htm, and http://booklistonline.com/.

This new online site for *Booklist* will be available in late spring 2006

Occasional features found in *Booklist* are bibliographies of "Books in Spanish from Spanish-Speaking Countries," "Books in Spanish Published in the U.S.," and "Recommended Reference Books in Spanish for Children and Adolescents." As mentioned above, the author of these columns, Isabel Schon, includes a helpful "Caveat Emptor/Inferior Translations" to assist librarians in building the best possible Spanish-language collections. Distributor addresses are included.

>   *CLIJ* (Cuadernos de Literatura Infantil y Juvenil), ISSN: 0214-4123, Editorial Torre de Papel, S. L., c/ Madrazo 14 6° 2a, 08006 Barcelona, Spain, Director: Victoria Fernández, Editor: Maria Victoria Fernandez, (34)93 238-8683, (34)93-415 6769 fax, e-mail victoriaclij@coltmail. com, http://www.revistaclij.com/.

This is the most important Spanish-language magazine regarding children's books. It began publication in 1988 and has as its purpose to dignify

---

Críticas Magazine

360 Park Avenue South, New York, NY 10010, 646-746-6853, 646-746-6734 fax, http://www.criticasmagazine.com.
Carmen Ospina, Senior Editor, 646-746-6853, cospina@reedbusiness.com.
Formerly a print journal, *Críticas* is now published monthly on the Web. The Web issues are supplemented by two print issues annually, in June and November. *Críticas* online is free, and does not require any registration. While the loss of *Críticas* as a monthly print journal was quite a blow, this is still perhaps the best and only place to find reviews of Spanish-language materials in English. It is still my favorite, and most highly recommended collection development tool. Online, you can click immediately to vendor sites to order a title, if you can log in and have password.

---

children's literature and to defend the cultural importance of reading from infancy. If you read Spanish, this is essential. CLIJ is published monthly, with one issue each year being devoted to various awards given in Spanish-speaking countries. An annual subscription is $120.

>   *Fondo de Cultura Económica,*
>   http://www.fondodeculturaeconomica.com/entradaFlash.asp.

>   *The Horn Book Magazine* and *The Horn Book Guide*, 56 Roland Street, Suite 200, Boston, MA 02129, 617-628-0225, 800-325-1170, and 617-628-0882 fax, e-mail info@hbook.com, http://www.hbook.com.

The Horn Book publishes occasional review articles by Isabel Schon under the title "Noteworthy Children's Books in Spanish." *The Horn Book Guide* is published semiannually, and includes "virtually every children's and young adult book published in the United States." I review Spanish and bilingual books for the guide.

Library Journal, "Spanish Bookshelf."
Libros de México (magazine),

Cepromex (Centro de Promoción del Libro Mexicano, Center for the Promotion of Mexican Books). Cámara Nacional de la Industria Editorial Mexicana (Caniem), National Center for the Mexican Publishing Industry, Holanda 13, col. San Diego Churubusco Del. Coyoacán 04120, México, D. F.
http://www.librosmexicanos.com/default.asp.
The online site for *Libros de México* is a link from www.librosmexicanos.
(52)5-688-2011/688-2021/688-2009,
(52)5-604-3147 fax.
Caniem's Web site: http://www.caniem.com/.
Also available from this organization is a booklet called *Cómo comprar libros y publicaciones periódicas de México/How to Obtain Mexican Books and Periodicals,* ISBN: 968-6276-03-3.

Libros en Venta (Books in Print),
National Information Services Corporation, NISC USA, Wyman Towers, 3100 St. Paul Street, Baltimore, Maryland 21218, 410-243-0797, 410-243-0982 fax.
http://www.nisc.com/factsheets/qlev.asp;
e-mail sales@nisc.com.
Available as an electronic database, this is the Spanish-language equivalent of *Books in Print.*

Multicultural Review, 14497 N. Dale Mabry Hwy, Suite 205N, Tampa, FL 33618, 800-600-4364, 813-264-2772, and 813-264-2343 fax,
203-226-3571,
203-222-1502 fax,
http://www.mcreview.com/.
This publication includes reviews from Isabel Schon.

PUBYAC listserv, http://www.pubyac.org
This is a discussion forum for Children's and Young Adult Librarians in Public Libraries. The Web site provides links to subscribe online or via e-mail.

REFORMA Newsletter/REFORMANET listserv,
http://www.reforma.org/
To subscribe to the REFORMANET listserv, go to
http://lmri.ucsb.edu/mailman/listinfo/reformanet
and follow the directions.
Reforma is the National Association to Promote Library Service to the Spanish-Speaking, and is an affiliate of the American Library Association.

The quarterly newsletter is available only to members. The listserv discusses a myriad of topics related to library services for Latinos. If you have a question about Spanish-language books, someone here can probably help you.

Nuevas hojas de lectura (New Pages of Reading),
a publication of IBBY Hispanicamérica.
Edited by Fundalectura, Colombian Section of IBBY,
Av. (Calle) 40 N° 16-46, Apartado 048902, Bógata, COLOMBIA, (57)1-320-1511, (57)1-287-7071 fax,
http://www.nuevashojasdelectura.com/p_resenaslibros.htm.

Fundalectura was created in 1990 with the purpose of supporting books and reading in Colombia, and is the Colombian section of IBBY, the International Board on Books for Young People. Contains reviews and informative articles about Latin American authors. In Spanish only.

School Library Journal,
Home Office,
360 Park Avenue South,
New York, NY 10010,
646-746-6759
646-746-6689 fax,
e-mail slj@reedbusiness.com,
http://www.schoollibraryjournal.com/.
Subscriptions:
800-595-1066,
515-247-2984,
712-733-8019 fax,
e-mail sljcustserv@cdsfullfillment.com.

School Library Journal publishes occasional reviews of children's books in Spanish.

Of course, the Internet is one of the first places to go, with new sources of information for Spanish-language materials appearing regularly. Publisher, vendor, and distributor catalogs, accessed either online or in print catalogs obtained by contacting the publishers or vendors, or by attending conferences are an important way of keeping up-to-date with new material releases. Other local sources that you may wish to explore are Spanish-language newspapers in your community as well as the review sections of mainstream newspapers.

INTERNET RESOURCES

The internet has been a boon to the teacher and librarian looking for Spanish-language books. International communication has been greatly facilitated through e-mail and Web sites. Many Spanish and Latin American publishers as well as children's book organizations are now on the internet. The internet addresses of distributors with an on-line presence are included with the distributor list under the individual distributor/vendor.

Due to the constantly fluctuating nature of the World Wide Web, this portion of the book is the most apt to become quickly out of date. I have done my best to ensure the accuracy of this information. These sites were all checked just before this book went to press. Hopefully most of them will be somewhat stable, or if they move, a holding page will be left behind to direct you to the new site.

Web sites

Amazon.com, http://www.amazon.com/exec/obidos/tg/browse/-/301735/ ref = br_bx_c_1_8/102-3063528-8028110.
Amazon has this page of Spanish-language books for children. I have found that virtually every Spanish-language book for children in print can usually be found at Amazon.

ARCE, http://www.arce.es/news/default.jsp.
The Association of Cultural Magazines in Spain.

Azteca Web Page, http://www.azteca.net/aztec/.
Useful mainly for its links to chicano-oriented sites. The literature section does not cover children's books.

Barahona Center for the Study of Books in Spanish for Children and Adolescents, http://www.csusm.edu/csb/.
Isabel Schon's site is the best one for a librarian or teacher looking for lists of recommended books. Schon gives complete bibliographic information and updates her list with recent titles.

Bilingual Books to Share, http://www.tsl.state.tx.us/ld/projects/ninos/ bilingual.html.
A list of bilingual books suitable for parent-child sharing from the Texas State Library.

Casa del libro, http://www.casadellibro.com/secciones/seccion/0,1022, 1,00.html?codigo=1.
A Spanish e-commerce site like Amazon.com devoted solely to books.

Cibercentro, http://www.cibercentro.com.
A yahoo-type search engine in Spanish, with the added feature of sections of links for individual countries.

CLNet Folklore/Customs/Traditions, http://latino.sscnet.ucla.edu/research/ folklore.html.

Includes links to sites about a great many aspects of Latino culture including Day of the Dead, the arts, festivals, foods, games, music, and religion.

¡Colorín Colorado!, http://www.colorincolorado.org/homepage.php.
This page is part of WETA Television's "Reading Rockets" project. It includes lists of recommended books and interviews with author Pat Mora and Francisco Alarcón.

Hispanic Online–Hispanic Links, http://www.hispaniconline.com/links/index.html.
This site has grown to be a gateway page, with news and links, including links to sites of interest regarding Latin literature and culture. The site is in English.

International Children's Digital Library, http://www.icdlbooks.org/.
This site dedicated to digitizing children's books from all over the world includes approximately 89 online books in Spanish.

Internet Familia, http://www.familia.cl.
A colorful site suitable for families with links of interest to both children and parents.

Jardin Mundial Kindergarten,
http://www.geocities.com/Athens/Acropolis/4616.
This is most helpful for links to articles on bilingual education.

Juegos y Canciones (Games and Songs), http://www.hevanet.com/dshivers/juegos.
Songs and games that can be used in an elementary school classroom from the Summer FLES conference in Forest Grove, Oregon.

Latin American Network, http://lanic.utexas.edu.
Another good set of links for individual countries and a number of links grouped by subject, which includes an excellent set of links for grades K-12. This is one of the best sites for teachers.

Latin World, http://www.latinworld.com.
A search engine and directory of resources for Latin American and the Caribbean.

¡*Leamos Amigos*! (Let's Read, Friends!), http://berkeleypubliclibrary.org/booklist/leamos.html.
A list of recommended books from the staff of the Berkeley California Public Library.

Learning Internet, Resources in Spanish,
http://lone-eagles.com/migcurr.htm.

Literacy Connections, http://www.literacyconnections.com/.

A site with resources for purchase on second language literacy and Latino literacy.

Multnoma County Library, Portland, Oregon (Spanish), http://www.multcolib.org/libros/index.html.

A great example of a public library Web site for the Spanish-speaking.

Mundo Latino, http://www.mundolatino.org/.

Includes "El Rinconcito" (The Little Corner) with links to educational and book-related Web sites for children. Also includes a selection of illustrated children's stories.

National Association for Bilingual Education, http://www.nabe.org/.

Information can be found here on the annual conference of this group, which draws publishers in the Spanish-language market.

Quepasa, http://www.quepasa.com/.
A Latino Web portal in English.

REFORMA Web Page, http://www.reforma.org/.

The Web site for this national association that promotes library service to the Spanish-speaking.

Serving Spanish-speaking Communities,
http://library.utah.gov/library_services/spanish_speaking/where_to_buy
.htm.

A site from the Utah State Library, listing some resources for acquiring Spanish-langauge materials.

Spanish Toys, http://www.spanishtoys.com.

An Amazon-type site based in the U.S. with a selection of children's books in Spanish.

Zona Latina, http://www.zonalatina.com/Zlchild.htm.

A fairly comprehensive set of links to Latin American children's resources.

ORGANIZATIONS

In the following sections, international phone numbers are listed in a standardized format: (Country Code) City Code-7-digit phone number. All city codes with the exception of Spain are 1 digit. All international calls from the United States must be proceeded by 011.

CERLALC (Centro Regional para el Fomento del Libro en America Latina y Caribe or the Regional Information Center on Books, Reading and Copyright in Latin America and the Caribbean). Based in Bogotá, Colombia, CERLALC is an international organization that promotes books, reading, and authors rights throughout Latin America.

CERLALC Calle 70# 9-52, Bogotá, Colombia, (57) 1-540-2071, 018000-912071 toll free, http://www.cerlalc.org/index.htm

e-mail libro@cerlalc.org.

CIDCLI

Centro de Información y Desarollo del la Comunicación y la Literatura Infantiles (Center of Information and Development of Communication and of Children's Literature),

Av. México, 145-601, Col. del Carmen, Coyoacán, México, D. F. C. P. 04100, (52)5-659-7524, (52)5-659-3186, http://www.cidcli.com.mx/.

IBBY (International Board on Books for Young People)

IBBY is an organization that has created a worldwide network of people who are dedicated to bringing children and books together. You can link to the Web sites of all the national sections, including those in Spanish-speaking countries from the IBBY home page: http://www.ibby.org/index.php?id=home&L=0.

The Spanish-speaking countries represented in IBBY, with their specific Web site if available, are Argentina, Bolivia, Chile, http://www.ibbychile.cl/. (the Chile site has a blog on children's books),

Colombia, http://www.fundalectura.org/, Colombia's site has a page of recommended books. Cuba, Ecuador, Mexico, http://www.ibbymexico.org.mx, Peru, Spain, http://www.oepli.org/ (this site is also where you can find a list of the winners of the Premio Lazarillo), Uruguay, and Venezuela, http://www.bancodellibro.org.ve/.

PUBLISHERS, DISTRIBUTORS, AND VENDORS

There are a growing number of distributors who deal either exclusively or extensively in Spanish-language books. Virtually all of these companies have catalogs from which materials can be selected and ordered. It is difficult, of course, to order sight unseen. Some vendors will bring materials to your location for first-hand inspection before your purchases are made. Some distributors will say that they can provide any title you request, but make sure they can fulfill their promises before you commit. You may be limited by the purchasing procedures dictated by your agency. Some agencies require contracts to be made with vendors and only allow purchases from those distributors with whom there are contracts.

Local Spanish bookstores, if there are any in your community, are a good source for actually seeing books before you buy. Larger chain bookstores such as Borders Books and Music and Barnes and Noble have begun carrying Spanish-language titles where the market and sales warrant. However, the bulk of books available in these stores are translations of books, which appeared originally in English. If you have the money or resources, the best option is to travel to conventions and book fairs. There are always a large number of Latino book publishers and distributors at the American Library Association meetings, and at some state library association conventions as well. The annual Book Expo American convention (http://www.bookexpoamerica.com) also devotes a significant amount of exhibit space to Spanish-language books, and is actually a better place than the American Library Association convention to see books. It is also possible to travel to a fair devoted exclusively to Latino books. The most prestigious of these is FIL, or the *Feria Internacional del Libro* (*International Book Fair*), held annually in Guadalajara, Mexico. This fair is an eye-opener in terms of the number and variety of books that can be seen. For anyone seriously interested in collection development and seeing books before making a purchase, FIL is the place to do it. It is not necessarily the best place to buy unless you work through a distributor. It is extremely helpful in negotiating FIL to have a relationship with a distributor who has a presence at the fair. Distributors can get catalogs, price lists, and other information from publishers who are reluctant to give the same to librarians. Distributors may also provide services such as personal consultation related to your collection needs and shipping to librarians shopping at the fair. This last issue is especially important given the complicated nature of importing books into this country. If you have a publisher ship directly to you and something goes wrong, you generally have no recourse, whereas you do have the possibility for resolution when working through a distributor who is based in the United States.

Information on FIL Guadalajara is available from the Information Center, Av. Alemania 1370, Colonia Moderna, Guadalajara, Jalisco, 44190, México, (52-33) 3810-0331 and 3268-0900, (52-33) 3268-0921 fax, e-mail fil@fil.com.mx, http://www.fil.com.mx/.

ALA Free Pass Program

The American Library Association as of this writing has partnered with the Guadalajara International Book Fair for the past nine years with a program that subsidizes American librarians in attendance and provides the following: 3 nights at the Plaza del Sol Hotel (six nights if you share a room with a colleague who is also part of the program), 3 continental breakfasts, Registration fee, and $100 toward the cost of airfare.

For more information on this program, check out the ALA's Web site at http://www.ala.org/ala/iro/iroactivities/guadalajarabook.htm.

You can also contact the program coordinator: David Unger, FIL New York, Division of Humanities NAC 5/225, The City College of New York, New York, NY 10031, 212-650-7925, 212-650-7912 fax, e-mail FILNY@ aol.com.

SPANISH-LANGUAGE BOOK AND MEDIA VENDORS AND DISTRIBUTORS

Astran, Inc., P.O. BOX 490274, Key Biscayne, FL 33149, 305-597-0064, http://www.astranbooks.com/

Baker and Taylor/*Libros Sin Fronteras,* 2550 West Tyvola Road, Suite 300, Charlotte, NC 28217, 800.775.1800, 704.998.3100, btinfo@btol.com, http://www.btol.com/.

Bilingual Educational Services, Inc., 2514 South Grand Avenue, Los Angeles, CA 90007-9979, 213-749-6213, 213-749-1820 fax, e-mail bes@besbooks.com, http://www.besbooks.com/.

This catalog includes the core bilingual materials lists prepared by the Los Angeles Unified School District, a separate list called "Focus on Books" from the Library Services Department of LAUSD, and the State of California Department of Education list.

Bilingual Publications Company, 270 Layfayette St. Suite 705, New York, NY 10012, 212-431-3500, 212-431-3567 fax, e-mail lindagoodman @juno.com.

Brodart/Books on Wings, 500 Arch Street, Williamsport, PA 17701, 800-474-9802, 570-326-1479 fax, e-mail support@brodart.com, http:// www.brodart.com/, http://www.espanol.brodart.com/, e-mail casalibro @aol.com.

Carvajal International, David A. Ashe, General Manager, 901Ponce de Leon Blvd., Suite 601, Coral Gables, Florida, 33134, 305-448-6875, 800-622-6657, and 305-448-9942, e-mail dashe@b2bportales.com, http://www.carvajal.com.co/.

Carvajal has a number of imprints; the most important for children's books is Grupo Editorial Norma.

Central Valley Video Distributors, 910 W. Yosemite, Madera, CA 93637-4555, 800-771-0671, 209-675-6827, and 209-675-3657 fax.

Children's Press (Scholastic Library Publishing), http://librarypublishing.scholastic.com

Chulainn Publishing Corp., 4875 DTC Blvd., No. 4-202, Denver, CO 80237, 888-525-2665.

Círculo de Lectores, and 1225 South Market Street, and Mechanicsburg, PA 17055, http://www.clubcirculo.com.

The Spanish-language Book of the Month Club, Publicaciones CITEM, Av. del Cristo No. 101, Xocoyahualco, Tlalnepantla, México, D.F., (55)5-238-0200.

Claudia's Caravan, Multicultural/Multilingual Materials, P.O. Box 1582, Alameda, CA 94501, 510-521-7871, 510-769-6230 fax.

Continental Book Company, 625 E. 70th Avenue, No. 5, Denver, CO 80229, 303-289-1761, 800-279-1764 fax, e-mail hola@continental-book.com, http://www.continentalbook.com.

Culture for Kids, 4480 Lake Forest Dr. No. 302, Cincinnati, OH 45242, 800-765-5885, 513-563-3100, e-mail info@cultureforkids.com, http://www.cultureforkids.com.

Del Sol Books, 6547 Edmonton Avenue, San Diego, CA 92112, 858-202-0235, 888-335-7651, and 858-202-0265 fax, e-mail ray@delsol-books.com, http://www.delsolbooks.com/. A distributor for the books of Alma Flor Ada, F. Isabel Campoy and the music of Suni Paz. Alma Flor Ada, http://www.almaflorada.com, F. Isabel Campoy, http://www.isabelcampoy.com; Suni Paz, http://www.sunipaz.com.

Donars Spanish Books, P.O. Box 32205, Aurora, CO 80041-2205, 303-343-7170, 303-343-7111 fax, e-mail donars@prolynx.com.

EBSCO Subscription Services, P.O. Box 1943, Birmingham, AL 35242, 205-991-6600, 205-995-1518 fax, http://www.ebsco.com. A good source for Spanish-language magazines.

Educal S.A. de C.V., Consejo Nacional para la Cultura y las Artes, Av. Ceylán No. 450, Col. Euzkadi, 02660, Mexico, D.F., (52)5-356-2815, (52)5-355-6772 fax, http://www.librosyarte.com.mx.

Fiesta Book Company, P.O. Box 490641, Key Biscayne, FL 33149-0641, 305-858-4843, and 305-858-9934 fax.

Giron Spanish Book Distributors, 2130 West 21st Street, Chicago, IL 60608, 773-847-3000, 800-405-4276, 773-847-9197 fax, http://www.gironbooks.com.

Howard Karno Books, P.O. Box 2100, Valley Center, CA 92082, 760-749-2304, 760-749-4390 fax, e-mail info@karnobooks.com, http://www.karnobooks.com/cgi-bin/karno/.

Latin American Book Source, 289 3rd Avenue, Chula Vista, California 91910, 619-426-1226, 619-426-0212 fax, http://www.latambooks.com/.

Latin American Book Store, 204 N. Geneva Street, Ithaca, NY 14850,

607-273-2418, 607-273-6003 fax, e-mail libros@americanbooks.com, http://www.latinamericanbooks.com/.

Lectorum Publications, Inc. (Subsidary of Scholastic), 557 Broadway (in Scholastic offices at Broadway and Prince) New York, NY 10012, 212-929-2833, 800-345-5946, 212-727-3035 fax, http://www.lectorum.com.

Librería Lectorum, 137 West 14 Street, (between 6th & 7th Ave.), New York, NY 212 741-0220, 212 463-8513 fax, e-mail librerialectorum@scholastic.com

Librería Martínez, 1110 N. Main Street, Santa Ana, CA 92701, 714-973-7900.

Librería Martínez (second location), Plaza Mexico, 11221 Long Beach Blvd., No. 102, Lynwood, CA 90262, 310-637-9484, http://www.latinobooks.com/.

Children's books Web site, http://www.mislibritos.com/.

Libros en Venta (includes the publishing output of twenty Spanish-speaking countries and Spanish-language titles from sixteen other non-Spanish-speaking countries), National Information Services Corporation, NISC USA, Wyman Towers, 3100 St. Paul Street, Baltimore, Maryland 21218, 410-243-0797, 410-243-0982 fax, http://www.nisc.com/fact-sheets/qlev.asp, e-mail sales@nisc.com.

Madera CineVideo, 311 South Pine Street, Ste. 102, Madera, CA 93637, 209-661-6000, 209-674-3650 fax, 800-828-8118, e-mail maderacvc @pacbell.net, http://www.mcinavideo.qpg.com/.

Mariuccia Iaconi Book Imports, 970 Tennessee Street, San Francisco, CA 94107, 415-821-1216, 415-821-1596, http://www.mibibook.com/, e-mail mibibook@earthlink.net

Multicultural Books and Videos, Inc., 28880 Southfield Road, No. 183, Lathrup Village, Michigan 48076, 248-559-2676, 248-559-5285 fax, e-mail service@multiculbv.com, http://www.multiculturalbooksandvideos.com/mcbv/ecom/controller.jsp.

Multicultural Connection, Libros Bilingües Para Niños, P.O. Box 653, Ardsly, New York 10502-1020, 800-385-1020 (fax also), e-mail bilngbk@mhv.net, http://www.mhv.net/~bilingbk.

Quality Books, Inc., 1003 W. Pines Road, Oregon, IL 61061, 800-323-4241, 815-732-4499 fax, e-mail info@quality-books.com, http://www.quality-books.com/.

Rainbow Book Company, 500 East Main Street, Lake Zurich, IL 60047, 800-255-0965, 847-726-9930, 847-726-9935 fax, e-mail sales@rainbowbookcompany.com, e-mail customerservice@rainbow

bookcompany.com, e-mail info@rainbowbookcompany.com, http://
www.rainbowbookcompany.com.

Spanish Book Distributors, 6706 Sawmill Road Dallas, TX 75252-5816, 1-
800-609-2113, 1-888-254-6709 fax, email sbd@sbdbooks.com, http://
www.sbdbooks.com

T. R. Books, 822 N. Walnut Ave., New Braunfels, TX 78130, 800-659-
4710, 830-625-2665, and 830-620-0470 fax, http://www.trbooks.com.

SPANISH-LANGUAGE BOOK PUBLISHERS/IMPRINTS

The publishers listed here represent those well known for publishing quality
children's books. The best way to obtain materials from foreign-based
publishers is through a distributor. I am providing the information for these
publishers should you wish to contact them directly. Some foreign-based publishers, like Santillana, have now established U.S. offices, to facilitate direct
contact.

Arte Público Press/Piñata Books, University of Houston, 425 Cullen Performance Hall, Houston, TX 77204-2090, 800-633-ARTE, 713-743-2847
fax, e-mail bkorders@uh.edu, http://www.arte.uh.edu/.

Barefoot Books, 2607 Massachusetts Avenue, Cambridge, MA 02140,
617-576-0660, 866-2151756, 617-576-0049, e-mail feedback@
barefootbooks.com, http://www.barefoot-books.com/us/site/pages/home
.php.

Charlesbridge Publishing, 85 Main Street, Watertown, MA 02472, 800-225-
3214, 617-926-0329, 800-926-5775 fax, e-mail books@charlesbridge
.com, http://www.charlesbridge.com/.

Children's Book Press, 2211 Mission Street, San Francisco, CA 94110,
415-821-3080, 415-821-3081 fax, e-mail orders@childrensbookpress
.org, http://www.childrensbookpress.org/.

Chronicle Books, 85 Second Street, Sixth Floor, San Francisco,
CA 94105, 415-537-4200, 800-722-6657, 415-537-4460 fax, e-mail
frontdesk@chroniclebooks.com, http://www.chroniclebooks.com/site/
catalog/.

CIDCLI, S.C. Centro de Información y Desarrollo de la Comunicación y
la Literatura Infantiles (Center of Information and Development of
Communication and of Children's Literature), Av. México, No. 145-
601, Col. Coyoacán, C. P. 04100, México, D.F. (52 55) 56 59 75 24,
(52 55) 5-6 59 75 24, (52 55) 56 59 31 86, (52 55) 56 59 75 24 fax,
http://www.cidcli.com.mx/.

Cinco Puntos Press, 701 Texas, El Paso, TX 79901, 800-566-9072, e-mail info@cincopuntos.com, http://www.cincopuntos.com/.

Clarion Books (a Houghton Mifflin Companies Imprint), 215 Park Avenue South, New York, NY 10003, 212-420-5883, http://www.houghtonmifflinbooks.com/clarion/.

Dominie Press, Inc./Pearson Learning Group, 5945 Pacific Center Boulevard, Suite 505, San Diego, CA 92121, 800-232-4570, 619-546-8822 fax, http://k12catalog.pearson.com/co_home.cfm?site_id=1181.

Ediciones Ekaré/Banco del Libro (Venezuela), Avenida Luis Roche, Edificio Banco del Libro, Altamira Sur, Caracas 1062, Venezuela, (58)212-264-7615/1421, (58)212-263-3291 fax, e-mail books@ekare.com.ve, e-mail editorial@ekare.com.ve, http://www.ekare.com/.

Ediciones Norte-Sur, North-South Books, 875 Sixth Avenue, Suite 1901, New York, NY 10001, 212-706-4545, 212-868-5951 fax, http://www.northsouth.com/.

Ediciones SM In Spain: Joaquin Turina, 39, 28044 Madrid, Spain, (34)91-422-8800, http://www.grupo-sm.com/.

In Mexico: Magdalena 211, Colonia Del Valle Del Benito Juárez, México, DF 03100, (55)1-087-8400, e-mail jperujo@ediciones-sm.com.mx, http://www.edicionessm.com.mx/.

Editorial Atlantida S.A. (Argentina), Azopardo 565, C. P. 1307 Buenos Aires, Argentina, (54)11-4346-0100, e-mail atlantidalibros@atlantida.com.ar, http://www.atlantidalibros.com.ar/.

Editorial Juventud (Spain), Provenza, 101, 08029 Barcelona, Spain, (34)93-444-1800, (34)93-439-8383 fax, http://www.editorialjuventud.es/.

Editorial Casals, s.a., C/ Caspe, 79, 08013 Barcelona, Spain, http://www.editorialcasals.com/esp/home/index.asp.

Note: One of Casals's imprints is Combel Editorial, publishers of some of my favorite new series for young readers, represented in the Core Collection.

Editorial Trillas (Mexico), General Administration: Av. Rio Churubusco 385, Col. Pedro María Anaya, Deleg. Benito Juárez, c.p. 03340 -México, D.F., (52)5-688-4007, (52)5-604-1364 fax, e-mail ftrillas@trillas.com.mx, http://www.trillas.com.mx/.

Sales Division: Calz. De la Viga 1132, Col. Apatlaco, Deleg. Itzalpalapa C. P. 09439, México, D.F., (52)5-633-6080/1122, (52)5-633-0870/2221 fax, e-mail laviga@trillas.com.mx.

Emecé Editores S. A. (Argentina), Av. Independencia 1668, CP 1100ABQ Buenos Aires, Argentina, http://www.koalaweb.com.ar/emece/.

Fernández Editores S. A. de C. V. (Mexico), http://www.tareasya.com/

Fondo de Cultura Económica USA, 2293 Verus Street, San Diego, California 92154, 619-429-0455, 800-532-3872, 619-429-0827 fax, e-mail sales@fceusa.com, http://www.fceusa.com.

Grolier Publishing Company
(see Scholastic)

Harcourt Brace Children's Books, 525 B Street, Suite 1900, San Diego, CA 92101-4495, 619-699-6431, 619-699-6220 fax, http://www.harcourt .com/.

HarperCollins, 1350 Avenue of the Americas, New York, NY 10019, 212-261-6500, http://www.harpercollinschildrens.com/harperchildrens.

Henry Holt & Co., 175 Fifth Avenue, New York, NY 10010, 646-307-5095, 212-633-0748 fax, e-mail publicity@hholt.com, http://www .henryholt.com/.

Hyperion Books for Children/Disney Press, 114 Fifth Avenue, New York, NY 10011, 212-633-4400, http://www.hyperionbooksforchildren.com/.

Lectorum Publications, Inc., 557 Broadway (in Scholastic offices at Broadway and Prince), New York, NY 10012, 212-929-2833, 800-345-5946, 212-727-3035 fax, http://www.lectorum.com.

Librería Lectorum, 137 West 14 Street (between 6th & 7th Aves.), New York, NY, 10011 212 741-0220, Fax: 212 463-8513, e-mail librerialectorum@scholastic.com.

Lee & Low Books, 95 Madison Avenue, Suite No. 1205, 212-779-4400, 212-683-1894, e-mail general@leeandlow.com, http://www.leeandlow .com/.

Little, Brown and Company, 1271 Avenue of the Americas, New York, NY 10020, 212-522-9333, http://www.twbookmark.com/children/ index.html.

Me+Mi Publishers, 128 South Country Farm Road, Suite E, Wheaton, IL 60187, 630-752-9951, 888-251-1444, 630-588-9801 fax, e-mail m3@memima.com, http://memima.com/.

Mirasol (imprint of Farrar, Straus and Giroux), Books for Young Readers, Farrar, Straus and Giroux, 19 Union Square West, New York, NY 10003, 212-741-6900, http://www.fsgkidsbooks.com/.

Northland Publishing/Rising Moon/Luna Rising, 2900 N. Fort Valley Rd., P.O. Box 1389, Flagstaff, AZ 86001, 800-346-3257, 928-774-5251, 800-257-9082 fax, 928-774-0592 fax, http://www.northlandbooks .com.

Penguin Ediciones (imprint of Penguin U.S.A.), Penguin USA Children's Books, 575 Hudson Street, New York, NY 10014, 212-366-2000, 212-366-2934, http://us.penguingroup.com/index-yr.html.

Puvill Libros S. A. U. S. office Dror Faust, One East Park Drive, Paterson,

NJ 07504, 973-279-9054, 973-278-1448 fax, e-mail drorpuvill@aol
.com, http://www.puvill.com/.

Raven Tree Press, 200 S. Washington Street, Suite 306, Green Bay, WI
54301, 920-438-1605, 877-256-0579, 920-438-1607 fax, e-mail raven@
raventreepress.com, http://www.raventreepress.com/index.html.

Rourke Publishing Group, P.O. Box 3328, Vero Beach, FL 32964, 800-
394-7055, 772-234-6001, 772-234-6622 fax, e-mail customerservice@
rourkepublishing.com, http://rourkepublishing.com/library/.

Santillana USA, 2105 N.W. 86th Avenue, Miami, FL 33122, 800-245-
8584, 800-248-9518 fax, e-mail customerservice@santillanausa.com,
http://www.santillanausa.com/.

Selector, Dr. Erazo 120 Col. Doctores, Mexico, D.F. 06720, (52)5-588-
7272, (52)5-761-5716 fax, e-mail info@selector.com.mx, http://www
.selector.com.mx/ingles/homefrm.html.

Suromex Ediciones SA, Distributed by Astran, Inc. (See Distributors above)

Susaeta Ediciones SA, C/Campezo, 13, 28022 Madrid, (91)300-9100,
(91)300-9118 fax, e-mail geneal@susaeta.com, http://www.susaeta
.com/htm/ppal.htm.

ONLINE BIBLIOGRAPHIC SOURCE

Spanish "Amazon.com" (formerly yenny.com): http://www.tematika.com.

Appendix

THE OAKLAND PUBLIC LIBRARY MULTI-LANGUAGE COLLECTION DEVELOPMENT POLICY

While I have said that general collection development policies stay the same regardless of language, it may be helpful, depending on the needs of your library, to have a policy that addresses the collection of materials in other languages very specifically. Because the best model for this kind of specific policy that I have found is from the "With the kind permission of the Oakland Public Library Collection Development Department," I am reprinting the entire policy here. While the policy deals with all the languages collected by Oakland Public, which serves very diverse ethnic communities, I felt that seeing the policy in its entirety would give a sense of how a specific library has responded to community needs in different languages. This policy can be used as the basis of developing your own local policy.

GOALS AND OBJECTIVES

MISSION STATEMENT

The Oakland Public Library, through its multi-language collections, values and reflects the diversity and changing needs of its diverse community. We strive to improve the quality of life in Oakland through excellence in library services and collections that delight, inspire, and inform.

GOALS

1. The language collections of the Oakland Public Library manifest, acknowledge and validate the diverse cultural heritage and experiences of the diverse communities.
2. The Oakland Public Library has a system-wide collection that supports the recreational, educational, informational, and cultural needs of all ages and reading levels within the diverse communities in Oakland, and

integrates its support of those needs into the services and operations of every branch.

3. The Oakland Public Library is responsive to changes in the multilingual community in Oakland by conducting periodic community analysis.

4. The Oakland Public Library has selectors and library staff who are informed, trained, capable and motivated to meet the special requirements of service to each linguistic community.

5. The Oakland Public Library provides appropriate access to its language collections in every branch. This includes—but is not limited to—bibliographic tools; bilingual library forms, notices, signs, and informational/instructional publications; and the physical location of multi-language materials within each branch.

6. The Oakland Public Library subscribes to the Library Bill of Rights, and adheres to its precepts when selecting materials in all languages.

OBJECTIVES

1. Determine budget guidelines for language collections and integrate these into the Oakland Public Library's budgeting process.

2. Determine and identify the levels and ranges of need for language collections in every branch.

3. Define and establish an appropriate level language collection ranging from core to reference collections for each branch or unit.

4. Solicit and encourage the participation of the multilingual community in the policy, planning, and acquisitions processes of the library's language collections.

5. Devise and implement a system-wide training plan for staff responsible for delivery of service to users speaking other languages.

6. Provide and purchase materials from different sources that reflect the diversity of cultures of the users of the language collections.

7. Select materials representing a variety of points of view; develop language collections on an inclusive rather than an exclusive basis.

8. Provide relevant, up-to-date materials of high quality, and establish procedures for maintaining currency of information.

9. Catalog and process all language materials in a timely fashion.

10. Develop clear and consistent signs for all locations where language collections and related services are available.

11. Establish and maintain systems of contact and exchange with other institutions; utilize and expand existing networks to share materials and information pertaining to multi-language collections.

12. Periodically review and evaluate all of the above points, and revise or redirect them as necessary.

COMMUNITY ANALYSIS

In the 1990 Census, nearly 93,500 Oakland residents over the age of five (27 percent of persons above age five) lived in households which spoke a non-English language at home. Ten percent of the total population were considered to be linguistically isolated, i.e., they live in households in which no person 14 years or older spoke English very well. Oakland is rapidly increasing in ethnic diversity, and is more diverse than Alameda County or California.

Library staff should practice continual analysis of the communities served, analysis for maintaining established language collections, for redeciding locations of these collections, and for establishing new language collections. Staff should first review bibliographies on multiethnic collection development. The primary method for assessment of a community is the use of demographics—the census, Oakland government documents, school statistics, and library circulation statistics.

1) The Census: From the 1990 census, one can select four displays of linguistic statistics, either by city or by each census tract: a) Age by language spoken at home and ability to speak English; b) Household language and linguistic isolation; c) Age, language spoken at home, and linguistic isolation; and d) Language spoken at home (this last giving a detailed list of the specific languages, rather than in broad groupings). There is no update of the language demographics between each decade's census. Branch service areas by census tract have been established. A list is available from the Branch Administrator or the Collection Development Librarian.

2) Local documents from Oakland government agencies are kept in the Science, Sociology, and Documents Section of the Main Library. Staff should also check the Oakland History Room for pamphlets and newspaper articles.

3) From the Oakland Unified School District, one can get the Language Census (form R30-LC) for each school, published annually in the spring. This is available at a Web site (http://www.cde.ca.gov), a graphics file. This lists primary language and number of students speaking it for each grade of the school. The charts show the number of LEP (limited English proficient) and FEP (fluent English proficient) students for each language. Staff can also call the schools and the adult schools in their area.

4) Circulation statistics can be pulled on the circulation of language materials in any given branch by asking the Automation Librarian. These statistics can also be broken down by fiction or nonfiction; adult or juvenile; or type of material. They can display the number of items circulated and the percentage of circulation for that category.

Secondary assessment methods involve contact with the given language community, as part of each librarian's outreach in the community. Focus groups can be set up, surveys of users given, and meetings with community leaders and organizations held. The Oakland History Room keeps a current list of neighborhood organizations, and the newsletters they publish. There are directories such as the Bay Area Directory of Clubs and Organizations, and the Encyclopedia of Associations (the regional, local, and state volume). Cityline's Community Information File lists many groups, as do the white pages of telephone books.

PROCEDURES FOR ESTABLISHING A NEW LANGUAGE COLLECTION

A minimum population must be present to warrant establishing new collections. At least 5 percent of the population in a branch area must speak the language to justify a new language collection at a branch for a language already collected in the Oakland system. If the language is not currently collected by the system, at least 2 percent of the city population should speak the language. The branch planning to establish the collection should be located near a significant portion of the population.

Once community analysis is completed, if it is determined that there is a need for a new language collection, the procedures for establishing a new language collection must be followed. These are: 1) New language collections must receive approval from the supervising librarian; 2) A minimum of $1,000 must be available for establishing a new language collection to ensure that it be adequate in size; 3) The selector must commit $500 a year from their materials budget to maintain each non-English language collection established; 4) Selectors who do not speak or read the language involved must select materials with the help of qualified staff who are knowledgable in the language; 5) There must be communication with the Technical Services department—as to where one can buy the books, and as to whether they can be cataloged properly for access. The availability of appropriate tools must be ascertained before the establishment of the new collection.

SELECTION

General Criteria

As with English language collections, quality is the highest priority for language materials. This includes not only the caliber of writing, but also the accuracy of reference data and translation where applicable, as well as the quality of illustration and overall production/packaging quality.

Since users of OPL's language collections are from dozens of countries of origin, represent diverse racial groups, and have different frames of reference for the various languages, materials should be selected from a variety of sources, and their content should reflect a range of perspectives. Since production values vary from publisher to publisher, selectors should base their decisions on first-hand examination whenever possible, especially with children's materials.

Hardcovers and special bindings, when available, are usually preferable over paperbacks; it may be necessary to reinforce most paperbacks before they are put out for the public. Durability increases cost-effectiveness.

Works in translation should be carefully evaluated for quality of translation. In children's materials particularly, an additional concern should be the appropriateness of illustrations. Selectors of materials for adults should be wary of extremes of literalness or generality that can render a translated work useless.

A related concern to selectors of multi-language materials is currency of information in nonfiction items. Errors and misrepresentations can slip past publishers just as easily as inaccurate translations; this is another factor in favor of personal examination of materials.

Similarly, selectors for both children's and adult multi-language materials should be especially mindful of the needs of "linguistically isolated" users who speak only another language. Just as there are different levels of reading skill, so are there different levels of English proficiency among users of multi-language collections.

Selection tools for materials in other languages differ from those for English language materials in one crucial factor: there are fewer conventional sources. Staff must be particularly alert not only for review sources, but also for selection tools appearing in the library literature, publishers' trade publications, reference resources, workshops, conferences, book fairs, and the expertise of colleagues. Some review sources include *Booklist, Nexos, Azteca, Boletín Internacional, Uno Mas Uno, La Opinión, Library Journal,* and *School Library Journal.* Profiles, vendor expertise, requests from the public, and community input are also important sources of information. High quality and cultural relevance in multi-language collections will foster repeated use and exploration of other collection areas.

Children's Materials

Emphases may vary according to content, age group or reading level, and availability of material, but there are some rules of thumb:

Of particular value at any level is the representation of a variety of cultures, and the absence of stereotyping.

Works at any level that enhance skills for coping in the "real world" outside home and family are also worthy of selection.

Picture books, folktales (including indigenous mythology, multi-language nursery rhymes, songs, riddles, tongue twisters and so forth) and easy readers are appropriate for preschool through third grade.

FICTION

"Moving up" fiction is appropriate up to about the third or fourth grade level; in the past, readers beyond this level have shown a preference for works in English, but more and more paperback fiction for older children is becoming available, and should be purchased.

Classics of children's literature should emphasize authors who write in the original languages.

NONFICTION

A basic language nonfiction collection should fill the informational and recreational needs of children from preschool to eighth grade.

Nonfiction materials in other languages for juveniles will be collected in the same areas as English, with emphasis on the subjects used for school assignments and recreational topics popular with children.

REFERENCE

Keeping in mind the nonfiction emphasis on school assignments, juvenile reference collections in other languages should include, if available, a bilingual dictionary aimed at juvenile users, an atlas, and one current juvenile encyclopedia.

MAGAZINES

There are a small number of juvenile magazines appropriate for multi-language collections. Some titles: *Colibri*, *Chispa*, *Espantapajaros*, *Hsiao hsiao t = en ti* (Chinese), *Baby Book* (Japanese), *Omma rang aki rang* (Korean).

NON-PRINT FORMATS

The juvenile language collections should include items in non-print formats such as kits, videotapes, and audiocassettes (emphasis on popular children's music, stories, and rhymes).

Adult Materials

All areas of adult materials should reflect the diversity within the linguistic community. Materials should reflect the diversity of educational backgrounds which commonly exist among the various populations. Materials should be provided at all levels of complexity, for a full range of interests. Community analysis will help establish the range of these collections.

Since users of these collections have demonstrated an interest in world literature and culture, fiction and nonfiction collections will be rounded out by high-interest works in translation. Emphasis in both areas, however, will be on works written in the original language.

FICTION

Adult fiction collections in other languages should cover the broadest possible range of subjects and should not be limited to traditional literatures or translations of English literature.

Both ends of the spectrum will be represented—from popular successes and contemporary styles to literary works and classics.

Fiction also includes genres like mysteries, romances, and science fiction.

NONFICTION

Adult nonfiction collections in other languages are general interest collections, and in this sense differ little from nonfiction collections in English.

Popular topics include sociology, history, economics, politics, folklore and folkways, all aspects of the immigrant experience, the occult, psychology and self-help, home and car repair [see Selection Subcommittee's current list of popular topics]. Selectors need to be aware of current popular trends.

REFERENCE

The Oakland Public Library is committed to maintaining extensive reference collections in other languages, particularly at the Main, Asian and the Cesar E. Chavez Libraries. Basic collections should include a bilingual dictionary, an almanac, an atlas, and encyclopedia, if these are available. Users of reference collections in all languages are interested in any information resources the collections can provide. General subject areas of frequently requested materials may include basic survival information to meet daily needs; information about the community, its resources and services; services developed by government agencies, and specialized dictionaries (medical, technical).

Reference information is also available in vertical file materials— pamphlets on demographics, folklore and other topics—and when these files are kept current, they are a significant reference resource.

PERIODICALS

Selected periodicals should reflect the diversity of the communities and include titles that both appeal to popular tastes and cover broad interests and various points of view.

Local newspapers and magazines in other languages are easily collected. National magazines in other languages should bear some topical or demographic relation to users of OPL's language collections.

Graphic novels are not an emphasis of the collection, but they are a popular form of fiction. Since graphic novels are usually published in magazine format, they are probably more properly collected as periodicals. Once a collection of graphic novels is established, it can usually be maintained through donations.

NON-PRINT FORMATS

Instructional and spoken word items in any non-print format may be of particular interest in multi-language collections.

Musical audiocassettes and compact discs should appeal to the same broad range of interests.

Videocassette holdings, though in line with OPL's general selection policy for this format, should reflect a similarly broad range of origins and subjects.

Cataloging

Oakland Public Library collects and catalogs materials in Spanish, Japanese, Chinese, Korean, Tagalog, Thai, Khmer, Hmong, Laotian, Russian, and French. Catalog librarians with language specialties catalog Spanish and Asian language materials.

Access to materials in languages other than English is the same as to English language materials with the following exceptions: Spanish language: All cataloged Spanish language materials are accessible by Spanish language subjects as listed in Bilindex or in OPL's local Spanish language subject headings file. The Spanish subjects are added as equivalents to the Library of Congress Subject Heading (LCSHs) assigned to the work.

Asian languages: Catalog cards with the vernacular characters for Chinese, Japanese, and Korean (CJK) titles are produced for those titles for which CJK is available on OCLC. If CJK characters are not available the vernacular script is transcribed for authors and titles. Diacritics are removed from Vietnamese language materials to enable searching in Dynix. Specific romanization systems are utilized for Chinese materials (Wade-Giles and Pinyin, authors and titles only), for Japanese materials (Modified Hepburn) and for Korean materials (McCune-Rischauer). ALA-LC romanization tables are used as necessary. The romanization systems applied to other languages, such as Khmer, Laotian and Thai, are dependant upon the available expertise of staff. Some book vendors such as Pan Asian provide romanized cataloging information for materials purchased through them.

A language designation appears in the call number of all Spanish, Japanese, Chinese, Korean, Vietnamese, Tagalog, Thai, Khmer, Hmong, Cambodian,

Laotian, German, Russian, and French language materials and in the call number of language instruction materials for a specific audience.

To further facilitate access to non-English language materials, adult bilingual materials are assigned the subject heading bilingual books. Juvenile bilingual materials are assigned the subject heading for the non-English language followed by the subdivision bilingual. As we add new language collections, new call number language designations are created. The utilization of romanization systems and the extent of cataloging information provided for new language collections are contingent upon the level of staff expertise, both within and outside the Catalog Section.

LONG-TERM COLLECTION MAINTENANCE

Oakland Public Library is committed to providing the community with materials in diverse languages. One of the ways the library does this is through the Multi-Language Committee. This committee acts as an advisory and information-gathering body. The Multi-Language Committee was formed in 1992 and was formerly the Spanish Language Committee. Its mission is to assure quality collections in non-English languages and to provide support for these collections.

As an advisory and information-gathering body, the committee assists in developing library-wide recommendations and guidelines concerning language collections.

To be most useful to the community, a language collection needs to include a basic level of materials, with a continuing budgetary commitment to keeping the collection current. Ideally, the material will be selected by staff conversant in the language.

Generally, a tiny collection established without this budgetary commitment and without staff who speak the language, although it may seem beneficial to the community, can actually be a disservice. These collections raise expectations in the community, are not usually current, and may dissuade patrons from using the larger, more current language collections established elsewhere. Like any subject collection, language collections need continued commitment and updating.

ANNUAL SURVEY OF LANGUAGE COLLECTIONS (USE OF THE COLLECTION AND DEMOGRAPHICS OF THE COMMUNITY SERVED)

The goal of this survey is to assist librarians in evaluating the demographics of their individual communities and the use of language collections. The survey is the committee's attempt to ensure consistency in establishment and maintenance of language collections. Librarians can contact the committee at any time with questions or concerns.

This survey is done annually, in May, for every language collection in the system. Oakland Public Library is committed to providing the community with books in various languages, and in order to do that well must continually assess use of existing language collections, and the possible need for dissolution or relocation of existing collections with changing demographics. This assessment may also indicate a need for more community outreach for a particular collection.

If demographic statistics indicate a need for relocation of a particular language collection, and if this change is accompanied by a corresponding drop in circulation statistics, the branch manager and branch supervising librarian will confer in the decision-making process. The Multi-Language Committee will also review any proposals for changes.

If circulation statistics for a certain language collection have dropped and demographics show the reason to be shifts in populations within Oakland, the branch librarian will most likely wish to reallocate the annual funding from that language collection.

There are several possible changes. A language collection might be moved to another branch which has experienced an increasing population of speakers of that language. The collection might be dissolved and given to another library system with more need for that language. The collection might remain at the original location, but as a frozen collection, with no more books being added. Further community outreach might be called for, and if so, the collection's use would be reassessed the following year.

BIBLIOGRAPHY

Census of Population and Housing. Washington, DC: U.S.G.P.O., Superintendent of Documents, 1990. (California data on CD-ROM.)

Cuesta, Yolanda, and Tarín, Patricia. "Guidelines for Library Service to the Spanish-Speaking." *Library Journal,* 103 (July 1978):1350–1355.

"Demographic Profile of Libraries to Receive Language Collections." Portion of Oakland Public Library internal document (1992).

Guereña, Salvador, ed. *Latino Librarianship: a handbook for professionals.* Jefferson, NC: McFarland, 1990.

Multilingual Materials Subcommittee (ad hoc), Adult Library Materials Committee, Reference and Adult Services Division, American Library Association. *Guidelines for Multilingual Materials Collection and Development and Library Services.* Chicago: American Library Association, 1990.

Scarborough, Katharine T. A., ed. *Developing Library Collections for*

California's Emerging Majority. Oakland: Bay Area Library and Information System, 1990.

Selection policies: Berkeley Public Library and Oakland Public Library (Children's Materials).

Tarín, Patricia A. "Books for the Spanish-Speaking : Sí Se Puede." *Library Journal*, 112 (July 1987):25–28.

Urban Strategies Council. *Overview of Collaboratives in Oakland.* November 1992.

Urban Strategies Council. Demographic data tables and maps provided to the Oakland Public Library. December 1992.

DEMOGRAPHICS

There are five branch libraries (plus the Main Branch) where use of Spanish language collections are particularly concentrated. Since most of these locations "straddle" two, three, sometimes four census tracts, further discussion of concentrations of the Spanish-speaking population (taken from a recent OPL internal document) is probably best done in the context of the service areas of these branches. Figures here concern percentages of Hispanic persons, AFDC recipients, and persons of limited English proficiency in respective census tracts of library branches.

Elmhurst
21% Hispanic
61% AFDC
19% Limited English Proficiency

In one recent six-month period, over 500 library card registrants listed Spanish as their primary language. Most Spanish-speaking patrons are recent immigrants and have limited English.

Latin American Library
50% Hispanic
38% AFDC
51% Limited English Proficiency

This is the primary resource for Spanish language materials; 48 percent of the 60,000 annual circulation is in Spanish. Requests are made for audiovisual materials and in reference materials for secondary school students.

Melrose
40% Hispanic
49% AFDC
40% Limited English Proficiency

Located one block from a high school whose student body is close to 50 percent non-English speaking. Referrals made daily to Latin American Library. Two Spanish-speaking librarians are regularly assigned to this branch library.

Main Library
62.3% Hispanic
N/A AFDC
47.5% Limited English Proficiency
Overall, the Main library represents the system's second largest Spanish language collection after LAL. As at LAL, the reference collection at Main is an important part of the service to Spanish speakers. A bilingual magnet school uses the Main Library's Youth Room as its principal library. Monthly library visits have increased the requests for materials in Spanish for the youngest children who have not developed their English skills.

Martin Luther King., Jr.
23% Hispanic
70% AFDC
25% Limited English Proficiency
Located on the same block with an elementary and junior high school and surrounded by a residential neighborhood that includes two large public housing complexes. Small Spanish collection is constantly in use. Specific requests for titles in Spanish.

Eastmont
11% Hispanic
53% AFDC
8% Limited English proficiency
The Eastmont Mall marketing department estimates 15–20 percent of the shoppers are Hispanic and mall management believe the numbers are growing. The Eastmont Mall advertises in Spanish and the number of Spanish language workers is increasing. Library staff who are Spanish-speaking borrow books each week from the Latin American Library for Eastmont Branch users.

GENERAL INDEX

AUTHOR INDEX

M

N

O

P

PROGRAMMING INDEX

TITLE INDEX

About the Author

A member of the 2006 Pura Belpré Award Selection Committee, Tim Wadham serves as Children's Services Coordinator for the Maricopa County Library District in Phoenix, Arizona. His undergraduate work was in Spanish literature, and he earned a Ph.D. in Comparative Literature from the University of Texas at Arlington. He also has an MLS from Brigham Young University. He is the author of *Programming With Latino Children's Materials*, published by Neal-Schuman in 1999.